The COCOS IS Mutiny

A significant World War Two mutiny took place on the night of 8 May 1942 in a lonely atoll in the Indian Ocean in a setting of intrigue, rebellion and the blood and tears of war. Japanese naval forces were at the peak of their southward thrust ....

While the battle of the Coral Sea raged, gunners of the Ceylon Garrison Artillery on the Cocos (Keeling) Islands off Australia's north-west coast attempted to arrest their British commanding officer and compel him to surrender to the Japanese. One soldier was killed and another wounded, but the mutiny failed and seven men were condemned to death. Ultimately three soldiers were hung, becoming the only Commonwealth troops to be executed for mutiny in World War Two.

Through extensive research over many years, Noel Crusz has uncovered an extraordinary story, one which the military had sought to keep secret. Certainly it is a story of the gravest of military crimes, but it is also a story of poor leadership, racism, and a seriously flawed court martial, against a background of changing attitudes to colonialism and the growing desire for self-government and independence throughout Asia.

The Cocos Islands Mutiny contributes a fascinating and unique chapter in the history of Pacific campaign in World War Two.

Noel Crusz was born in Sri Lanka and came to Australia in 1974. He holds a BA from the University of London, an MA from the University of New South Wales and a Diploma of Education from Armidale and Fordham University (USA).

Trained in broadcasting at the BBC London, he broadcast on London's Home Service programs, and from Radio Eireann, Hilversum, Cologne and Berne. He has been a newsreader for Vatican Radio and has broadcast on the 'Voice of America'. In Ceylon (Sri Lanka) he was Director of Radio Ceylon's 'Catholic Hour Programme'. He produced radio features, plays and interviews on all Radio Ceylon's services and was also a scriptwriter for the Ceylon government film unit's weekly newsreels. He has also directed and filmed many features and documentaries.

Noel Crusz has taught for seventeen years in Sydney's high schools, and at present teaches Special Religious Education at State high schools. As a puppeteer he belonged to the New South Wales Puppet Guild and worked with the doyen of puppetry Edith Murray.

As a freelance journalist Noel Crusz has contributed to the major Australian and international press. *The Cocos Islands Mutiny* is his first book and was completed with the assistance of a writers grant from the Literature Fund of the Australia Council.

The Cocos Islands Mutiny

Noel Crusz

FREMANTLE ARTS CENTRE PRESS

First published 2001 by
FREMANTLE ARTS CENTRE PRESS
25 Quarry Street, Fremantle
(PO Box 158, North Fremantle 6159)
Western Australia.
www.facp.iinet.net.au

Consultant Editor Allan Watson.
Production Coordinator Cate Sutherland.
Cover Designer Andrew Allingham.

Typeset by Fremantle Arts Centre Press
and printed by PK Print.

National Library of Australia
Cataloguing-in-publication data

Crusz, Noel, 1921– .
    The Cocos Islands mutiny.

    ISBN 1 86368 310 0.

    1. World War, 1939–1945 — Participation, Sri Lankan. 2. Mutiny — Cocos
    (Keeling) Islands. 3. World War, 1939–1945 — Cocos (Keeling) Islands.
    I. Title.

940.54595493

The State of Western Australia has made an investment in this project
through ArtsWA in association with the Lotteries Commission.

Publication of this title was assisted by the Commonwealth Government
through the Australia Council, its arts funding and advisory body.

for
Tirzah

The way it actually was. The endless ocean. The infinite specks of coral we called islands. Coconut palms nodding gracefully toward the ocean. Reefs upon which waves broke into spray, and inner lagoons lovely beyond description … The waiting. The timeless, repetitive waiting …

James A Michener, *Tales of the South Pacific*

Contents

Maps

Foreword

As the officer who led the Ceylon forces on the Cocos (Keeling) Islands in World War Two, I have always been interested in the military history of that period. I was then, at the age of twenty-four, a captain in the Ceylon Defence Forces (1940) and holder of an emergency commission in the British army (1941).

During my tour of duty we were attacked on 3 March 1942 by Japanese naval forces. We survived the ordeal. At the time I was privileged to be in command of the Ceylon Garrison Artillery's Rowe Battery and Ceylon Light Infantry, whose loyalty and courage remained unquestioned.

After a British Officer, Captain George Gardiner, had taken over from me there took place a mutiny of Ceylon troops on 8 May 1942. It is one of the three known mutinies by British Commonwealth forces in World War Two and the only one in which perpetrators were executed. This event has not been subject to serious research until now. The revolt posed many questions and not a few answers. Today there has been a sudden and renewed interest in this campaign of the war.

I have known Noel Crusz for many years, and he has done monumental work for over three decades in documenting the facts and eliciting the causes of this event. It is fortunate that he has been able to interview the officers and others who were on Cocos at that time.

He spent many hours at the Imperial War Museum in London and at the Public Record Office in Kew, where he acquired the files of the Field General Court Martial and both statements of the mutineers and loyal soldiers.

There are some who consider the Cocos mutiny as a slur on the Ceylon Garrison Artillery, but this opinion becomes untenable in the light of the author's careful sifting of the causes of tension on the atoll at the height of the Japanese advance in the Indian Ocean.

There is significant relevance to Australia in this story, not only because the Cocos Cable and Wireless station was manned by Australian and British personnel, but also because the station was a critical part of a vital communication link with Britain during the war. Furthermore it was Australia that planned the defence of Cocos as fears grew of Japan entering the war. It is also the case that many relatives of the mutineers and loyal troops have settled in Australia.

The fact that many Asian youth were trapped in the web of Japan's 'co-prosperity' propaganda was understandable, especially given Ceylon's changing attitudes to colonialism and the growing desire for self-government and independence both in Ceylon and India. What I cannot understand is why the loyal troops were not awarded campaign medals — the 1939–1945 Star and the Pacific Star.

This book will certainly interest the general reader as well as military historians. Stripped of all the myths and legends that have so far been circulated, it is a fascinating story which adds an important chapter to the annals of the Pacific War. We owe a debt of gratitude to the author, whose consistent commitment and careful scholarship have given us a true picture of this wartime uprising.

Lyn Wickramasuriya
Lieutenant Colonel, officer commanding troops
on Cocos (Keeling) Islands in World War Two

Preface

A significant World War Two mutiny took place on the night of 8 May 1942 in a lonely atoll in the Indian Ocean. It occurred in a setting of intrigue, rebellion and the blood and tears of war. Japanese naval forces were at the peak of their southward thrust, and the Ceylonese contingent on the Cocos (Keeling) Islands was restless. The Ceylon Garrison Artillery on Horsburgh Island, under the command of a British officer, Captain George Gardiner, and the Ceylon Light Infantry on Direction Island were the sole defenders of Cocos and its strategic cable station.

The intention of the mutineers was to seize Gardiner, gain control of the defences of Cocos, signal the Japanese High Command and proceed to finalise surrender. The plan was elaborate but the mutiny failed. A Field General Court Martial found seven men guilty, and but for the intervention of General Archibald Percival Wavell, Commander-in-Chief of the Allied Forces in the Far East, they would have been executed at dawn. It was his wish that the mutineers be sent back to Ceylon, where in the end only three were hanged. These were the only executions of Commonwealth servicemen for mutiny in the history of World War Two.[1]

According to the 1966 census there were living in Australia nearly fifty thousand migrants who had been born in Ceylon. Among them were a few mutiny survivors and many relatives of those who were involved in the events at Cocos. Their desire to know the real story has not abated over time.

An underlying factor in the Cocos uprising was the impact of the Japanese 'co-prosperity' propaganda on Asian youth, who were beginning to feel the force of the slogan 'Asia for the Asians.' The political upheavals that were simmering in India and Ceylon prior to the war with regard to independence and self-government found a ready response among young soldiers, many of whom were convinced that the Japanese war machine would inevitably succeed, and thus strike a first blow for decolonisation. In this climate, any form of racism perpetrated by British commanders would be bound to have repercussions.

To understand the causes of the mutiny, it is necessary also to see it in the context of the war in Asia. The advance of the Japanese naval forces into the Bay of Bengal, within striking distance of Ceylon, marked the beginning of a new era for the soldiers on Cocos, and their morale was affected still more when an air raid was launched on Colombo on Easter Sunday, 5 April 1942. Another factor is the role Cocos played in the Indian Ocean, and whether the Japanese were really intent on acquiring it.

The Cable and Wireless company's station on Direction Island, in the Cocos group, was a vital communication link between the Malay Peninsula, Australia and Britain. In spite of intensive bombing by Japanese naval and air forces, it remained in action throughout the Pacific War, and its successful role was one of the best kept secrets of World War Two.

I was in Colombo in April 1942 and experienced the ordeal of the Japanese air raid; I was in personal contact with the chaplains and prison authorities who were present at the execution of the three mutineers; I was a product of the same school system that produced loyal soldiers on the one hand and rebellious troops on the other. These were some of the factors that prompted me to embark on the task of uncovering the details of the uprising, no serious attempt having been made by military writers to research this field. They could have been deterred by the secrecy surrounding the event, the paucity of documentation and the wish of a country to hide its military shame.

Investigating an event about which there remain few written records has not been easy. Though it was clear that some military documents existed, securing right of access was a slow process. The task also involved tracing the surviving men in Ceylon, Australia, Malaysia, Singapore, India, the United States, England and Europe. Only some were prepared to talk, and many of these gave accounts that did not inspire confidence. The family of the man who planned and led the mutiny, Bombardier Gratien H Fernando, was willing to provide photographs, correspondence from Cocos and all the documents they had gathered in their efforts to stay his execution.

Among those who agreed to be interviewed were some who had been in the inner circle of the mutiny, namely Gunners Mark Hopman, Gerry Anandappa, Kenneth Porritt and Alfred Edema. Lance Bombardier M T Ousmand of the Galle Face Battery produced the cable secretly sent by Fernando from Cocos. The sister of Gunner Carlo Gauder, Totsy Collinson, traced to the Sydney suburb of South Strathfield, produced photographs of her brother and gave detailed accounts of his last days prior to execution and her desperate pleas for a reprieve.

In spite of wide research and investigation, no contact could be made with Captain George Gardiner, who returned to England after the war. His second-in-command, Lieutenant Henry Stephens, though a personal friend, was for a long time unwilling to offer me more than scanty information; when eventually he gave his version of the mutiny in several long sessions, it was obvious that some facts were being concealed.

In Colombo Lieutenant Colonel Lyn Wickramasuriya provided background to much of what happened at the atoll after he handed over his command of Rowe Battery to Captain Gardiner. Interviews with Lieutenants Owen Wambeek, R D C Jonklaas, Henry de Sylva and I D M Van Twest, and with Captain George Koch, all of whom were on Cocos at different stages of the war, were of invaluable aid in assessing the state of army morale.[2]

With the release of a section of the war records after thirty years, efforts were made to get at the files of the Field General Court Martial, but access was blocked. Surprisingly, Captain Koch informed me in September 1970 that he had some relevant files, including one of the court martial proceedings, but that he was not prepared to release them. A similar situation arose when Henry de Sylva, who was in charge of the Ceylon Light Infantry on Direction Island, said that he alone knew the cause of the mutiny. Many of these men carried their supposed secrets to the grave; what they did not know was that the dog-eared files in London at the Public Record Office would eventually divulge them. Many papers were handed over to General Wavell's Asian Command in India, and British officers removed them from Ceylon's Army Command.

My quest turned to London, but I drew a blank in the Public Record Office in 1979, and also in the Imperial War Museum. No history of the Ceylon Garrison Artillery covering World War Two was found in the latter, and the published history of the Ceylon Light Infantry did not record any details beyond 1940 in spite of the work being published in 1944 and meticulous coverage being given of events during the first year of the war. The only reference to the Cocos Islands to be found in the War Museum's collection of Ceylonese unit histories was that nine officers and non-commissioned officers of the Ceylon Medical Corps were posted there in the early part of the war.

Among the original correspondence of the Straits Settlements, the Public Record Office found mention of the defence arrangements for Christmas Island and the Cocos Islands in 1942, but there was no reference to the mutiny.

Amazingly, the War Museum in Canberra advised that it had no reference to the mutiny in its holdings, and the Australian Archives in Melbourne had only a 'top secret' military reconnaissance report on Cocos prepared by the Australian Department of Defence prior to the outbreak of war. Mr John Clunies-Ross, the former hereditary ruler of Cocos, told me in correspondence that he 'found nothing written about the mutiny in the Cocos papers of the time, and all the files were removed by the military when they left the islands at the end of the war.'[3]

An approach to the Director General of War History in Japan was unsuccessful, and nothing was forthcoming from Japanese sources in Ceylon or Canberra.[4] The Mitchell and Dixson Library of New South Wales provided most of the Australian newspapers of the war years, and Ceylonese newspapers from 1939 to 1945 were found in the National Archives of Ceylon.

Correspondence with Ceylonese and other Commonwealth troops afforded various accounts of the events, many of which had to be assessed for accuracy. Articles on the Cocos mutiny appeared in many of Ceylon's English-language newspapers after the war, including scrappy versions from some of the surviving men.

As editor of an English-language evening daily, the *Star*, I ran a seventeen-part serial on the mutiny in 1970, with material collected from interviews with the men involved, but it was clear that their memories were tainted with bias and the wish to keep the events secret. A fictional serial by Marie Tirzah, 'The Cocos Island Mutiny,' was published in 1973, stimulating many soldiers to surface and give more information or correct inaccuracies.

The situation with regard to documentary evidence changed dramatically in May 1994 when the Public Record Office opened more files. Then in June 1998 I succeeded in getting at the full reports of the Field General Court Martial held on Cocos and the subsequent appeal papers, along with the Judge Advocate General's review findings and the sworn statements of the mutineers. The evidence and reports were enthralling, and brought a tremendous sense of realism to the story.

Nonetheless the key primary sources for this study are my personal and exclusive interviews with officers and men who were directly involved in the events. It would not have been possible to reconstruct the sequence of the uprising or assess its causes or importance without this evidence. The benefits of oral history are that individuals are seen in the context of the forces that shape their lives. It may be subjective and anecdotal, but it adds a dimension to a story, and, considered along with documentary sources, can contribute to a fairly accurate picture.

Ceylon became the Republic of Sri Lanka in 1972, but throughout the narrative I use the former name, which for centuries referred to the resplendent isle and which was of course still the name of the country when the mutiny occurred. I make no excuse for this usage, nor for dealing at length with the strategies and outcomes of some aspects of the Pacific War, since the rapid advance of the Japanese in the Indian Ocean and the air raids on Ceylon moulded in no small way the thinking and motivation of the overseas contingents. It certainly brought a sense of urgency on Cocos.

The Cocos Islands mutiny is an important event in the annals of the Pacific War. Those who have paid it any attention have been inclined to dismiss it as a flash in the pan, or a badly planned coup that had no chance of success. Nothing could be further from the truth, as I will attempt to show.

I am reminded of a day in 1942 when, as a young seminarian, I overheard some army prison chaplains talking in whispers. They were making arrangements to attend the execution of three Ceylonese soldiers who had been involved in a mutiny on Cocos. More than half a century later my quest nears its end, and I hope that these pages tell the true story.

PART ONE

MOONRISE

1

War Clouds Gather in Ceylon

When Great Britain declared war on Nazi Germany in September 1939, Ceylon became a belligerent in World War Two. Though a crown colony, it was by and large loyal to Britain, and the war aims of the dictators Hitler and Mussolini were universally condemned. The leader of the State Council, Sir Baron Jayatilake, assured the king and the British government of support in the war by contributions of men and materials.

British soldiers and sailors had been in Ceylon from Queen Victoria's days, and its defences were adequate for the time. The Royal Navy's East Indies Squadron had a presence in Colombo on the west coast and in Trincomalee, 161 miles away on the eastern shore. From 1937 assistance had been provided by the Royal Ceylon Navy Volunteer Reserve. The fixed land defences at Colombo consisted of coastal artillery batteries at Galle Face, Mutwal, Battenburg and Colombo harbour. In Trincomalee there were batteries at Ostenburg, Hoodstower, Diamond Hill, Elephant Point and Clappenburg.

The army comprised British and Ceylonese troops, the latter being all volunteers. There were a coastal artillery regiment of the Ceylon Garrison Artillery, an anti-aircraft regiment, a Ceylon Engineers unit, a battalion of the Ceylon Light Infantry, the Ceylon Planters Rifle Corps, Army Service Corps units and the

Army Medical Unit. At that time there were no armoured units or field artillery.[1]

In Colombo and the coastal towns there was feverish preparation against air raids when the war broke out. A blackout came into immediate force and air-raid drills were conducted. Most of the schools were obliged to close when the armed forces commandeered their buildings. The overseas broadcasts of the BBC, heard in many Ceylonese homes, had the effect of cementing the population's sense of solidarity with Britain and the empire as a whole.

This pro-British sentiment had been fostered most strongly by the flourishing education system, which inculcated the ideals of doing one's duty to God and country. Schooling in both the denominational and state schools was based on the British system, and the medium of instruction was English. Education was almost an obsession with the middle classes, and, outside Japan and the Philippines, Ceylon had the highest literacy rate in Asia, rising from 39.9 per cent to 57.8 per cent between 1921 and 1946. In the 1930s thousands of students sat for London external examinations, which were geared to a syllabus that had little relevance to the history, culture and aspirations of the people of Ceylon. Warner and Marten's *Groundwork of British History* was a bible in Ceylon classrooms.

Mr W G A Ormsby Gore, British MP and Under-Secretary of State for the Colonies, who toured the British colonial empire in 1928, remarked on 'the denaturalising, de-ruralising and intellectually and socially cramping results of the system of education, and the tyranny of an external and distant examination wholly out of touch with the needs, traditions, mental gifts and aptitudes of the people.' He condemned in no uncertain terms the 'anglicising and denationalising tendencies of academic or clerical education in the colonial schools.'[2] In Ceylon at least, this was still as true ten years later.

The imperial heritage was especially evident in some of the big schools, many of whose headmasters had studied in England and brought back with them the spirit of Eton and Rugby. One result of this intense connection was that platoons of cadets — units of the Ceylon Cadet Battalion (CCB) — were involved in regular parades and an annual camp at Diyatalawa, a health resort in the central mountainous region of Ceylon. It enhanced a school's reputation to have its platoon accredited as a reserve of the army, and this status was eagerly sought after by principals. The cadets were aged between thirteen and eighteen years. At Trinity College, Kandy, if you were not a cadet you had to join the Boy Scouts, so there was no escape from the inculcation of empire values.

There was a healthy rivalry between schools, not only in the academic field, in regard to which the results of the Cambridge Junior and Senior and the London Matriculation examinations were all-important, but also in sport. Rugby football, cricket, soccer and athletics featured prominently in intercollegiate competitions. Buddhist colleges like Nalanda and Ananda were prominent in all areas of interschool competition but, interestingly, none of the mutineers were former students of these. Nowhere was status more contested than at the senior and junior cadet camps at Diyatalawa, where British officers were in charge of training.

The achievements of Ceylonese who had volunteered for service in World War One were praised widely at school assemblies on Remembrance Day. Oscar M Abeyratne in his *History of the Ceylon Light Infantry* refers to Private Jacotine of the Ceylon Light Infantry (CLI) who was killed in action at the Battle of Lys on 13 April 1918. He quotes Sir Arthur Conan Doyle who, in his official history of the British campaign in France, wrote:

> After severe mixed fighting the attack was driven back. At 0915 hours it was renewed with greater strength, but again it made no progress. It is typical of the truly desperate spirit of the men, that when every man save one on an outpost had been killed or wounded, the survivor Private Jacotine carried on the fighting alone for twenty minutes before he was blown to pieces by a grenade.[3]

Such folklore would have been part of the background that inspired a rush of school leavers to enlist when war was declared. The Ceylon Garrison Artillery(CGA) and the CLI were volunteer corps that young bloods were keen to join. One student's decision to join the CLI was said to be that he 'knew that the Prince of Wales was the Honorary Colonel, and there was the plume of feathers on the helmet and cap with the German words "Ich Dien" (I serve).'[4] Others realised that an overseas posting was a way of seeing the world — as well as fighting for a cause. Many applied for training with the RAF in England when, in September 1940, recruitment opportunities were announced.

Ceylon prior to the war had had only one battalion of the CLI, two hundred of the thousand men being regularly stationed in Echelon Barracks in Colombo. One of the buildings was occupied by British soldiers and another by the Royal Engineers, while the Ceylonese troops occupied the upstairs sections of two other buildings. Although the members of the CLI and CGA were all volunteers, and so not subject to conscription, the oath they took did in fact commit them to serving overseas should they be called upon to do so. As civilians the CLI and CGA members had to attend at least eight parades a year and the annual camp in Diyatalawa, which lasted for seven to ten days. During the war the CLI grew to four battalions, the commanding officers being J G Van der Smagt, A Martenstyn, C P Jayawardena and Harold Van Langenberg.

The volunteer armed forces went under training according to the British military tradition, and many imbibed the spirit of British officers. Recruitment followed the British pattern, second lieutenants buying their commissions and then being able to rise to the rank of lieutenant, captain and major. Non-commissioned officers (NCOs) were appointed to their positions by their commanding officers on the basis of their general ability and leadership qualities. NCOs could rise from lance corporal (one stripe) to corporal (two stripes), sergeant (three stripes), regimental sergeant major and company sergeant major.

While it is true that there was broad support for the British war effort, there were other factors at work. Within the CLI and CGA there was some resentment over treatment of Ceylonese troops by British officers and perceived favouritism in the promotion of NCOs. In the broader political arena radical elements had been at work throughout the 1930s with an agenda far beyond that of the moderates who had secured constitutional reform — and the institution of a largely elected State Council with some executive powers — in 1931.

Collectively known as the 'leftist movement', these elements took a radical stance against British imperialism. From 1935 the LSSP (Lanka Sama Samaja Party) was under Trotskyite influence and in 1940 became a frankly Trotskyite organisation. Its members in the State Council openly challenged the war aims of the colonial administration. There was uproar when the Chief Secretary of State wanted a substantial supplementary allocation of money to buy land for an RAF base, the *Times of Ceylon* of 29 May 1940 reporting one member as saying:

> Was the RAF retreating East? They were always clever at retreating according to plan ... What the British need is not equipment or money but courage. The British are running away, retreating ... They are a declining and decrepit empire.

Their abstention from voting for war supplies led to the arrest of the leaders of the LSSP and their imprisonment on 17 June 1940.[5]

Meanwhile the influence of the LSSP had been seeping into the island's educational institutions, especially the secondary denominational schools from which the ringleaders of the Cocos mutiny came. While the doctrines of the Marxists made little impact on the country as a whole, the Western-educated youth, such as were to be found in the University College and the top forms of secondary schools, were greatly influenced by them.[6] This was evidenced by a smattering of yellow Suriya flowers among the red poppies worn by schoolboys on 11 November, Remembrance Day. There was nothing inherently political about the yellow flowers — they were sold by Buddhist organisations at this time to help local charities — but choosing to wear one at a non-Buddhist school, rather than a poppy, was a not so subtle political gesture.

The leaders of the Cocos mutiny came from four Roman Catholic and two Anglican colleges and one state school. Royal College (Colombo) was the state school; the Catholic institutions were St Joseph's College (Maradana), St Benedict's College (Kotahena), St Anthony's College (Katugastota) and St Sebastian's College (Moratuwa), while the Anglican schools were St Thomas College (Mount Lavinia) and Trinity College (Kandy).

The leader of the mutiny, Bombardier Gratien H Fernando, studied at St Thomas College. The others involved were Gunners Gerry D Anandappa (St Anthony's), Kenneth R Porritt (Royal College), Carlo Augustus Gauder (St Joseph's), G Benny de Silva (St Sebastian's), R S Hamilton (Trinity) and A Joe L Peries (St Joseph's), and Lance Bombardier Kingsley W J Diasz (St Benedict's).

Wathumullage Gratien Hubert Fernando was born in 1915. His Sinhalese Buddhist parents, Wathumullage Daniel Fernando and Porowaka Arachchige Margaret Silva, were delighted at the birth of their son, whose horoscope identified him as a person of destiny. The third child in the family, he had three brothers (Hector, Gordon and Patrick) and three sisters (Eva, Leena and Helen). His father was a respected superintendent at the Ceylon Telegraph Office.

Gratien grew up with loyalty and respect for his parents and family, and became a keen student of comparative religion. As a young adult he read widely about the new trends in Asia and the strong spirit of nationalism that was taking hold. He was fascinated by the Marxist LSSP program, but did not fall for it. He expressed distrust of the dictators and hatred for totalitarianism, and was ready to volunteer for active service when the war came.[7] It cannot be doubted, however, that like many of his generation he had mixed feelings about the turn of world events, and that he would have read the widely circulated anti-war pamphlets, some of which openly advocated sedition:

> We should not support in any way this mastery over coloured people. Rather we should seek to overthrow the system and work for the day of our freedom that must arise from the downfall of contending forces.[8]

On 2 September 1939, a day before the outbreak of war, the CLI and CGA were mobilised. The CLI men were sent to Trincomalee and to Boosa and Galle in the south. The three hundred troops who went to Trincomalee under Lieutenant Colonel C P Jayawardena occupied the esplanade in tents. From there they were sent to Ostenburg, below the eastern hill, which to that point had been manned by the newly formed CRA (Ceylon Royal Artillery). The latter went on to Diamond Hill (China Bay) in Trincomalee, where they guarded the aerodrome and especially the large oil tanks.[9] Like the British, the Ceylonese troops enjoyed the privilege of buying their chocolates, tobacco and cigarettes at duty-free rates.

Ceylon was soon to see the arrival of about a hundred thousand soldiers and air personnel from all parts of the Commonwealth in addition to the coming and going of many thousands of navy personnel. For defence purposes small groups were tactically dispersed all over the island, particularly anti-aircraft units and teams of RAF observers. Some of the untiring efforts of the leftist propaganda machine were directed at British servicemen:[10]

> You have been brought all this way to die defending Ceylon when the Ceylonese masses themselves refuse to lift a finger in its defence. We are not interested in the defence of a country which does not belong to us. This country does not belong to you either. It belongs to the Imperialist bosses who exploit us here just as they exploit you at home. They are our

common enemies. It is a shameless lie of the imperialists that this war is being fought for Democracy and Freedom, because every worker in India and Ceylon knows that there is not a trace of democracy in these countries …

Our opposition to the war of the British Imperialists against Japan and Germany does not mean that we intend to welcome the armies of the Mikado with open arms. We are not the fifth columnists of any Imperialism. To the rising sun of Japan and to the setting sun of Churchill we oppose equally our own blood red banner of revolt. It is only under this banner, the banner of the revolutionary workers of the world, that fascisms whether it be Hitler's fascism or Churchill's can be fought and done to death.

In spite of the leftist onslaught, Ceylon remained with Britain in the war, and the volunteers of the CLI and CGA had before them the highest ideals of loyalty, fidelity and courage. They also wanted to defend the reputations of their own units.

With the entry of Japan into the war, and its early successes, there was perhaps some shift in sentiment. S A Pakeman refers to a 'little anti British feeling that cropped up here and there, perhaps a feeling of sympathy with Japan … as an Asian nation, having made things very hot for the British at any rate for a time.'[11] On the other hand, there is evidence that Fernando and others were worried by news of Japanese atrocities. He stressed to his friends that the Japanese had never signed the Geneva Convention of 1929 with regard to the rules of a just war. Furthermore, to the Japanese surrender was the ultimate ignominy, and so prisoners of war would have no chance of survival.

If the leaders of the mutiny were obsessed with the notion of an impending Japanese victory, one might ask whether it was fear of capture and ill-treatment, a desire to share in the spoils or a hatred of the foreign yoke that really motivated them.

As war clouds gathered in Ceylon it was time for the first overseas contingents to leave, and there were feverish preparations at all the Ceylon batteries. The destinations were Seychelles and Cocos. The Galle Face Battery, to which many of the mutineers belonged, had two big nine-inch guns which, according to former gunner Ernie Dabrera,[12] had a range of 10,000 to 15,000 yards. The Battenburg Battery at Mutwal had nine-inch and six-inch guns with a range of 8000 to 12,000 yards. There was a friendly rivalry between these batteries, but the relationship was to sour on Cocos. It was one of the factors that led to mutiny.

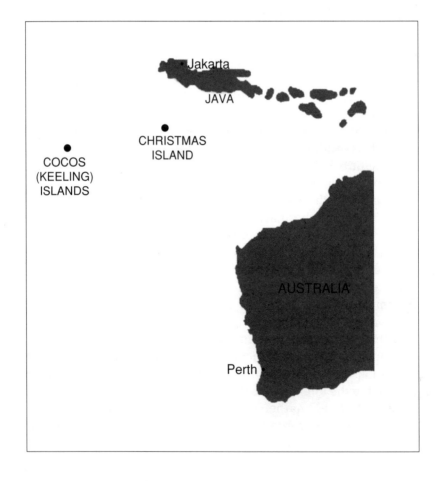

2

For King and Country

The honour of providing the first contingent of Ceylonese troops to be sent on overseas service in World War Two went to the Ceylon Garrison Artillery, and many volunteered.[1] Some went to the British colony of Seychelles, a group of about a hundred islands to the north of Madagascar,[2] and others to the Cocos (Keeling) Islands, on the other side of the Indian Ocean, all expenses borne by the Imperial Government.

Captain George Koch of the Ceylon Garrison Artillery was in charge of the first volunteers to go to Cocos, while Lieutenants R D C Jonklaas and J A Pye headed up the Ceylon Light Infantry and the Medical Corps contingents respectively. The Ceylon army headquarters posted the names of the CGA men to depart:

Captain G E G Koch, Lieutenant J A Pye, Battery Quartermaster L Wewala, Sergeants A H Hunter, D J R Kulatunga, Lance Sergeants B F Grigson, G N Antony, Bombardier B I Loyola, Lance Bombardiers F M D Dhanapala, O M D W Perera, Gunners M J Dominic, R Y Perera, A L P A de Silva, F T Joseph, K W J Dias, T Le Mercier, C A Porritt, H Morris, W R Weerasuriya, F A Gunawardena, T M Morfeth, W A Karunaratna, W W Silva, F H Bartholomeusz, J J S Fryer, D H Perera, W A F N Dias, M L C Direckze, V H Pietersz, C N Hesse, V R S Ebell, F S Sebastian, D B Kulasekera, R D C Pereira, V D D

Lieutenant (later Lieutenant Colonel) Lyn Wickramasuriya, who commanded Rowe Battery on Cocos until relieved by Captain Gardiner.

Guinan, R S Hamilton, L T A Foenander, L Le Mercier, J A Raymond. With them were the following members of the Ceylon Engineers: Lance Corporal D J Z Lampra, Sapper S Ebert, CASC Sergeant W Weerasinghe, CMC Lieutenant A de Mello, Private A D Tanner.

In August 1941 a second contingent left Ceylon on the SS *Capetown Castle*, which was carrying two thousand RAF personnel to Singapore. On this ship was Lieutenant Lyn Wickramasuriya, who had received his commission as early as March 1940. After a five-day journey alongside the *Viceroy of India* as escort, they arrived at Singapore. Then, in early September, the Cocos contingent embarked on the SS *Islander* and proceeded to its destination via the Sunda Straits and Christmas Island.

With Wickramasuriya were Lieutenant Douglas Aluwihare of the CLI and Lieutenant S K Menon of the Ceylon Army Medical Corps. Aluwihare relieved Jonklaas and Wickramasuriya relieved Pye, both of them serving under Koch, who remained as commanding officer. On 21 November 1941 another relief came from Ceylon, with Second Lieutenant Henry Stephens relieving Koch. Wickramasuriya was promoted to captain and took over the command.

Towards the end of 1941, with Japan well and truly involved in its southward thrust, there was a feverish upsurge in enlistment for overseas assignments with the Ceylon Defence Force. A contingent that was about to leave for Seychelles in early January 1942 under Major H J C Spurrier and Lieutenant Leslie Pereira met the Governor of Ceylon, Sir Andrew Caldecott, in the ballroom of Queen's House, Colombo. He inspected the troops with Brigadier J O Thurnburn, the officer commanding all troops on the island.[3] Much of the Governor's address was remembered by the men. He first addressed the matter of why they were being sent overseas:

> I want to say a word of thanks to the regiment to which you belong. Why are you going? The reason is the place to which you are going needs your protection against sea wolves in sheep's clothing. You have read quite recently in the newspapers what happened at Nauru, a peaceful island in the Pacific which was bombarded and where a great deal of damage was done by these sea wolves ...[4]
>
> I am glad to think I can rely on you to do your bit in the great fight, for the cause of liberty and decency against piracy. The life of a watch guard is an exacting and exciting one. No one could tell whether it will be your good fortune to meet these sea wolves. But let me tell you that we in Ceylon are very proud that our gunners are protecting not only our shores, but the shores of others as well.[5]

Roman Catholic soldiers recalled a service at St Philip Neri's Church in Pettah (Colombo) where the men were farewelled.[6] The Anglican troops assembled at St Paul's Church in Kynsey Road, Colombo, for a similar ceremony.[7] The names of the men in this contingent were issued by military headquarters: Battery Quartermasters K D van Sanden, C L Perera, Sergeants G R F Perera, J E V Othen, Lance Sergeants G E Melder, V C V de Zilwa, Bombardiers F A Weber, G M Dhason, V Ratnam, I V Jacob, F V Swan, Acting Bombardier G V Swan, Lance Bombardiers M T Ousmand, T S White, A Ratnayake, F R Pereira, Gunners K W G Abeywickrema, G D Anandappa, E G Anderson, A L W Amerasekera, D J Cramer, A V Collinson, A C de Alwis, E R A Dias, D A S Devanamune, Q de Silva, H O de Alwis, V N David, G B de Silva, W F Dias, S A de la Harpe, J H T E Elders, S P Fonseka, K V A Fernando, I G P Gay, C A H Gauder, M A Hopman, S G Jackson, D P Kulatunga, V F Keegel, E B Labrooy, B C La Freneis, T R Nugara, I P C Overlunde, G W Palewaandram, H R Porrit, K H D Perera, W D Rodrigo, E Raju, U A Sugathadasa, C V P Tillekeratne, S R Van Twest, H S Van Cuylenberg, C M G Walles, H G de Zilwa.

A number of these troops went on to Cocos later, among them Carlo Gauder and Benny de Silva, who were to be involved in the revolt. Some of the seeds of the revolt were to be sown in the luscious French-patois-speaking islands in which they were first stationed.

The commanding officers, Major Spurrier and Lieutenant Pereira, both of the CGA, were soon facing problems of indiscipline.[8] For their part the Ceylonese troops felt the British officers were discriminating against them and exploiting them. According to Mark Hopman, the men came to believe that there was a colour bar operating, with British soldiers given privileged and preferential treatment.[9] There can be little doubt that this had a lot to do with their unruliness. Spurrier sharpened the disaffection of his men by constantly reminding them of the achievements of the Ceylon Planters Rifle Corps in World War One. During that 'Great War to end War,' eight officers and 221 other ranks from Ceylon were sent to the Western Front, where eighty died and ninety were wounded. At the height of ill feeling in the camp a cable was sent to Major Mervyn Joseph of the Galle Face Battery in Colombo, who looked after the interests of the CGA men. The cable read: 'Major stigmatises Battery,' the reference being of course to Major Spurrier.

According to Spurrier, these Ceylonese had to learn the hard way, and he did not pull his punches. He even sent some of the gunners back to Ceylon, labelling them as 'plain stirrers.'[10] His tough line with the men followed an incident in which Ceylonese troops and Seychelles policemen were involved in a serious fight after a soccer match at the capital, Victoria, on the island of Mahé. The underlying cause of the confrontation appears to have been resentment on the part of the police over favours being bestowed on the local girls by the visitors. Gunner Harold Van Cuylenberg told me that it seemed both sides had been at fault: the policemen waylaid the gunners, who came back later with weapons and engaged them in a free-for-all. Spurrier could not condone this behaviour, but when he confined the men to barracks there was an outcry. Army Command in Ceylon was not impressed, and Spurrier decided to join the British commando force in Malaysia, where he was killed in action.

With regard to the business in hand, two six-inch guns were mounted at Seychelles and manned for six months. The contingent saw no enemy action — unless one were to include under this heading the confrontations with Major Spurrier.

A cyclone-prone group of specks in the Indian Ocean, the Cocos (Keeling) Islands are situated roughly halfway between the south-west corner of Australia and Ceylon, approximately 2300 miles west of Darwin. All but one of the twenty-seven islands lie in the horseshoe configuration typical of a coral atoll, the other — North Keeling Island — being the only part of a second, more northerly, atoll to stand above the ocean's surface. The lagoon is six miles long by five miles wide and the total land area a little more than five square miles.

Though discovered in 1609, Cocos was not inhabited until 1826, when an Englishman named Alexander Hare settled on one of the islands, bringing with him a Malay harem and slaves. He was followed the next year by Captain John Clunies-Ross, a business partner, who took up residence on another island and set about converting the natural coconut groves into plantations, bringing in further Malays to harvest the coconuts for copra. Formally claimed as a British possession in 1857, the islands were placed under the Governor of Ceylon in 1878. Control shifted to the Straits Settlements in 1886, and in that same year Cocos was granted in perpetuity to the Clunies-Ross family, the Crown reserving power to resume land and to use the territory for cable communications. In 1903 control was transferred to the British colony of Singapore, but it reverted to Ceylon during World War Two when Singapore came under Japanese domination.

Island women at work in a copra shed, 1960s.

It was to this tiny outpost that the first batch of Ceylonese troops headed off on 1 March 1941 under Koch, Jonklaas and Pye.[11] The men came principally from the middle classes. There were Sinhalese, Burghers, Tamils, Moors and Eurasians, the Burghers being descendants of Portuguese, Dutch and British settlers. The rank-and-file soldiers were educated men who spoke English fluently and had been well exposed to all the influences of Western culture. Many had good educational qualifications and some were among the cream of the products of Ceylon's colleges, where a classical education was an integral part of the system. Most were urban dwellers, although a few came from rural areas; almost all found the challenge of overseas assignment with the army too tempting to refuse.

One of the CLI men who went to Direction Island under Lieutenant Barry Jonklaas was Private Callistus Seneviratne. When speaking with me in April 1999 at the age of 83 he recalled details of his stay there. His first real task came about when the Cable and Wireless station received information that a petrol storage tank had been built secretly by the Japanese on North Keeling Island. He was in a group that went there by motorboat and destroyed it.[12]

After a three-month stay in Cocos Seneviratne was selected, with eight others, to go to Singapore in company with a group from the CGA. Upon arrival they were ordered to proceed to Kuala Lumpur to get information about the Japanese advance. There they were told the enemy was about ten miles away and heading south. Panic was spreading all around them as they withdrew. Five days before Singapore was captured the group was put on a warship but told nothing about where they were going. They ended up being nearly a month at sea as the ship took circuitous routes to avoid mines and suspected Japanese submarines. There were several alarms, and their state of apprehension was such that they either wore lifebelts or carried them all the time.

Their story gave rise to understandable fears among the troops on Cocos of what the Japanese might have in store for them. The islands in the Indian Ocean were assumed to be prime targets.

3

Horse Shoe Lagoon

With war brewing in 1939, Australian and British eyes had turned to the Cocos Islands because of their strategic importance in three respects — as an aircraft refuelling depot, as the possible site of an air base and, most crucially, as the location of a vital communications station.

During 1939 Captain P G Taylor went on a series of exploratory flights across the Indian Ocean on an Australian government mission to select and survey possible sites for air bases. He nominated West Island in the Cocos group as a suitable location. As it turned out no action was taken until 1944, when the RAF built a runway there at the expense of thousands of coconut palms.[1] Towards the end of the war hundreds of sorties were launched from it against Japanese targets.

The cable station on Direction Island dated from 1901. It was a vital element in a globe-encircling telegraphic cable system connecting all the major parts of the British Empire, completed in the following year. It was linked on the west to South Africa via Mauritius and on the east to Cottesloe in Western Australia. A telegraphic signal degenerates over distance, and the function of a relay station such as the one on Cocos was to amplify it before sending it along the next section of line. Had the cable been laid directly from South Africa to Australia the signal would have

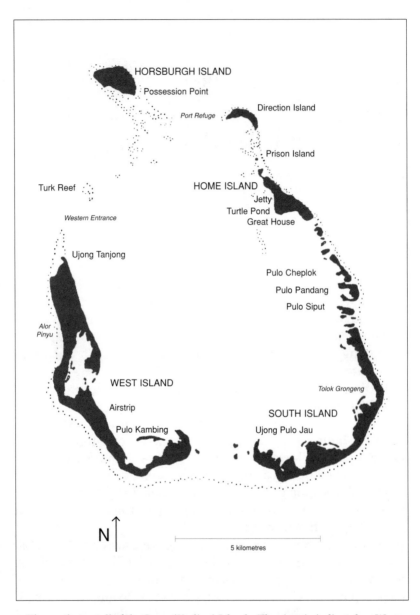

The southern atoll of the Cocos (Keeling) Islands. The airstrip indicated on West Island was built towards the end of the war.

faded too much to be recoverable.

By 1939 the station, now operated by Cable and Wireless London Ltd, had been for many years also a radio base, enabling communication with passing ships. Another development had been the installation

Cable station, Direction Island, 1965.

of a cable from Cocos to Batavia (now Jakarta), which linked to Australia via Darwin.[2] Despite developments in international radio communications, the cable remained very important in strategic terms because the signals were not susceptible to jamming or interception by an enemy, nor to the vagaries of atmospheric conditions. It was chiefly to defend the Cable and Wireless installation that the Ceylonese troops were sent to Cocos. What did they find there?

The soldiers were deployed to the two northern islands. The crescent-shaped Direction Island, where the Ceylon Light Infantry contingent was stationed, is half a mile long and two hundred yards wide, and rises about eight feet above mean sea level. Forty acres in the central section of the island were occupied by the cable station, and in 1940 twelve Europeans, most of them Australians, twenty-one Chinese and six Malays worked there. Horsburgh Island, which is a little higher and considerably larger, was the location of the Ceylon Garrison Artillery. The other main islands in the Cocos

Cable station staff quarters, Direction Island, c.1930.

group are South, West and Home, the last being where Clunies-Ross and the bulk of the population lived.[3] The simple, peaceful lifestyle of the locals was a matter of some fascination to the visitors. The tropical climate is tempered by a south-east wind that prevails throughout the year.

The only passage into the lagoon is between the two islands where the troops were stationed, at which location there is also an area of deepwater anchorage known as Port Refuge. The relatively calm waters of the lagoon are navigable only by small boats and launches.

There was no natural soil on the islands, but the coral sands had sustained a couch-like grass and a heavy growth of coconut palms before settlement. The supply of fresh water was limited. It came from twenty shallow wells on Home Island and others on South, West and Horsburgh Islands. These were three feet in diameter and six to twelve feet deep, held fifty to a hundred gallons of water and filled in half an hour to an hour. The staff of the cable station had a plant on Direction Island to supply distilled water from seawater and a roof-water storage tank with a capacity of 120,000 gallons. Even so, during the dry season there was water rationing. The station functioned with its own engines and generators.

At this time the Cocos islanders of Malay descent numbered about fourteen hundred, of whom seven hundred were children. There were relatively few residents of European descent. Copra was exported, and many of the islanders' needs were met by fishing and engaging in crafts. Their timber-framed houses were thatched with coconut palm leaf. Rice and other essential supplies came from Singapore three times a year on the Christmas Island Phosphate Company's SS *Islander*, which was chartered for the purpose.

Every attempt was made to conserve the natural resources of fish, coconut trees and coral, a limited catch of mullet and cod being netted from boats in the lagoon. Paw-paws and bananas were grown on Home Island, and some vegetables on Direction and Horsburgh. Soil brought from Christmas Island many years previously had made these exotic gardens possible. Pigs thrived.

Before the army came, Horsburgh Island was out of bounds to the villagers as it was occupied by young girls who had been sent there for a year's domestic training. They also took care of some poultry and the vegetable patch. On Home Island the islanders had a carpentry shop with a lathe, drill and power saw. There were two 28-foot motor launches and two smaller ones, and a number of barges for unloading stores from the supply ship. About 150 islanders were employed as tradesmen and labourers.

The Clunies-Ross administration did not support a doctor, but medical attention could be sought from the cable station, where an elderly practitioner was employed. There was, however, no hospital and there were no facilities for taking X-rays, among other deficiencies. Hereditary syphilis was prevalent — this was supposed to have been communicated to the Malays at some earlier time by Chinese 'houseboys' — and amoebic dysentery was endemic, as were pulmonary tuberculosis and roundworm infection. Mosquitos and copra bugs could make life miserable, and Direction Island had its quota of termites, centipedes, hunting spiders and scorpions.[4]

In this environment recreation was important. The Cable and Wireless station had two hard tennis courts, a billiard room and a library, but these were not available to the garrison. A soccer ground within the precinct was, however, made available to the troops for football, hockey and cricket. There was good swimming along the lagoon beach of Direction Island, though ear problems could result from bathing. Troops were also warned against coral abrasions, which could be very slow to heal. On Horsburgh were a hockey field and two swimming pools that were filled from roof run-off. Rainfall averaged seventy-seven inches a year, with the least fall between September and January.

Some of these observations about Cocos are taken from a 'Most Secret' report that had been made by two Australian army officers following a reconnaissance mission conducted in October–November 1940 for the Australian Department of Defence.[5] There was, understandably, considerable concern in

Australia about the defence of the cable station, and in those early days it was envisaged that Australian soldiers were likely to be deployed there. The officers went from Melbourne to Perth by air on 25 October 1940 and headed for Cocos two days later on HMAS *Perth*, which was escorting an Australian Infantry Force convoy.[6] The flag officer commanding the Australian squadron had meanwhile agreed to secure air photographs of the Cocos group with the object of producing a mosaic to supplement the existing admiralty chart.

When the *Perth* arrived off Cocos its captain, Sir P Boyce Smith, and gunnery officers offered their assessment of likely modes of attack against the cable station. Rear Admiral J G Grace, who was in command of the convoy, agreed to make a sweep round the western and southern sections of the perimeter to get a view of the target presented by Direction Island from all feasible bombardment locations. The land-based reconnaissance was carried out with assistance from S R Acton, secretary to John Clunies-Ross, in the form of water transport within the atoll.

The report prepared by the officers on their return covered a wide range of concerns. Strategic considerations were foremost, but ancillary matters were also addressed. For example they made some strong recommendations in regard to medical services. All medical, dental and hospital facilities would have to be provided by the Australian army. They went on to say: 'It is not recommended that nurses should be sent to the islands at present, owing to the isolation, restricted areas and absence of other women.'[7]

Regarding transport, no road vehicles would be needed, but it was suggested that the cable company's existing 2' 6" tramline be extended to both ends of Direction Island. The report went on: 'In comparison with troops serving on the mainland, a garrison on Cocos would suffer the additional disadvantages of isolation and congestion, and it is considered that the scale of accommodation and facilities should not be less than that provided for camps in Australia.'

It was recognised in the report that enemy action against the

Cable and Wireless station could come in any of three ways: bombardment by a raider with or without spotting aircraft, a bombing attack by a raider's aircraft, or an attack by landing parties with supporting fire from a raider. Owing to the small size of the atoll, naval bombardment could be launched from any point outside it.

The radio mast on Direction Island reached more than a hundred feet above the coconut palms and, as it was located immediately adjacent to the operating room, it was an ideal ranging mark in a locality that did not have any other conspicuous features. A bombarding vessel would almost inevitably use it for range-finding, and action would have to be taken to induce the Cable Company to remove it.

The close grouping of buildings on Direction Island also presented a logical target for low-level bombing by aircraft operating from a raider. But, while an accurate attack from the sea or air would destroy the buildings on the island, it would not necessarily destroy the cables. These passed into the lagoon through the entrance between Direction Island and Horsburgh, the latter known in code as 'Island X', and then to the beach immediately in front of the Cable and Wireless buildings. They were buried between this point and the operating room, which was approximately a hundred yards from it.

Inevitably, war preparations were influenced by memories of an attack carried out on the cable station early in World War One by the German light cruiser *Emden*. This would have devastated the station had it not been for the appearance of the Australian cruiser *Sydney*, which, having been in the close vicinity, was able to respond quickly to a distress call the staff had managed to broadcast before the transmission facilities were destroyed. Serious damage was done before the *Emden* and her landing party withdrew, but not enough to put the facility out of action for long.[8]

Accordingly, the cable company staff had located the more vital instruments in protected locations. Such a strategy could only accomplish so much, however. The most effective method of disrupting transmissions would be to cut the cables at the shore end, where they were easily seen through the clear water of the lagoon. The ends could then be towed a short distance out to sea, where they would be lost in deep water.

The army report stated that, since a demolition party must either land on Direction Island to destroy the cables or drag for them in the shallow water adjacent to it, an infantry garrison had to be located there. The task of dealing with such an eventuality could not be allotted to the personnel of an artillery garrison. From suitably located firing positions, an effective defence could be provided by two platoons armed with rifles and light automatic weapons.

It was believed that, with the balance of naval power in the Indian Ocean as it was in November 1940, a raider could not afford to undertake any operation against Cocos beyond conducting a brief raid aimed at inflicting maximum damage in the short time available before British naval forces could arrive. A relatively modest artillery installation would therefore be adequate to the task, and the officers accordingly recommended that a battery of two six-inch guns be installed. Their location would need to be determined by the two modes of attack an enemy ship might engage in.

As had been the case with the *Emden*, a landing party would approach Direction Island from the lagoon side, and this could not be reached by ships' boats without extreme risk except through the northern entrance, between Horsburgh and Direction. This region therefore had to be guarded. If an enemy's intention was, on the other hand, to bombard the installation, such an operation could be mounted from any position outside the atoll within the range of a ship's guns. This made it important for the battery to have a wide arc of fire. One factor that could be discounted in the search for an optimal gun-emplacement location was height advantage, since no site on any of the islands was higher than about ten feet.

To ease the administrative burden and to reduce the garrison's requirements in personnel, its artillery and infantry components would have to be located on the same island. The implication of this, however, was that the addition of the artillery barracks to the cable station buildings, already augmented by the barracks of the infantry garrison, would offer a fair-sized target to the enemy. This line of argument led to the observation that Horsburgh had some advantages over Direction as a location for the battery. There was a greater area available for administrative and barrack buildings, soil suitable for cultivation and a reliable water supply.

Nonetheless the inexpedience of separating the artillery and infantry was seen to be of overriding importance, and the report's recommendation was that the battery should after all be installed on Direction Island along with the infantry unit. There was the added advantage of it being the nearest practicable site to the enemy's objective and one that afforded the closest approach to an all-round arc of fire. The team chose as the most suitable site some cleared ground on the north-west extremity which covered the approach to the inner lagoon at short range by direct fire and still conformed to all the other tactical requirements.

There were, however, two further problems with locating the artillery on Direction Island. A naval direction-finding cell with four short masts was located about a hundred yards west of the site selected for the left-hand gun. While it offered no obstruction to the arc of fire of either gun, there was concern on the other hand that the battery might affect this installation. They argued, however, that should naval and military interests conflict, it was a matter of decision whether the coastal defence requirements should be paramount. Resiting the direction-finding station on Horsburgh Island was an option. The other problem was finding sufficient elevation to cover the area to the south, since a grove of coconut palms was in the way. Nonetheless there were a few rises that were sufficiently high and at the same time met requirements in regard to arc of fire.

Foundations for the actual gun emplacements would require special attention, since coral was not sufficiently robust. It would be necessary to construct a pit to contain sand for the bed of a platform. If for any reason a retaining wall for the sand could not be built, the gun platform could be anchored to steel piles driven through the coral to take the thrust.

Owing to the absence of any high ground it was recommended that a tower be built for both observation and range-finding. This tower, which was to play an important part in the mutiny, was not to be of such a height as to provide the enemy with a ranging mark, and it had to be strongly braced so as to offer a firm platform for the instruments. Given the physical character of the island, a below-ground magazine was out of the question, and they recommended the construction of one above-ground fireproof magazine with two shell stores, one for each gun. Electric lights on the north-east flank of the battery would adequately illuminate the approach to the entrance channel. The installation of anti-aircraft guns was also envisaged.

The report on Cocos and its defence was submitted to the Chief of the General Staff at army headquarters in Melbourne on 10 November 1940. Action was to follow fairly quickly, although of course the defence of the Cocos Islands was not of exclusive concern to Australia. In the end, Australia was responding to urgent requests for troops to oppose Rommel in the Middle East, and the decision was taken to deploy Ceylonese troops on Cocos. Orders were given that the recommendations of the Australian reconnaissance report were to be followed.

A few months after the report was tabled, Captain George Koch and Lieutenant J A Pye were sent from Ceylon to Cocos to install the guns.[9] The first batch of men from the Ceylon Light Infantry and the Ceylon Garrison Artillery No. 11 Coast Battery followed soon afterwards, on 1 March 1941. The new-type six-inch guns had a range of fifteen thousand yards. It seems Koch was well aware that they did not provide adequate defence against enemy raiders armed with long-range guns, but that they could be used to advantage at short range.

A major deviation from the recommendations of the report was the decision to site the battery on Horsburgh. According to Koch, this was to give the guns a better field of fire against approaching battleships. In August 1941 he decided that the hundred-foot wireless mast on Direction Island should be dismantled because of its potential as a ranging point for warships, just as the report had suggested. When he instructed the manager of the Cable and Wireless station to take it down, this was done without any question.

Lieutenant Lyn Wickramasuriya was drafted with about fifty other gunners, infantrymen and signalmen — personnel of the Army Service Corps, Ceylon Engineers and Ceylon Light Infantry — to relieve the servicemen who had been on Cocos from March 1941. The contingent left Ceylon in August of that year on the SS *Cape Town Castle*, which was carrying RAF personnel to Singapore. For the second leg of their voyage, the men embarked on the *Somawathie*. The journey was far from peaceful, as German submarines were prowling the Indian Ocean, and all on board were often in a high state of alertness.

In addition to being commissioned by the Ceylon defence force governor, Captain Wickramasuriya and the other officers who served overseas were granted emergency war commissions in the British army — 'King's Commissions.' This goes some way towards accounting for the unusual situation on Cocos — when Koch, then Wickramasuriya, then Gardiner was the officer commanding the troops, each of them a mere captain, he was also commander of the region, there being no superior military officers in the area. Furthermore, he had all the codes and ciphers entrusted to him. The commander's authority over the civilian staff of the Cable and Wireless station and the Malay inhabitants was a sore point with some. And this state of affairs was also to have great importance in the aftermath of the mutiny.

It was a critical time when Captain Wickramasuriya took over. He had been informed that second degree alertness had been ordered for most of the RAF and RAAF stations in Malaya. The troops he and his men had relieved had seen no action at all, but that might well change. Before long he was warned via a ciphered signal from the British War Office in London that, as war with Japan was imminent, a strict blackout was to be imposed in the zone, along with other security precautions.

Two days after this instruction was sent, on 6 December 1941, an Australian airman, Flight Lieutenant J C Ramshaw, was piloting a Lockheed Hudson over the South China Sea when he saw a Japanese convoy of thirty-five ships, twenty-two of them transports with thousands of soldiers lining their decks.[10] As it was heading for the east coast of Malaya, he radioed back to the RAAF station at Kotabaru for permission to shadow it. This was refused. What he was not told was that the British Commander-in-Chief of Allied forces in the Far East, Air Chief Marshal Sir Robert Brooke-Popham, had ordered that no attack was to be made against any Japanese invasion force heading for Malaya or Thailand.

Within forty-eight hours the Japanese troops had landed on the Malayan coast and taken the British and Australian defenders by surprise. The Pacific War had started.[11]

4

The Rising Sun

It was February 1942, and pressure was building on the commander of Ceylonese troops in the Cocos Islands, Captain Lyn Wickramasuriya. The Japanese had taken Singapore, Darwin had been attacked and he had received instructions from Army Command in Singapore that all ships moving into the vicinity of Cocos were to be attacked and destroyed if they did not identify themselves.

On 10 February he saw from the sixty-foot observation post a merchant ship about fifteen miles away. As he put aside his range-finding instruments and looked once again at the broad scene, he was startled to see three destroyers with black rings on their funnels. This appeared to be shaping up as an encounter with the enemy. Then came an even bigger surprise: 'I couldn't believe it — a huge aircraft carrier was cruising in at about ten knots, … and was not more than five hundred yards from the big guns on Cocos.'

There had been no advice from Singapore regarding Allied shipping, so things were not looking good. He ordered the signaller to challenge the aircraft carrier, which was decked with a vice-admiral's flag. The five ships turned course, raced off for about five hundred yards and stopped. 'My gunners were awaiting orders from me to fire, but I hesitated,' said

Wickramasuriya. The aircraft carrier responded with the signal 'GBC', which meant nothing to him. In fact it was the British naval recognition signal for the day, but he had not been advised of it. Immediately he sent a naval cipher to army headquarters in Singapore inquiring whether part of the Japanese fleet might be in the Indian Ocean. To the commander's relief a reply came from the ship: 'We are a British aircraft carrier. We shall remain here overnight.' A few hours later Singapore Army Command replied: 'They are British ships. Sorry we forgot to tell you. Thanks.'[1] They might have added: 'Hope you haven't sunk any of them.'

A few weeks later, on 3 March, a Japanese aircraft flew over the atoll. Since it was by no means the first enemy plane to visit Cocos, it wasn't paid much attention. But things began to look very different late that afternoon when Wickramasuriya saw some vessels west of Port Refuge: two Japanese destroyers and a submarine were approaching. Feeling very much alone as he pondered the situation, he was not helped by the fact that night was falling and visibility was poor. Then it happened: a light cruiser that had joined the other vessels began to bombard Direction Island from about a thousand yards off. As it would have been dangerous to return fire with the six-inch guns on Horsburgh, he decided that no action was the right action and ordered that there was to be no response from the battery or the infantry unless Japanese troops attempted to land. The bombardment of twenty rounds lasted for fifteen minutes. Lieutenant Stephens, Wickramasuriya's deputy, and Gunner Bob Harvie observed all this with some concern that their commander was doing nothing.

Meanwhile Wickramasuriya had another serious matter on his mind. The intelligence ciphers of the British government and the British navy, the interdepartmental codes and the Anglo-Dutch codes were in the commanding officer's hands. To destroy or not to destroy was the question. He made his decision, and with the help of the medical orderlies rushed the heavy intelligence and cipher books to the shrubs and buried them. Their destruction would have meant the total isolation of the contingent.

The initial results of the Japanese naval attack were that the servants' quarters on Direction Island were set on fire, as were the bonfires that were kept in readiness to burn the secret documents if there was an enemy landing. Yet another fire was started by the cat of an overanxious cook, which knocked over a kerosene oil lamp in a storage shed. The smoke and the fire convinced the Japanese that the communications station had been destroyed. In fact, while minor damage was inflicted on some instruments, all the vital cables were untouched.[2]

Lieutenant Henry Stephens, second in command on Cocos, another target of the mutineers.

With the consent of the British Admiralty, Wickramasuriya then foisted on the enemy one of World War Two's most successful bluffs. The Cable and Wireless station was ordered to send a message in plain language that the Cocos facility had been permanently put out of action.[3] The Japanese intercepted the signal and accepted it at face value. The next day Radio Tokyo announced: 'Last night our naval forces operating in the Indian Ocean attacked the island of Cocos and split it in two.' From then on Cocos was always referred to in communications by various code names in order to disguise its identity. It was fortunate that the shelling of Direction Island did not ignite a holocaust — the island held a large stock of aviation spirit on behalf of the Royal Netherlands Air Force. Five thousand gallons were stored close to the wireless station headquarters and the soldiers' barracks.

A few weeks later all men were on alert following another alarm, but the approaching aircraft turned out to be a Catalina flying boat of the Dutch Air Force, one of the last to leave Java. It flew around for a few minutes and then landed in the calm waters off Direction Island. Summoned under escort, the captain of the Catalina said: 'I am Captain Mueller of the Royal

Netherlands Navy, and this is Flight Lieutenant Wilholt of the Royal Netherlands Air Force.' He explained that their plane, which had sixty-six people on board, was the last to leave before Batavia fell. They were proceeding to Sydney, and needed a thousand gallons of aviation fuel from the stock being held on Cocos for the Netherlands Government.

Just as Mueller was signing a receipt on behalf of Queen Wilhelmina, Wickramasuriya received a message from Australia that Japanese naval units were in the seas north of Cocos. It was thought best that the Catalina take off immediately, but in attempting to do so it struck a coral reef and began to sink. Mueller wanted to destroy the plane but army engineers and technicians were able to repair it, and soon it was on its way to Sydney.

In March 1942 Captain Wickramasuriya was relieved by Captain George Gardiner of the CGA, the latter having sought an overseas posting. Stephens was to continue as deputy. A British citizen who had obtained his commission in Ceylon, Gardiner resided in Havelock Town, a fashionable district within

Captain George Gardiner, against whom the mutiny was directed.

Colombo. He was a chartered accountant with a leading business, and his marriage to Nancy Gilliat, just a few months before the outbreak of war, had been a social event to which the *Times of Ceylon*, a newspaper targeted at Englishmen, gave much publicity. Some wondered at the recently married Gardiner opting to serve overseas, and he later admitted that what prompted his move was the difficult situation he was confronting in his marriage.

When Wickramasuriya handed over his command, he gave Gardiner a few words of advice on how to treat Ceylonese soldiers. He had long observed Lieutenant Stephens's manner of interacting with the men, and his early impressions were that Gardiner's attitude was similar. To put it bluntly, both were tainted with an unusually virulent strain of racism.

Mutiny leader Bombardier Gratien Fernando.

According to some who knew him, Stephens was an enigma. His outrageous jibes at his own Burgher, Sinhalese and Tamil friends were both inexplicable and intolerable. He had grown up in Ceylon's hill country and later in the low-country rubber district of Horana, where his Eurasian father, Alick Stephens, and his mother, Olga Smith, were the cream of the planting society of that day.[4] Young Henry and his elder brother Alick Junior (known as Jumbo) attended St Joseph's College in Maradana (Colombo), where they were boarded. Living in the same school hostel was Carlo Augustus Gauder, who was later to come into a collision course with his former boarding mate. Stephens flaunted his English ancestry even during his school days. He gained his military commission at the young age of nineteen.

On Cocos, Stephens had no answer to Bombardier Gratien Fernando's arguments that the early British administration of Ceylon had changed the property laws so as to deny land title to Sinhalese and allow British settlers to flock into the country and grab land for planting. The point was not lost that Stephens had benefited greatly from this act of theft.

Gardiner was a disciplinarian bordering on being a martinet, but that judgement needs to be given some context. In the first place it must be said that he took his command seriously. It was his responsibility to have a disciplined unit ready to respond to whatever situations might confront it, and a number of factors were combining to make the troops somewhat restless. In the first place there was the isolation, of which many were acutely conscious. The lack of fresh vegetables was so serious as to give rise to concerns about beri-beri. Since there were no sanitary provisions the ground was fouled, the water was polluted and in consequence illness among the troops was not infrequent. The fact that the officers monopolised some of the sporting facilities did not go unnoticed. And some of the men complained that there were 'no women' — though sales of perfume and handkerchiefs at the troops' canteen[5] suggest that some of the more enterprising found this to be not completely true.

With Captain Gardiner settled in as commander, tensions began to run high. There was a serious breakdown in communication between officers and men, especially where the gunners were concerned, and the attitudes of young bloods in the batteries curdled into the formation of Galle Face and Battenburg factions. While reasons for the unrest could be readily discerned in the local dynamics, it was being fuelled by an external factor — what the Sri Lankan writer Somasiri Devendra called 'the faint crackle broadcasts from Japanese-held Singapore calling our brothers and sisters in India and Ceylon.'[6]

Reception was much better on Cocos. Not only were the Japanese-operated Radio Manila and the 'Tokyo Rose' broadcasts received loud and clear on the atoll, they were exerting a fascination over many of the troops. No censorship or regulation discouraged the men from tuning in to the broadcasts; indeed, as Lucian Koch remembers: 'The camp woke up each morning at 05.30 hours to the music of "There's no Place like Home" on the radio beamed across by the Japanese ... and ending with "Americans Go Home."' They brought a message of freedom to Asians who would accept the challenge of a grand Asian vision.

In January 1942, a month after the attack on Pearl Harbor, General Hideki Tojo[7] made his first policy speech as Prime Minister, which was reported in English on short-wave radio:

> The cardinal point in the war of Greater East Asia, which our empire is now prosecuting, is to secure strategic bases in Greater East Asia, and to bring regions with important

resources under Japan's control, thereby augmenting our fighting power and, in close co-operation with Germany and Italy, to extend increasingly vigorous operations, and fight on until the United States and British Empire are brought to their knees.[8]

The notion of a 'Greater East Asia Co-Prosperity Sphere' was proclaimed as Japan's military achievements began to astound the world. The nation's rulers had the vision of a new Asia, within which countries to the south would provide raw materials and food while Manchuria and northern China would be the source of basic materials for heavy industry. The plan saw the Japanese Empire as a manifestation of 'morality', its special characteristic being the propagation of the 'Imperial way.'[9] It strove for the achievement of the principles of 'Hakko Ichiu' (Making the world one big family) and 'Kodo' (Loyalty to the Emperor). Only by fostering the power of the empire could East Asia shake off the yoke of Europe and America and return to its original state of independence and co-prosperity. Thus would its countries and peoples be enabled to develop their respective abilities in peaceful cooperation and secure livelihood.

One Ceylonese soldier who listened very intently to these broadcasts was Bombardier Gratien Fernando. He was enthralled by the plan, and often discussed it with others in the camp at Cocos. He was also stirred by the attacks on the colonial powers — notably including Australia — that perpetuated racist policies. Well known for his anti-white sentiments, Fernando was among those who suspected that for the white man the Asian soldier was only cannon fodder, as the broadcasts were suggesting.

The co-prosperity plan envisaged the states, citizens and resources of the Pacific, Central Asia and the Indian Ocean being formed into one general union, established as an autonomous zone of 'peaceful living and common prosperity of the peoples of the nations of East Asia.' The area included Japan, Manchuria, North China, the lower Yangtze River and the Russian maritime provinces, which were to form the nucleus of the East Asiatic

Union. As leader of this union, the Japanese Empire had a duty to emancipate East Siberia, the rest of China, Indochina, the South Seas, Australia and India. Burma was to be captured as a flank for the conquered countries and as a source of rice and oil.

Of great interest to the troops was the notion that the Ceylon Governor-General was to be a Japanese appointee in control of Ceylon, the southern part of India and certain islands in the Indian Ocean.[10] The East Indies, British Borneo, Labuan, Sarawak, Brunei, Cocos (Keeling) Islands, Christmas Island, the Andamans, Nicobars and Portuguese Timor were to be purchased.

Radio propaganda about this ambitious plan was intensified after the fall of Singapore, a victory widely publicised in both radio and print. A report in the Japanese newspaper *Asahi Shimbun* of 16 February 1942 typified Japan's elation:

> To seize Singapore island in as little time as three days could only have been done by a Japanese army … Japan is the sun that shines for world peace. Those who bathe in the sun will grow and those who resist it will have no alternative but ruin. I solemnly declare that with the fall of Singapore the general situation of the war has been decided. The ultimate victory will be ours.

In a telegram of congratulations to Tokyo, the Japanese commander of occupation forces in Vietnam said: 'I pray that we may without delay accomplish the second stage, the capture of Australia and Colombo.'[11]

About six months after the start of the war Japanese radio propaganda reached its zenith in terms of volume of broadcasts. As Lucy Meo has pointed out, 'it was essentially a tactical weapon, and a great deal of it was intended to pave the way for the Japanese forces in Asian countries and at the same time fan the apprehension of European listeners.'[12]

It was a crucial time for the British Empire in the East. India and Ceylon, not least the overseas volunteers in Seychelles and

Cocos, followed with amazement and some fear the achievements of General Tomoyuki Yamashita's well-trained and all-conquering XXV Japanese army. Years later Captain Wickramasuriya recalled the impact of the Singapore debacle on the morale of officers and men as Radio Manila went on telling and retelling the story, which was indeed astonishing. As H P Willmott put it, 'a mere eleven Japanese divisions overran the whole of South East Asia, defeating and in the process humiliating much larger forces than themselves.'[13]

The Japanese wasted no time in giving Singapore a new name, Syonam, 'the light of the East.' Tokyo Rose made much of this while she seduced her listeners with Western pop music. I remember well the impact these broadcasts had on me as a teenager in Ceylon.

Taking his cue from the radio propaganda, Fernando kept insisting that the Japanese could arrive at any time. He was familiar with the chant 'We do not execute at sunset, but at sunrise' and impressed by the story that the troops landed in Malaya with a month's supply of ammunition but only a week's rations, and were expected to gather the rest of their food off the country.

Australia and New Zealand were included in the Japanese plan from the earliest days. It was during the Japanese drive on Singapore that Tokyo tried to sound out the Australian attitude to its plan for the region: 'All that Japan asks is that Australia sever its ties with Britain and cease resistance against Japan, and that Australia co-operate with Japan in the construction of the sphere of common prosperity.'[14] This broadcast was repeated on 16 February, after Singapore had fallen. Tojo wanted Australia and New Zealand 'to avoid a useless war, cease to depend on Britain and America and seek happiness in trying to understand Japan's real intentions and take a fair and just attitude.'

The tone changed as the campaign continued: 'Australians, we warn you! The Americans are there only for show and are not much for the two million directed against you. This is the voice of your enemy warning you …' 'The doom of Australia is sealed.

There is no way left for her but to be destroyed by Japan ...'[15] '[Australia will] have to face a terrific onslaught by the massed might of Nippon.'[16] Messages like these found fertile soil in Australia, where fear of the Asian hordes was part of the national inheritance.[17]

Listening to the broadcasts did have its lighter moments, however. Lucy Meo recalls some of the howlers:

> The remaining planes took to their heels. (Tokyo, August 1943)
>
> With the exception of the dead, all in the exchange ships were in the best of spirits. (Tokyo, October 1943)
>
> We are all anxiously awaiting brilliant results. (Singapore)
>
> Britain is worried by a scarcity of silk. The British Government contemplates taming the wild silk worms of Liberia ... but first they must be domesticated.
>
> Japanese men look furious, but they are sweet inside. (Tokyo, 7 July 1944).

In January 1942 Tokyo Radio propaganda directly aimed at promoting revolt in India and Ceylon.[18] Tojo declared as a Japanese aim the elimination of British influence in India, but mentioned nothing of what the torturers of the dreaded Kempei-Tai might do in the process. Snippets of information had brought some awareness of Japanese atrocities to the Cocos camps, and Kempei-Tai methods became a talking point — the water treatment, burning, electric shocks, knee-spread, suspension, flogging and being forced to kneel on a sharp instrument.[19] Fernando took all this as grist to his own mill: just as the Japanese onslaught offered hope to Asians, it was also to be feared. But in embracing 'Asia for the Asiatics' it seems he was unable to see what was in the soul of Japanese propaganda.

Of course not all Asians were seduced by the Japanese blandishments. Rabindranath Tagore rejected them utterly,[20] and Pandit Jawaharlal Nehru declared that 'India was anti-British and not Pro-Jap' as he urged Indian opposition to Japan.[21]

Lucy Meo explains that propaganda-making is dependent for its success not only on the propagandists' understanding of the art, but on their knowing the enemy country and its people, and what is influencing them at a given moment.

> In most of these respects the Japanese propagandists were at a disadvantage. If this had not been so, there is no knowing with what greater benefit to themselves the propagandists (and Japan itself) could have turned such a powerful slogan as 'Asia for the Asiatics' ...[22]

The main reason for the seeming ineffectiveness of the later Japanese broadcasts was, she says, that after the first six months of victories the Japanese were steadily losing the war: 'You can hardly win a war on radio when you are losing it on the battlefields.'[23]

And there was another huge factor at work: 'the observed behaviour of Japanese in Asia'.[24]

5

Waves of the Indian Ocean

Any sense among Ceylonese that they were well insulated from the conflicts of World War Two was dissipated over a few weeks early in 1942. The Japanese emerged from the remote China Sea firstly to capture Singapore and then, much more ominously, to take over the Andaman and Nicobar islands. The shock to Australia had come even more rapidly, the fall of Singapore being followed just a few days later by an aerial attack on Darwin involving seventy-eight Japanese bombers escorted by twenty-seven fighters.

Winston Churchill called the loss of Singapore, on 15 February 1942, the 'worst disaster and largest capitulation in British history.'[1] It was not, however, Britain's first humiliation at the hands of the Japanese. Hong Kong was not nearly as significant strategically, and it was far from the Indian Ocean; nonetheless Lieutenant Henry Stephens remembered animated discussions on the threat to the Far East colony between Bombardier Gratien Fernando and Gunner Gerry Anandappa in the recreation room at Cocos. It was the autumn of 1941, the Japanese 38th Division was massed on the Kowloon waterfront of Hong Kong and Britain was responding to the situation with customary hauteur. An official communique from Government House stated:

This colony is not only strong enough to resist all attempts at invasion, but all the resources of the British Empire, of the United States of America and of the Republic of China are behind us ... Those who have sought peace can rest assured that there will never be any surrender to the Japanese.

Across the water on Kowloon Colonel Tanaka was closer to the truth when he said: 'The Hong Kong campaign will be a historic one ...'[2] Meanwhile Japanese loudspeakers broadcast the routine message: 'Give up and the Japanese will protect you. Trust in the kindness of the Japanese Army.' The response of Hong Kong's Governor, Sir Mark Young, was to urge his defenders: 'Fight on. Hold fast for King and Empire. God bless you all in this your finest hour.' Within the thirty-one square miles of Hong Kong the British, Canadian and Indian defenders did hold fast — for a while. One British soldier wrote:

Behind the mountains grim and bare
Like a wounded lion we lay,
Oh that the Mother Lion was there
To help defend her peaceful lair
And win the hard fought day.[3]

The battle for Hong Kong saw two thousand British soldiers killed along with four thousand civilians. Jan Morris has noted that this was the first armed conflict ever between the Japanese and the British.

Of course Singapore would be different: it was well defended against attack from any direction. Except, as it turned out, the north. By the simple expedient of cutting off the island's water supply at Johore, General Yamashita rendered Singapore indefensible. The Singapore debacle exacted a high price in men and materials, the cost to Australia alone being 1789 men killed, 1306 wounded and 15,395 captured, of whom nearly one-third were to perish in captivity.

In February 1942, after further devastating Japanese advances,

Admiral Geoffrey Layton with Ceylon Governor Sir Andrew Caldecott and Sir John Kotelawala, April 1940.

the defence of Ceylon had assumed great importance in the mind of the British prime minister. On 27 March, in a note to the Chiefs of Staff Committee, he said: 'Nothing must be taken from Ceylon which endangers the naval base or deters the fleet from using it.'[4] Admiral Geoffrey Layton had meanwhile visited Ceylon and reported on 'the state of unreadiness and unjustified complacency in all circles.' A few weeks later Churchill appointed the admiral as Supreme Commander of All Forces and Civil Authorities in Ceylon.

The garrison of Ceylon at that time consisted of the 34th Indian Division. This comprised one Ceylonese and two Indian brigades, with only one battery of field artillery; there were 116 anti-aircraft guns. One brigade group of the 70th British Division was expected to arrive in mid-March.

It happened that three Australian divisions were at the time returning from the Middle East to shore up Australia's defences against the Japanese advance, and Prime Minister John Curtin was asked to provide some of those soldiers to reinforce Ceylon's defences until the British brigade came. Though initially reluctant to agree, he advised Churchill early in March that two brigade groups of the 6th Division would be made available. Curtin wanted an assurance of adequate air support in Ceylon and a proper escort to Australian waters after their tour of duty. The 16th and 17th Brigades duly landed in Ceylon during March and in the end remained for sixteen weeks rather than the few weeks envisaged.[5]

General Wavell, the commander-in-chief (CIC) of Far East forces, was livid. It was his conviction, one that he had conveyed to the Chiefs of Staff on 28 February, that Ceylon could only be saved by more naval and air units.[6] Yet all that was happening was that more army contingents were being brought to the island. The British War Cabinet however insisted that the defence of the naval bases in Ceylon by ground troops must have priority.[7]

Admiral Layton took over the Ceylon Command on 15 March 1942. He was a submarine expert who had temporarily succeeded Sir Tom Phillips as CIC Far Eastern Fleet when Admiral Phillips was lost in HMS *Prince of Wales* off Malaya.[8] Layton was a colourful and flamboyant figure who I met in the most improbable of places: the sanctuary of a Catholic church. The admiral and his entourage were the unwilling guests of a rather eccentric French priest, Fr L M V Thomas, whose long sermon in the parish church of Veliveriya in Ceylon irritated the navy man to the point that he was heard to utter some very spicy naval epithets under his breath. Stephen Roskill has told the story of how the Ceylon Defence Commissioner, Sir Oliver Goonetilleke, complained to the governor that Layton had called him a 'black bastard'. The governor replied: 'That is nothing to what he calls me.'[9] Layton was asked to take all the measures necessary to keep Ceylon and to ensure the proper coordination of military and civil resources. The new CIC soon informed Churchill that he had succeeded in boosting morale in the country among both the civilian population and the military.

On 3 March 1942 the HMS *Kelantan* set off from Colombo for Cocos with Captain George Gardiner of the CGA and Lieutenant Henry de Sylva of the CLI plus a complement of troops. They were to relieve Captain Wickramasuriya and Lieutenant Aluwihare. The level of tension and apprehension on the Indian Ocean journey may be gauged from the somewhat laconic notes of Corporal Lucian P Koch of the Medical Corps:

> While leaving Colombo harbour at dusk, we were ordered back and left later in deep darkness as our destination was being shelled by the Japanese.[10] While at sea the ship's crew

spotted a submarine and gave a warning signal. The submarine surfaced and signalled in code that it was a USA submarine on patrol.

Koch said that on 10 March at 5.20 a.m. they saw a group of islands, and by 7.30 four large sailing boats had come alongside the ship and the troops began to disembark.

> At 8.30 we were at the pier of Horsburgh Island, which was the second largest in the Cocos basin and nearest to the deep part of the Indian Ocean.[11] The crew consisted of Capt Gardiner of the CGA, one BQMS, two Sergeants V Ratnam and O M D W Perera, two bombardiers and the rest were gunmen. There was also one Sergeant and a Private from the CASC, one Corporal [De Mello of the Medical Corps], one Sapper from the Ceylon Engineers and myself.

With the Japanese supremely confident after a series of stunning victories on land and sea, Vice-Admiral Chuichi Nagumo, who was in command of the Japanese armada, had sailed into the Indian Ocean.[12] The Japanese plan was to seize Ceylon after a westward offensive across the Indian Ocean. Oil supplies from the Persian Gulf were to be cut, and eventually there would be a link-up with the Axis powers in Egypt.[13] The taking of Ceylon by Japan was anticipated also on the other side of the globe by German Grand Admiral Erich Raeder, commander of the German navy. In a message to Hitler on 13 February 1942 he said:

> Japan plans to protect her front in the Indian Ocean by capturing the key position of Ceylon, and she also plans to gain control of the sea in that area by means of superior naval forces. Fifteen Japanese submarines are at this moment operating in the Bay of Bengal, in the waters of Ceylon and in the Straits, on both sides of Sumatra and Java. Once Japanese battleships, aircraft carriers, submarines and the Japanese naval air force are based in Ceylon, the British will be forced

to resort to heavily escorted convoys, if they desire to maintain communication with India and the Near East ...[14]

British naval forces had already taken a battering. Most notably, the battleship *Prince of Wales,* which Churchill had told Stalin could destroy any Japanese ship, had been sunk along with the battle cruiser *Repulse.* He admitted that 'over all this vast expanse of waters Japan was supreme, and we everywhere were weak and naked.'[15] In Vice-Admiral Nagumo's view, the strategic importance of Ceylon, even to the less grandiose Japanese aim of annihilating the British Far Eastern Fleet, was beyond question. It must be noted, however, that the Japanese thrust into the Indian Ocean did not have complete support within its own ranks. One of the most brilliant air tacticians of the age, Mitsuo Fuchida, who directed the carrier task force under Nagumo, saw the priorities as lying elsewhere, and argued against the diversion of energies into the Indian Ocean. He believed targets there, including Ceylon, could easily have been handled with one aircraft carrier, and maintained that the strength of the carrier task force should have been concentrated on defeating the United States fleet.

On 23 March 1942 Admiral Sir James Somerville was on his way to Colombo when Japanese forces occupied the Andaman Islands. These lie in the Bay of Bengal about 120 miles west of the southern part of Burma and 600 miles from India. This action came as no surprise, as the capital, Port Blair, had been bombed by Japanese planes a month earlier, merchant shipping in the Bay of Bengal had been sunk and there had been many reconnaissance flights over the islands. Indeed so certain did invasion seem that Allied forces had been withdrawn a few days before it took place. Japanese occupation of the Andaman brought the whole of the east coast of India and Ceylon within two and a half hours' bombing range of a Japanese land base.[16] Meanwhile, on Cocos, Bombardier Fernando was losing no opportunities to brief his colleagues on the successes of Japan's onslaught, which he did with remarkable intensity.

A definite pattern was emerging: it now seemed certain that the Japanese were intent on capturing most of the islands in the Indian Ocean. Christmas Island had been bombed on 4 March and captured eight days later. This was after Indian soldiers from the Hong Kong and Singapore Artillery had mutinied and killed the British commanding officer, Lieutenant Senior.[17] Thirty-three men and four NCOs raised the white flag of surrender to the Japanese when they found that no Allied relief was forthcoming.[18]

This turn of events was, however, exceptional. According to Lawrence James, 'over 3,700,000 Indian troops served with the Allied forces during the Second World War. It was a splendid response, which seemed to affirm the old soldier's faith that the warrior classes of Indian society had been untouched by twenty years of nationalist agitation.'[19] Churchill, he said, had been troubled by fears that political agitation might turn Indian soldiers against Britain, but these anxieties proved groundless: in spite of efforts by nationalists to subvert troops, there were hardly any outbreaks of disloyalty.

The Japanese were more than pleased with the progress of the war. Commenting on the occupation of the Andamans and the smaller Nicobar group to the south, a Japanese news agency stated:

> The capture of the islands has placed the Japanese armed forces within dangerous striking distance of the vital British military bases of Calcutta, Madras and Ceylon. Utilisation of the islands as a naval and air base for extensive forays would permit the Japanese forces to wreak havoc on British communications with India and Australia.[20]

Admiral Somerville arrived in Colombo on 24 March and began to assemble a British Eastern Fleet, capital ships having been withdrawn already from the Atlantic and Mediterranean and sent east. The fleet had the flagship *Warspite*, four slow old poorly protected battleships (*Royal Sovereign, Ramilles, Revenge* and *Resolution*), two modern aircraft carriers (*Formidable* and *Indomitable*), one small elderly carrier (*Hermes*) and nine cruisers, including the modern *Cornwall* and *Dorsetshire*. There were sixteen destroyers — a mixed lot — and seven submarines.

Somerville had been in Ceylon scarcely any time before he began to move the Eastern Fleet away and concentrate it near Adu Atoll, a coral island lagoon in the Maldive Islands six hundred miles south-south-west of Ceylon in the north Indian Ocean.[21] He had been under Admiralty instructions to move the fleet away if an enemy air attack appeared imminent, and this now seemed to be the situation. The Japanese had landed in the Andamans just the day before his arrival in Ceylon, which was therefore now well within striking distance of the enemy's bombers. Furthermore a powerful Japanese armada was lurking in the ocean.

Remaining in Colombo harbour for the time being were forty-eight ships of the East Indies Fleet under their commander-in-chief, Vice-Admiral Sir Geoffrey Arbuthnot.

Somerville decided to meet Nagumo's thrust by forming his fleet into two battle divisions as well as by taking it to a secret base. From his flagship *Warspite*, with Rear Admiral Danckwerts as chief of staff and Rear Admiral Boyd as Rear Admiral Aircraft Carriers, Somerville commanded the carriers *Indomitable* and *Formidable*, the cruisers *Dorsetshire* and *Cornwall*, the old light cruisers *Emerald* and *Enterprise* and six destroyers.[22] Vice-Admiral A V Willis, in the 21-knot battleship *Resolution*, commanded the *Revenge*, *Ramilles* and *Royal Sovereign* and the old aircraft carrier *Hermes*. As G Hermon Gill has said, 'the Eastern fleet, still in process of formation and at best an ill-balanced force, lacking in tactical exercising, was materially inferior to what the Japanese could oppose to it.'[23] Vice-Admiral Nagumo had five aircraft carriers — *Akagi*, *Hirya*, *Soryu*, *Shokaku* and *Kaikaku* — which were escorted by four fast battleships, three cruisers and twelve destroyers. The British carrier-borne aircraft were antiquated, while the five Japanese aircraft carriers had a complement of two hundred light bombers and a hundred fighters, all of them effective, modern planes.

Vice-Admiral Nagumo had no definite information about Allied air strength in the region, and believed that he might have to face more than three hundred Royal Air Force planes. Had he known the actual count was less than one-third of that, he might have taken a much bolder approach to pursuing the Japanese Indian Ocean campaign. Furthermore the RAF aircraft consisted of the old slow-moving Blenheims and the Wildebeests ('flying coffins'), with a few Catalina flying boats and sixty fighters — RAF Hurricanes and Fleet Air Arm Fulmar fighter reconnaissance planes. These included thirty-six Hurricanes that had been diverted to Ceylon by Admiral Layton.

The most recent batch of CGA and CLI men to arrive on Cocos had observed urgent work being done to prepare Ceylon to meet the Japanese advance. There was feverish construction of airfields at the Colombo Racecourse, Ratmalana, Katunayake, Vavuniya, Kankesanturai, Sigiriya, China Bay, Kekirawa, Hingurangoda and Koggala (Galle). Australians, New Zealanders, Canadians, South Africans and Rhodesians in a Ceylon-based squadron awaited the Japanese raids. Some of these airmen had taken part in the Battle of Britain in 1940. Air Vice-Marshal John D'Albiac prepared the air forces while Layton went all out to install anti-aircraft and radar equipment.

All this activity reflected an accurate reading of Japanese intentions. Nagumo realised that if the British Far Eastern Fleet was to be annihilated, a useful Indian Ocean base was necessary. Professor S A Pakeman, who I interviewed in Ceylon in 1948, found it difficult to understand 'why the Japanese did not bother to take over Cocos Keeling Island, which would have been a perfectly simple matter.'[24] The atoll could have been seized and held by just a few men, and would have provided an adequate base for their purposes. He argued that eventually the Japanese did not attempt anything more because, following their failure to locate the British fleet, a more conservative strategy supervened and their military efforts were concentrated in the Pacific.

H P Willmott has argued that, had Japan instead risked everything on a major military and land effort in the Indian

Ocean, both Britain and the United States of America might well have been forced out of the war. The Japanese would have needed significant land forces to secure Ceylon, but India could have been bypassed, since the mere proximity of enemy forces would likely have brought about the collapse of the defences in that country. Furthermore the British positions in the oilfields of the Persian Gulf could have been attacked from Ceylon.[25]

The Japanese radio propaganda was intensifying. Lucy Meo says that part of the strategy was to attempt to induce fear by repeating bad news several times over, as in the news service of 21 February 1942, two days after the first bombing of Darwin: 'Port Darwin bombed! Port Darwin bombed! Thirteen enemy vessels sunk and twenty-six planes shot down!' This was repeated by the announcer, in a fearsome voice, three times. She gives us other examples from propaganda broadcasts of 1942: 'The air raid sirens in Australia were afraid. They did not sound. They squealed.' (3 September 1942, 10 p.m.). 'The nerve of the Allied leaders was shattered' (18 April 1942). 'MacArthur is now a nervous wreck in Canberra' (31 May 1942). 'Dr Evatt had the jitters' (17 July 1942, 7.23 p.m.). 'The Japanese troops were ingenious, brave, valiant, daring, intrepid, brilliant, spectacular, formidable, death-defying' (12 August 1942).

Meanwhile Japan was about to strike in the very heart of the Indian Ocean, carrying out the Imperial Rescript of Emperor Hirohito when he declared war on the United States and the British Empire, 8 December 1941:

> We by the grace of Heaven, Emperor of Japan, seated on the throne of a line unbroken for ages eternal, enjoin upon you, our loyal and brave subjects ... To ensure the stability of East Asia and to contribute to world peace is the far sighted policy which was formulated by Our Great Illustrious Imperial Grandsire ... To cultivate friendship among nations and to enjoy prosperity in common with all nations has always been the guiding principle of Our Empire's foreign policy.

6

Zero Hour for Ceylon

In spite of Admiral Layton's efforts to prepare Ceylon to meet a Japanese invasion, Winston Churchill and General Wavell knew that the situation there was precarious. For the British prime minister the Battle of the Java Sea had been 'the forlorn battle', and now there was every prospect of another debacle.

As it turned out, he was right to be concerned. Admiral Yamamoto had been persuaded by the chief of the Operations Division of the Japanese Combined Fleet, Captain Kameto Kuroshima, to launch an offensive against Ceylon and the Indian Ocean region generally with the aim of linking up with their German and Italian allies.[1] A week after Admiral Raeder told Hitler that Japan was about to capture Ceylon, on 21 February 1942, the German naval attaché in Tokyo handed over photographs of the island's coastline at Galle, Mount Lavinia, Wellawatta, Negombo and other locations where Japanese forces might land. When this story came to light after the war, it brought back memories of the supposed activity of a Japanese former resident of Colombo named Numano who had run 'Ono and Company', a bicycle and toy shop located in the main street of Pettah. A year before the war he had closed the shop, and was reputed to have returned to Japan with maps, photographs and other information that would help a Japanese invasion — but this may have just been wartime paranoia.[2]

War preparations were proceeding apace in Colombo, Trincomalee and other coastal areas of Ceylon. Among the new airstrips built on Admiral Layton's orders was one that involved the appropriation of a racecourse in the Colombo residential area of Cinnamon Gardens and the bulldozing of many adjacent mansions, including the Chief Justice's residence. Another sporting venue to be sacrificed was a golf course. Trincomalee saw a new airstrip built at China Bay. In Ratmalana, near the aerodrome, the Royal Air Force commandeered Sir John Kotelawala's upstairs bungalow for use as an officers' mess.[3] As these changes to the landscape were being effected, Ceylon received two squadrons of Hurricanes (Nos 30 and 261), which had been brought from North Africa in the *Indomitable*. These were followed on 28 February by an RAF squadron of Blenheim medium bombers (No. 11) and the No. 413 Squadron of the Royal Canadian Air Force. Two squadrons of Fleet Air Arm Fulmars (Nos 803 and 806) and another of Albacores arrived at Ratmalana. At the seaplane base at Koggala on the south coast, which was manned by the RAF and the Dutch air force, three Catalina long-range flying boats were added to the strength of the naval air station's eastern theatre.

On 21 March 1942, following Prime Minister John Curtin's undertaking to supply troops to Ceylon for a short time, the Australian contingent arrived at Colombo on the HMT *Otranto*. The troops then went by train to Koggala on the south coast,[4] which was protected by the 34th Indian Division. The vigil there had its moment of drama. Quentin Tilley, a company commander, recalled the Intelligence Section advising that Japanese amphibious vehicles had landed on the coast — 'there were vehicle tracks four to six feet from the beach to the sea,' one member had announced. The enemy eventually turned out to be an eight-foot sea turtle that had come ashore to lay its eggs![5] Centipedes, snakes and mosquitoes bothered the troops, but these irritations — and the real danger — were forgotten among the cool breezes and coconut palms of the southern beaches, where catamarans sailed and many received sexual favours from shapely village girls.

Meanwhile the short-wave listening post on the Cocos Islands was receiving Colombo Radio loud and clear when Commander-in-Chief Admiral Geoffrey Layton delivered a broadcast speech, in a strident staccato voice, from the broadcasting organisation's ramshackle Cotta Road studios — the sort of grave speech leaders deliver when a country is perceived to be facing serious danger. His final words were:[6]

> There is no need for fear or panic. We are faced with a very obvious danger of attack by an extremely efficient enemy. We must prepare for that in every detail that human ingenuity can conceive with a sure knowledge that if that attack comes, then we shall meet it with confidence.

On 23 March, three days after the Japanese occupied the Andamans, the commander of the Eastern Fleet, Sir James Somerville, informed all the services and his superiors in Britain that the Japanese sea and air invasion of Ceylon would possibly take place on 31 March.[7]

The enemy fleet was certainly in the region: Japanese Vice-Admiral Chuichi Nagumo had entered the Indian Ocean on 26 March with the aim of finding the British Far Eastern Fleet and destroying it, as he had the US fleet at Pearl Harbor. He expected to find it in Colombo or Trincomalee. Unfortunately for him — though he was not to learn this for a little while — by this time the British Admiral had taken the fleet off to its secret location.

Somerville's predicted invasion date came and went with no Japanese attack. With the heat off, the admiral instructed the two cruisers *Dorsetshire* and *Cornwall* to return to Colombo harbour for refitting. Also to undergo a refit was the old aircraft carrier *Hermes*, which was sent to Trincomalee on the east coast in the company of the Australian destroyer *Vampire*, captained by Lieutenant Commander W T A Moran.

Before long, however, the tide was to change: the Japanese

fleet was heading for its quarry. There were the aircraft fleet carriers *Akagi* and *Kaga* (both 26,900 tons), able to take fifty to sixty aircraft, and the new carriers *Syokaku* and *Zuikaku* (completed in 1941) of 17,000 tons, each taking forty-five aircraft. The *Hiryu* (Blue Dragon), *Koryu* (Flying Dragon) and *Soryu* (Shining Dragon), each of 10,650 tons, carried forty aircraft, while the *Ryuzyo* and *Hosyu* were smaller vessels — 7000 tons — taking about twenty-five aircraft each.[8] Completing the fleet were the battleships *Haruna*, *Hiei*, *Kirishma* and *Kongo*, two heavy cruisers and ten escorts from the First Destroyer Flotilla, along with seven submarines to help with the rampage.

It was a vastly superior force to the British armada, but for Admiral Isoruku Yamamoto, Chief of the Combined Fleets, this was not the complete story.[9] According to his belief system, there was always the potential for material resources to be overcome by 'spirit' alone. The British historian Stephen Howarth referred to this as 'Japan's bewitching dream of blood and steel, a dream of power in which spirit overcomes any material superiority.'

As events unfolded, the initial move in the Japanese grand plan was spotted by a 24-year-old Canadian pilot, Squadron Leader Leonard J Birchall. He and his crew had landed at Koggala air base in a Catalina on 2 April, having flown from the north of England via the Shetland Islands, Norway and Karachi. They were not to have much rest. Birchall was instructed to refuel for a 36-hour four-hundred-mile reconnaissance flight, and on 4 April they took off from Koggala. The early hours of reconnaissance proved uneventful, but then the 27-year-old navigator, Warrant Officer Bart Onyette, saw a speck in the ocean at the southern horizon. They flew towards it at a height of two thousand feet and soon were able to confirm that they had located the Japanese fleet.

As Sergeant F C Phillips transmitted his message to Ceylon, six Japanese Zero-sen fighters from the *Hiryu* flew at the Catalina. Birchall and his crew were attacked with explosive shells and compelled to ditch the plane. Alternate wireless operator Sergeant L A Calorossi, who had one leg blown off by a shell, went down, as did turret gunner J Henzell and Sergeant I M Davison, who were unable to get out of the sinking aircraft.[10] Having survived strafing by Zeros in a choppy sea, the remaining six members of the crew were taken prisoner by the Japanese destroyer *Isokaze* four hundred miles from Ceylon. Birchall, who survived the war, later explained that they were picked up with two aims: to find out whether they had been able to send a warning message and to obtain information about the defences of Ceylon and the location of the Royal Navy ships. Michael Tomlinson has carried out what is perhaps the most extensive and best documented research on the Japanese raids on Ceylon.[11] In regard to this event he wrote:

> Few members of the Catalina detachment had even had the chance to meet the lost crew. 'All I ever saw of Birchall,' said one, 'was his kit left in the corner of his mess.' Their loss was mourned, but at least we now knew where the Japanese fleet were. Calculations were made and it was estimated that Ceylon would be attacked early next morning. No time was wasted in regaining contact with the enemy ships, and darkness had scarcely fallen before Flt Lt Jock Graham in the 205 Squadron Catalina was sent off, armed with the sighting position radioed by Birchall, to shadow the enemy fleet. Between midnight and 1 a.m. he signalled that he had sighted an enemy destroyer some 200 miles well to the south east of Ceylon, heading north west. Ominously the message was not repeated. No further word was ever heard from Graham and his eight other members of the crew.[12]

Flight Lieutenant W Bradshaw, in a Catalina from Squadron 240, took over from Graham, maintaining surveillance of Nagumo's movements every hour. He reported the approach of four battleships with an unknown number of carriers and destroyers. Sir Geoffrey Arbuthnot hurriedly ordered all forty-eight of his ships out of Colombo harbour to the west and north-west coasts, while twenty-one merchant ships remained in the harbour. Admiral Somerville had already taken his fleet and what he called his 'untrained boys' and hidden in the Adu Atoll.

On 5 April 1942, Easter Sunday, at 4 a.m. in Ratmalana, the Hurricane pilots and ground crew of No. 30 Squadron were awake and having breakfast, enjoying bacon and egg-hoppers prepared according to a new recipe that Sir John Kotelawala's chef had taught their cook.[13] At the Colombo Racecourse aerodrome the Squadron 258 men were also on full alert.

Commander Mitsuo Fuchida of the *Akagi* gave the order to attack when the fleet was two hundred miles from Ceylon. From the five aircraft carriers *Akagi*, *Shokaku*, *Zuikaku*, *Hiryu* and *Soryu*, Ceylon was to face an enemy of 125 planes with 36 Type 99 dive-bombers (Vals) each with their crew of two, 53 type 97 Attack Bombers (Kates) with a crew of three, along with a fighter escort of 36 Zero-sen (A6M2) fighters. Fuchida went as an observer in Lieutenant Mitsuo Matsuzaki's aircraft.

The Japanese air armada, led by Commander Shigeru Itaya, reached landfall at Galle on the southern coast at 7.15 a.m. and flew along the coastline for half an hour at eight thousand feet. People in the towns of Hikkaduwa, Galle, Maggona, Beruwela, Kalutara and Moratuwa ignored the air-raid sirens and gazed at Fuchida's planes droning steadily along with no opposition. The astounding fact, still unexplained, is that British Fighter Operations, which was in direct telephone communication with Ratmalana and the Colombo Racecourse, did not know what I and many other Ceylonese were witnessing directly: that Fuchida's invasion force was very much in town.[14]

Had the RAF contingent in Ratmalana received only visual warning, the Hurricanes would have had at least half an hour to get into the air ready for Fuchida's planes. But they were still on the ground when the Japanese aircraft came. It has since been revealed that Ratmalana missed the Japanese arrival because for some unknown reason its radar was unmanned during the crucial period. The radar installation was of a very indifferent standard and scheduled for replacement, but the new equipment was still on its way from Karachi. Had the radar operatives been at their posts, it would have been possible to lament the late arrival of the new equipment if images of the enemy planes had been late in appearing on the screens. But even good equipment is not much use if the consoles are not manned. (For their part the Japanese had no radar at all, a fact of which neither Somerville nor Layton was aware.[15])

While Squadron Leader G F Chater's No. 30 Squadron crews were looking up from Ratmalana airstrip at Fuchida's bombers, the Japanese pilots could not believe their luck, and flew serenely on after delivering their loads. When the enemy dive-bombers came along a little later and released their bombs at five hundred feet, the British Hurricanes were still on the runway trying to take off. At the racecourse a similar scenario was unfolding. Fighter Operations was asking Squadron Leader Peter Fletcher whether there was an enemy force in sight. 'Yes,' he said, 'they are right over us and we are taking off now' — a remarkable reversal of the usual situation, in which operations control alerts the squadron!

The primary targets of the Japanese attack on Colombo were the British warships, but, whether or not they were actually expecting the harbour to be full of them, they were disappointed. Their attack bombers severely damaged the railway workshops at Ratmalana and the oil depot in Kolonnawa. Seven were killed at the Angoda mental hospital when it sustained a major hit, the Japanese bomber crews having at first mistaken it for the oil installation. Even without Somerville's fleet there were plenty of targets in Colombo harbour, and the armed merchant cruiser *Hector* and the *Tenedos* were among the many ships sunk.[16] The *Hector* burned for a fortnight, one of the longest marine fires in history. Many other fires raged at installations around the harbour, which were bombed ruthlessly.

In the heart of Colombo what were left of the British Hurricanes were now in the battle. Flight Lieutenant P G Paxton and Warrant Officer L A Owens fought bitter dogfights with Zeros until they were shot down. Owens died instantly; Paxton bailed out at sixteen hundred feet and landed in a coconut tree, from where he was rescued. He died of severe burns two days later. A wrecked plane that I saw on Colombo's Galle Face Green had been a victim of friendly fire from the anti-aircraft battery. The pilot, Canadian D A Macdonald, bailed out at sixteen hundred feet, walked to the Colombo Club and asked for a double Scotch.

The Easter Sunday air raid on Colombo lasted for twenty minutes. The results were never accurately assessed, and even the extent of British casualties remains unclear. In Colombo alone twenty-seven aircraft were lost, seventeen airmen killed and eleven seriously injured. After the engagement No. 7 Squadron had only seven aircraft left that could fly; at the racecourse nine of the fourteen Hurricanes did not return; only nine serviceable planes remained in No. 258 Squadron. Overall, and taking into accountforces stationed in Trincomalee, fifty-one of the RAF and Fleet Air Arm personnel taking part in the operations over Ceylon were killed. The civilian casualties amounted to eighty-five dead and seventy-seven injured, many of whom were in the Colombo harbour, where East African troops were unloading food ships. All of this was a high price to pay, particularly when judged in terms of the Japanese losses, which were minimal.

Three Japanese planes fell over land: one went down at Horana, another (which I saw) at St Thomas College in Mount Lavinia and the third at Pita-Kotte, an outer suburb.[17] The first of these was accounted for by Sergeant G T Brown and the other two by an Australian, Flying Officer G E Caswell of No. 30 Squadron RAF, who was killed later in the battle. The Japanese admitted these losses and a further two over the sea. Admiral Layton claimed that twenty-seven Japanese planes had been destroyed, no doubt an exercise in bravado and exaggeration thought necessary to boost local and international morale.

One account of these events has it that the engagement ended when Mitsuo Fuchida recalled his bombers after receiving a hoax radio message to the effect that Somerville was about to launch a sea attack on the Japanese armada. While the bombers left, the Zero-sen fighters remained in the Colombo skies to deal with the British Hurricanes. At 8.30 a.m. the last of the Japanese aircraft departed to join their carriers. At 1.55 p.m., two hundred miles south of Ceylon, the Allied forces suffered yet another loss when the *Dorsetshire* and *Cornwall*, the two cruisers sent by Somerville to Colombo at the end of March, were attacked and sunk.[18]

The officer commanding, Air Vice-Marshal John D'Albiac, was shattered by the Easter Sunday debacle. 'I shall never get over this,' he said.[19] There had been other bungles apart from those already mentioned. Early in the day the enemy force had been sighted by an RAF crew under Flight Lieutenant Bradshaw in his Bismark Catalina. But, astonishingly — this was one of the men who had alerted the British forces to the approach of the Japanese fleet — he thought they were friendly planes. And in a dawn patrol on that same day six Fulmar planes saw Japanese aircraft near Bentota, but they neither identified them nor reported the observation. One important reason for these 'let-offs' for the Japanese was that a radio silence had been imposed to guard the secrecy of Somerville's rendezvous in Adu Atoll. And a complicating factor was that the airmen had been given reason to believe that British planes from two of Somerville's ships — the *Indomitable* and *Formidable* — were in the area, and the Japanese aircraft they saw were mistaken for these.

After the air raid there was a huge exodus from Colombo, the mood of which bordered on panic and hysteria. Rumours of the horrors of Japanese occupation in other countries, with the wholesale massacre of civilians, had spread in the city. One story circulating was that in Singapore and Hong Kong patients and staff in hospitals had been bayoneted. I stood outside the gates of St Francis Xavier Seminary at Bambalapitiya and witnessed the flight: cars, bullock carts, bicycles, rickshaws, hand carts and buggies all filled with people and goods fleeing along Colombo's famous Galle Road.

Later on that Easter Sunday the contingent on Cocos heard a broadcast by Admiral Layton. It had a noticeable impact on some of the CGA men — they saw through Layton's bravado and became very fearful of a Japanese attack. He was of course concerned about the panic in Colombo and the consequent mass exodus from the city. Setting aside any inclination he might have had to tell the whole truth, he delivered a message that was a blend of praise, reassurance and bombast:

> Facing a first air raid the people of Colombo set an example of courage and calmness, which is second to none, rivalling that of Great Britain, who have set a high standard. It is not a matter of luck that we got off so lightly. It is entirely due to the manner in which we have prepared ourselves to meet this danger, and so long as we do not relax, and continue to work together with grim determination to succeed, and avoid all signs of panic, we need have no fear as to the future. I sympathise with the relatives of those who have lost their lives. You can feel proud in the fact that these lives have not been wasted but have been given in the defence of their beloved country.[20]

Nobody knew when or whether the raiders would be back, but they did not have to wait long before finding out. On 8 April, three days after the attack on Colombo, a patrolling Catalina warned that three of Nagumo's battleships and a carrier were making their way to Trincomalee. The harbour there had by now been largely cleared of ships, the main exception being Captain Richard Onslow's *Hermes*, which had arrived several days earlier. The delay in the aircraft carrier's departure was due to the recall signal taking a long time to register with the crew members, who were being entertained by Burgher girls at a dancing party. It was 7 p.m. when the carrier finally weighed anchor and sailed into a choppy and dark sea.

At 6.20 a.m. Fuchida led ninety-one bombers and thirty-eight fighters into attack, just as he had in Colombo. Radar communication was better at Trincomalee however, and Fuchida was surprised to find a squad of Hurricanes ready for him. The defending fighters were engaged in dogfights by the efficient, fast-moving Zeros, allowing them little chance to attack the Japanese bombers. Squadron 261 suffered severe losses, eight Hurricanes being shot down, and a Fulmar from 273 Squadron was also lost. The *Erebus* (a very old warship) and the *Sagaling* (a merchant ship carrying a cargo of whisky) were scuttled in flames. The Japanese bombers then struck at the China Bay aerodrome, which was guarded by two anti-aircraft regiments from the Marines and the 55 Light AA Regiment. Ammunition dumps were blown up, and for the first time a Kamikaze attack was witnessed: a Japanese plane headed straight into the navy's massive fuel tanks, which burnt for many days. When the action ended, Fuchida had lost five bombers and six fighters. Among many Allied casualties, eleven Australian RAF officers from Squadrons 261 and 11 had been killed in action.[21]

There was more to follow — the tragic demise of that toothless old tiger, the *Hermes*. After heading out to sea the previous evening, she had met up with her inadequate little escort, the destroyer *Vampire*, with which she had arrived several days previously. The carrier had been scheduled to undergo a refit before sailing to Australia for further duty. Originally a cruiser, the *Hermes* was very far from being a state-of-the-art aircraft carrier, and she had been patrolling the Indian Ocean between Simonstown, Mombasa, Mauritius, the Persian Gulf and the Maldive Islands.[22] As she was not in combat mode at Trincomalee, all her planes were neatly parked at nearby aerodromes, sitting ducks for the impending Japanese forays.

The movements of enemy planes told Captain Richard Onslow that the *Hermes* had been spotted. He altered course to head for Trincomalee, while his futile radio signals for help were monitored by the Japanese air force. There was no escape. Five miles from the coast of Ceylon she was turned into a blazing inferno, and Onslow died in his cabin. The aircraft carrier sank at 10.55 a.m. on 9 April in thirty fathoms of water. The Japanese had 'won the dubious distinction of sinking … the first and only British Carrier sunk by enemy action during World War II.'[23] The brave little *Vampire* also went down in this battle, as did the British *Sergeant Athelstane* and *Hollyhock*.

The hospital ship Vita took in the survivors of the *Hermes*, while local fishermen recovered many of the bodies that were floating in the sea. Others were cast up on the eastern Ceylon beaches of Potthuvil, Batticaloa and Kalkudah, some of them mauled by sharks.[24]

What did the brief Japanese foray into the Indian Ocean amount to? Major General Anton Muttukumaru has written that 'the reason for the two air raids on Colombo and Trincomalee by the Japanese has been argued in service circles ever since they were undertaken, and the fact that there was no major follow-up has led to the conclusion that the raids had a reconnoitring role.'[25] To which it might be responded: Could the Kamikaze pilot have been imagining he was on a reconnoitring trip? And what could the Japanese conceivably have observed in their action against Ceylon that deterred them from doing whatever they had in mind? It must have looked to them like a pushover.

John Deane Potter tells the story that after the Colombo raid the five Japanese carriers, with their escorting battleships and cruisers, sailed around and deliberately allowed themselves to be seen by RAF reconnaissance planes as a ploy to entice Somerville's fleet into a decisive daylight battle. Potter says that Somerville refused to fall into the trap: he knew that if he engaged in a daylight battle, hundreds of Japanese planes would pound his ships into the Indian Ocean. He wanted what his opponents also often tried to achieve — a night surface action.[26]

It can be speculated that a key factor in the outcome was the decision to keep the British Far Eastern Fleet disengaged. If we take seriously the possibility that the Japanese intended to capture Ceylon and use it as a base for a westward thrust, we can see that it would have needed to commit a large military force to defend its positions on the island against a possible British naval attack for as long as Somerville continued to play hide and seek. Not only this: any further westward move by the Japanese would have looked a much riskier exercise with a viable enemy fleet hovering in the region.

Tomlinson has another observation on the retiring role played by the British fleet:

The Eastern fleet had not made a single offensive move against the Japanese. It was scarcely a situation Somerville could relish. Had it been otherwise, historians of the future would not be able to aver, as they doubtless will, that the last major action ever to be fought by the Royal Navy with a fleet of comparable size was at Trafalgar. For such a fleet will never sail again under the White Ensign and the only opportunity for such a battle to present itself in World War Two was here in the Indian Ocean.[27]

The progress of the Pacific campaign and the raids on Ceylon were carefully monitored by the soldiers on Cocos. Some of the messages came from the Ceylon Royal Naval Volunteer Reserve ship *Okapi*, which was out at sea during the Japanese action. Commanded by Lieutenant Meredith Monnington, it was a 365-ton vessel on anti-submarine patrol duties. On board were several Ceylonese: Lieutenant A V Frugtniet, Alexander Smith, P O Jainudeen, Clair Roeloffz and leading signalman Benny Ambrose, who saw the first Japanese planes approaching Ceylon on Easter Sunday. They claimed that they saw HMS *Hector* go down when a bomb went through its funnel.

On 11 April Winston Churchill made a statement to the British House of Commons on the Japanese attack on Ceylon:

On April 4th superior Japanese naval forces which had entered the Indian Ocean were observed going towards Ceylon. These forces comprised at least three battleships, including one of the modernised 16 inch guns Magato type, and five aircraft carriers together with a number of heavy and light cruisers and destroyer flotillas.

Severe air attacks were delivered in the harbours of Colombo and Trincomalee. The cruisers *Dorsetshire* and *Cornwall* and the aircraft carrier *Hermes* were sunk in the sea by an air attack. I must admit to the House that it is true that while the attack on Colombo was being delivered by the Japanese, our torpedo aircraft sailed out to attack the carriers from which the Japanese attack had been delivered, but owing to thunder storms and low clouds in that vicinity, they did not make contact on that day.

With regards to Trincomalee very violent attacks were made by the torpedo aircraft which we possessed and also by fighter bomber aircraft on the spot in such numbers as were available.

As already published one of the Japanese carriers is said to have near misses. But whether damage was done I have no knowledge. Practically all aircraft taking part in the attack were shot down or seriously injured or became unusable.[28]

Canadian Prime Minister Lester Pearson recalled how, at a dinner at the British Embassy in Washington hosted by Lord Halifax in honour of Churchill some time after these events, someone had asked the wartime leader what he felt had been the most distressing and dangerous moment of World War Two. They thought he would refer to the events of June and July 1940 or to the time when Rommel was heading towards Alexandria and Cairo or when Singapore fell. To their surprise he replied that what had caused him the greatest alarm was receiving news that the Japanese fleet was heading for Ceylon and the British naval base there. The capture of Ceylon, the consequent control of the Indian Ocean, and the German conquest of Egypt, all of which then seemed possible, would have closed the ring and the future would have been bleak.

He went on to refer to Squadron Leader Leonard Birchall. 'We were saved,' said Churchill, 'from this disaster by an airman on reconnaissance, who spotted the Japanese fleet, and though shot down was able to get a message through to Ceylon, which allowed the defence forces there to get ready for the approaching assault.'[29] In the *London Daily Telegraph* and *Morning Post* of 1 May 1943 there was a headline 'DFC Pilot Who Saved Ceylon.' The news item under it read in part: 'When Birchall failed to return from the reconnaissance in the Indian Ocean, he was presumed lost. Two months ago his wife in St John New Brunswick learned that he was a prisoner in Yokohama.'[30] All credit to Birchall, but the extent of the bungles and the feebleness of the response on that Easter Sunday must leave us wondering how much difference it would have made if his message had not got through.

The Japanese task forces retired to a location between the Nicobar Islands and the Andamans.[31] Much damage had been inflicted on Ceylon, a population had been terrorised and British air defences had been humiliated; nevertheless it was the case that, for the first time since the beginning of the war in Asia, a major offensive of the Japanese had not advanced.

Admiral Somerville and his fleet left Adu Atoll on 10 April and proceeded to Bombay. Not long afterwards Admiral Nagumo withdrew his carrier force, which had ruled the Indian Ocean for four months, and returned to the Pacific. Within a month of the attack that he had launched on Colombo, grim mutiny was brewing on the Cocos Islands.

PART TWO

ENCOUNTER

7

Seeds of Mutiny

Events in the Indian Ocean, culminating in the Japanese attack on Ceylon, had strengthened Gratien Fernando's belief that Japan was on the verge of fulfilling her dream of Asian domination. After the Singapore debacle there had followed the fall of Burma, the capture of the Andamans, the Nicobars and Christmas Island, and the attack on Direction Island. While all this pressure had been building up, his urge to fight white domination had been strengthening.

By April 1942 the morale of the soldiers on Cocos had slipped to the point that their capacity to defend the outpost was seriously in jeopardy. Many of them believed — not without reason — that Japanese commandos might land on the island at any time. Partly due to Fernando's insistent prodding and questioning, many had come to the conviction that the days of British imperialism were at an end, and some were beginning to toy with the notion that it would be better to hand over the island to the Japanese should they make a move on it. Beneath the particular influences at work there was the peculiar orientation in the outlook of volunteer soldiers — their boredom, their disgust, their flashes of intense fear, their satisfaction at being still alive and their wonder at the folly of obligatory killing.

It is not possible to understand Fernando without appreciating the strength of his belief in Buddhist-influenced concepts of fate and karma. On 28 February 1942, a few days before he left for Cocos, he had written to his father thus:[1]

Dear Father,
I don't know what am I to write. I feel so guilty. Everything seems right with me, yet everything is wrong. I don't know how mother will feel. I am trying my best not to even imagine her feelings. Everything is a matter of fate. Believe me, I don't know what made me sign, being so conscious of the reaction at home. It is all fate. Please bear up everything cheerfully, for I assure you that I am going to a place far safer than Ceylon and will [probably] be back by August.

It's not in my power to like or hate. For everything is laid down to Fate. Tell mother and explain a soldier's life is always that. Everything I am sure will turn out for the good.

Excuse me: I can't write any more. I can't think. Best and sincere wishes to everyone: Father, you mother, sisters, brothers. I stole all the snaps from sister when I came home the other day. Believe me everything I am doing is in the interests that some day I might be able to bear the burden of responsibility when I come back.

Your loving Son,
Gratien

It might be observed that the sense of foreboding in this letter is at least as strong as the expression of certainty about his return to the family, while underlying everything is his conviction about the role of fate. This would not in itself undermine the validity of particular notions that have been proposed as to his motivation, which must be judged on their merits. For example a British author has accused the bombardier of allowing a broken love affair to spur his actions;[2] another story has it that his stormy relationships with the 'tuans' on Malayan rubber plantations fostered racial attitudes on his part.[3] There is some evidence for the first of these notions, although the family has categorically denied that there was any broken love affair or that he ever worked on Malayan plantations.

The core discontent of Fernando and those who ultimately aligned themselves with him centred on the issue of racism. Apart from their own direct experience of it, they were perceiving with increasing clarity the inherently racist character of colonialism.

Fernando has been remembered as recalling train journeys in a second-class compartment of the Ceylon Government Railway, on which the bulk of the first-class accommodation was taken by white planters like Gardiner and Stephens. All the troops knew of the exclusive 'white only' Colombo Club, where Scotch and soda, gin and lime and other colonial tipples flowed freely. The same segregation applied at the Colombo Swimming Club, the Darawella Club and the Hill Club at Nuwara Eliya.[4]

Among the Ceylonese troops in general there was some awareness that they shared a common lot with Indian soldiers. These had always been regarded by their British commanders as auxiliaries and moppers-up who came in after the British shock troops had, with their superior qualities, spearheaded an assault. Extolling the fighting prowess of the British soldier was a common theme of British military rhetoric, one that could be irritating to those outside the fold. Fernando in particular was very conscious of the lack of acknowledgement accorded to Asian soldiers. Since being deployed overseas, Ceylonese soldiers had experienced many humiliations, even though their particular status had in many instances privileged them beyond the general run of Asian and African troops serving under the British flag.

It was not only Asians who were seeing this mindset for the myth that it was. In the course of World War Two General William Slim began to note that his divisional commanders were now calling for Indian battalions in place of British. He said that the Asian fighting man was equally brave, usually more careless of death, less encumbered by mental doubts or humanitarian sentiment, and not so moved by sights of slaughter and mutilation.[5] Slim did not hide his instinctive sympathy for the

Indian middle classes, having regard to the humiliation that the British inflicted on them, if often unconsciously.[6] He understood the emotional importance of nationalism, not only in politics but in every aspect of Asian middle-class life. Captain Gardiner could have taken a lesson from him.

In summing up the Malayan campaign, Gilbert Mant spoke of the segregation between officers — mostly British — and non-British troops, who had different clubs and drinking places assigned to them. The latter were defending their own country, not just the rubber plantations of the *tuan besar*, but found themselves barred from European clubs and from the Raffles Hotel in Singapore.[7]

Mark Hopman and other volunteers often recalled the experiences they encountered when they went overland to Bombay to embark for Seychelles. One they remembered vividly was a visit to the Bombay Services Canteen, which was a vast place with dance halls, library, restaurant and billiard tables. Here titled European women helped to entertain the troops, and one of Asia's well-known impresarios, Donovan Andree, and his Ceylonese 'Red Tail Minstrels' performed. When Hopman and his comrades fronted up they were refused entrance and directed to another canteen that had been set up for the use of coloured troops.

But they had a card to play, and play it they did. Unlike their fellows from India, Malaya and Africa, the Ceylonese soldiers had their British Other Rank status, and so they flashed their passports at the doorkeepers. This caused some consternation. There were frantic phone calls and interventions by British top brass; then, eventually, they were allowed in. They got what they wanted, but it had been a humiliating procedure.

Those who had been at Seychelles fuelled resentments further by relating what happened after the *Bismarck* was sunk close by and the *Dorsetshire* limped into the port for repairs after picking up German survivors. The British officers feted the prisoners with visits to the beach, joy-rides, picnics and dances, and they were given lodgings in the best hotels in Seychelles. It was clear that a white prisoner got better treatment than a coloured ally.

There was also a story from Mombasa, where a Ceylon contingent of eighteen soldiers under Sergeant Jem Melder had been refused admission to theatres reserved for whites. Much worse was the fact that they were taken to a camp for African coloured soldiers and accommodated 'like cattle and given a bucket of mealies — ground nuts boiled with rice.'[8] Although he had at first ordered his men to accept the conditions, this treatment became too much for the pro-British Melder, who went to the commandant and demanded that the Ceylon men be housed in the 'British Other Ranks Camp' next door, which was their entitlement. It was also the last word in luxury.

The commandant declared that coloured troops had never been allowed there, but was stopped in his tracks by the passports. There was a deadlock and much questioning as to how the Ceylonese troops had been accorded their unusual status. The outcome in this case was not as happy as the Bombay resolution: the commandant ruled that, 'British Other Ranks or not,' coloured troops would not be allowed to live with whites in Africa. After telegrams were sent to Colombo, the soldiers were asked to seek accommodation in a hotel for 'coloureds'. These events were vividly and repeatedly recounted in the camps at Horsburgh.

A deep sense of comradeship had developed among the ten CGA gunners who had been sent on to Cocos from Seychelles, breeding ground for a growing resentment against white officers. Gunners Benny de Silva, Carlo Gauder and Mark Hopman were members of this group, which had created trouble for Major Spurrier in Seychelles and whose transfer to Cocos had been put into effect for disciplinary reasons.

On Cocos the main representatives of British authority were Captain George Gardiner, his second-in-command Lieutenant Henry Stephens and Sergeant Major A H Perera, who was also battery quartermaster and widely regarded by other Ceylonese as a bootlicker. Gardiner, whose racist attitude and authoritarianism have already been mentioned, was quite blatant in showing that he had absolutely no regard for his men. For his part, the Eurasian Stephens openly flaunted his notions about British superiority, especially as it was reflected in the glories of its colonial empire. In doing so he made it clear that he regarded the 'coloured' soldiers as his inferiors. He was prone to hammer this theme in the canteen, and surprisingly believed his men were happy enough to put up with it.

Given this situation, it is not to be wondered at that communication between officers and men was deteriorating and relatively minor problems and complaints were beginning to blow out of proportion. While it was true that living conditions were not good, what came to be much more important was the perception of unfair treatment.

The nub of this latter complaint was that Perera, in his role as quartermaster, was giving preferential treatment to the men in his own unit, the Battenburg Battery, to the detriment of members of the Galle Face Battery. In particular he was providing the Battenburg troops with more generous rations of cigarettes, beer and tinned food.[9] It is of some significance that Bombardier Fernando was a Galle Face man, and one thoroughly convinced as to the reality of this state of affairs — on one occasion he reminded Perera that there would be no distinctions between the batallions when Japanese forces landed on Cocos and they had to fight. Perera, who was a calm but calculating individual, told me that he heard no complaints from either the new arrivals from Seychelles or the gunners of the Galle Face Battery.

Very likely it was

Some of the men from the CGA Galle Face Battery. Standing: Sarap, Daniels, Kronemberg, Edema. Seated: Weber, Porritt, Gratien Fernando, Sahadevan, De Rooy.

because of this perception of unfairness that there was also growing rivalry and animosity between the volunteer gunners of the respective batteries, especially between the key individuals in the two groups.

Through witnessing some verbal clashes Fernando came to realise that homosexual relationships in the camp were also a cause of tension. (This did not concern him personally — his interest lay with the women from the other islands who, in spite of the risks, were available at a price.[10]) Henry de Sylva argued that the failure to organise the younger soldiers for homosexual favours was one of the causes of the discontent.[11] This was never substantiated from oral evidence or any of the files of the mutiny at the Public Record Office in London.[12]

Fuelling the volatility of the situation on Cocos were the very real fear of a Japanese invasion on the one hand and the history of British colonialism in Asia on the other. One aspect of Gratien Fernando's growing sense of Asian identity was his heightened awareness that a large number of the Cocos soldiers were Burghers, who enjoyed a relatively privileged status in Ceylon, and he often unkindly asked them to justify their European ancestry.[13] Nonetheless he mixed with them well and won their respect, friendship and confidence. They were by no means the main targets of his resentment: apart from white authority figures there were the 'coloured' stooges who managed to enjoy some of the privileges that the colonial system offered.

As adjacent countries that had shared the status of British colony for centuries, Ceylon and India shared much, including independence movements, but gestures towards independence had been much more evident in India. These had been observed very keenly from the island, and the Ceylonese knew of their bloody foreshadowing in the Sepoy Rebellion — better known as the Indian Mutiny — of 1857–58, when certain princes, fearing the confiscation of their lands, encouraged unrest among Bengalese troops. These were further inflamed by being issued with cartridges coated with what they believed to be beef grease, the handling of which violated Hindu law.

The Indian fight for independence, and in particular the efforts of Mahatma Gandhi and Jawaharlal Nehru, had found a quick response in Ceylon. Indeed Gratien Fernando had led school debates on such subjects, in which he voiced his opinion that only deeds could drive the white man away. On Cocos he often made references to Gandhi's Quit India Policy — and to the leader's imprisonment. In the context of such reflections the question often arose: Why were Asians fighting wars on behalf of their foreign colonisers?

The fall of Singapore had created a deep impression on various countries that were concerned with the fortunes of the Empire. According to Ravindra Varma, 'the Singapore debacle brought to an end four centuries of Western dominance of Asia ... exposing Asian nations to a new colonial rule by an Asian race of Imperial Japan.'[14] The surrender of British forces in Singapore had no doubt puzzled the Chinese, who with fewer resources had held the Japanese back for four and a half years. Varma pointed out that the speed of the defeat, and the sight of undisciplined European soldiers in flight, shattered the myth of Pax Britannica in South and South-East Asia.

This was the mood and the thinking of the soldiers at Cocos. They were influenced in part by the Australian staff of Cable and Wireless on Direction Island, who, whatever their political loyalties, were coming to terms with the realisation that their country could no longer imagine that Britain was able to defend her. Prime Minister Curtin had referred to the British surrender at Singapore as 'Australia's Dunkirk' when he announced the opening of the 'Battle of Australia.'[15] This shift in attitude had not happened all at once. On 18 December 1941 the *Sydney Morning Herald* had recorded a growing feeling that defence needs in the Pacific carried insufficient weight with the British War Cabinet.[16] The Melbourne *Age* wanted a minister to go to Singapore to direct policies from Australia's viewpoint and inquired 'whether the Pacific was regarded almost exclusively from the U.K. angle.'[17] The trend of thought was that the Australians had nailed their colours to the wrong mast.

At some point Fernando's reflections on the war, his sense of grievance, his visions of the end of British dominance and his mixed feelings about the onward march of Nippon tipped over a line: the idea of mutiny began to form and then to elaborate in his mind. With whatever degree of trepidation and after what delay we can have no way of knowing, but at last he began to voice this bold notion, firstly with those he knew shared his views and some of his passion, then with the wider circle of his Galle Face colleagues, and at last with some of the Battenburg men. If he had any notions about approaching the CLI troops, these did not come to fruition.

Of course there would be no bloodshed. If everything was carefully planned and properly carried out, that would not be necessary. Meanwhile he continued with his insistent indoctrination. One thing he quietly hammered was the real possibility of a Japanese invasion and the likely consequences of that for the Ceylonese men. Brave the enemy army was — but also barbaric, cruel and insensitive to suffering.

In my numerous interviews with surviving former soldiers who had served on Cocos, the loyal and mutinous alike, there was an agreement that Fernando spoke frequently on a particular theme: there was no reason why Asian soldiers should be exposed to defend British interests.

Gunner Ken Porritt, who shared many of Fernando's views, recalled that the mutiny leader was stirred by radio broadcasts emanating from Japan and the annexed countries.[18] The bombardier had yet to sift the genuineness of Nippon's promises of co-prosperity, and had no way of knowing, for example, what the nationalist Burmese leader Aung San found out the hard way when he and the Burma Independence Army co-operated with the Japanese: 'If the British sucked our blood, the Japanese ground our bones.'[19] He was not naive about their intentions, however. One thing Fernando had emphasised, according to Porritt, was the segregation of white officers and coloured men, not only in the Malayan conflict but also in most of the campaigns in World War Two; the Asian soldier was neglected and his fighting qualities not acknowledged. Nationalism and humiliation were consistent themes.

As Fernando floated the idea of insurrection among his colleagues, they responded in various ways. A few were very positive and very enthusiastic, and these became the main plotters. Their names were Benny de Silva, Carlo Gauder, Ken Porritt and Gerry Anandappa. As plans for the mutiny began to solidify, Lieutenant Stephens was given veiled hints that trouble was brewing. These came from Mark Hopman, whose own attitude to the plotting was equivocal. Stephens reported these intimations to his superior, but Gardiner assured him there was nothing to be concerned about.

Fernando and his core supporters had a clear idea as to what their mutiny was about. They were waging war against British colonialism — and against Gardiner and Stephens. These two might well have stewed in the juice of Viceroy John Lawrence's famous words: 'We are here by our own moral superiority, by the force of circumstances and the will of Providence. These alone constitute our charter of Government, and in doing the best we can for the people, we are bound by our conscience, not theirs.'[20]

George Gardiner would have had every reason to recall the Parthian shot delivered to him when he took over the Cocos command on 23 March 1942. As Captain Lyn Wickramasuriya ended his tour of duty he said to his successor: 'These are Ceylon volunteers who are part of the war machine. Do not ever treat them like black cattle. They must never be driven. They must be led. Treat them as equals in the common cause. Be firm, be ruthless but above all be fair and they will be loyal to you to a man.'[21]

8

'Eggs' for a Password

The mutiny plan was basically this: to place the commanding officer and his second-in-command under arrest, disarm the loyal troops on Horsburgh, turn the big guns against Direction Island to keep the infantry detachment at bay and contact the enemy. It was an ambitious agenda, but one that was not by any means beyond realisation. One advantage they had was that, as Guard Commander, Gratien Fernando managed the sentry roster and had access to the ammunition stores.

Essentially it was Fernando's plan, but on more than one occasion he discussed it in secret with Benny de Silva, Carlo Gauder, Ken Porritt and Gerry Anandappa. These were the core mutineers; others enlisted by Gratien were R S Hamilton, Joe Peries, F J Daniels and Kingsley ('Chicago') Diasz. Recruitment exercises took place at secret coastal beach meetings. Groups from the battery often went to the beach to play cards, sing — 'Whispering Hope' and 'Danny Boy' were favourites — and generally relax, so there was nothing suspicious about a few people getting together there. Overall Fernando found that thirty men out of fifty-six were in sympathy with his plans. In the process of determining this, he of course had conveyed to the other twenty-six at least part of what he had in mind. Charles Wijenayake was to recall, however, that most of the troops did not take the mutiny talk seriously.

One man Fernando was very keen to enlist to his cause was a thirty-year-old gunner, Mark Hopman. The part that Hopman played in the affair has been clouded with conjecture, to the extent that he has been accused of betraying his colleagues by giving evidence against them to save himself. The rancour and heartache have not diminished even after so many years. As his Field General Court Martial evidence will later show, Hopman did, at the least, play a rather ambiguous hand.

Initially Hopman had been sent to Seychelles, but in January of 1942 he had gone back to Colombo on compassionate leave because his mother was seriously ill — the army did have a heart after all. While there he had been offered a commission, which surprisingly he did not accept. Instead, he volunteered to go to Cocos. Volunteers were hard to find, especially for the Indian Ocean outposts — by now obviously vulnerable to Japanese attack — and his request was readily granted.

Hopman had a quiet admiration for Fernando. He responded to him as a dynamic character and as an intellectual soldier who had brought with him to Cocos 'not a bagful of clothes but a bagful of books,' which he read deep into the night by the light of a torch. The books were slim paperbacks on philosophy, religion and history, some of them yellow with age and in tatters. Hopman was also interested to notice Fernando writing: he kept a diary and made notes for a book he was working on called 'Island of Fate.' It is not possible to know what Gratien understood Hopman's position to be in relation to the mutiny plans, but he was certainly not under the illusion that he was a committed ally.

Charles Wijenayake was another soldier whom Fernando could not win over.[1] He came from an upper-class Sinhalese family and had been listed to leave Cocos with the March 1942 batch. But his relief had not come, and he had been obliged to stay back. Years later he recalled that, like many of the other soldiers, he had failed to recognise how explosive the situation was.

Much though he would have liked to have these two men on side, Fernando believed he had enough support to pull off the mutiny. There were no guarantees, of course, and so he had a contingency plan. If everything fell apart, they would seize a motorboat and proceed to Christmas Island with the intention of surrendering to the Japanese. Two Malay boatmen, Puria Bin Amin and Dubney Bin Bohin, ran launches for the army between the islands,[2] and Fernando had decided on one of these, *The Wangle*, as their getaway boat. The bombardier was certainly aware that Indian troops had mutinied on Christmas Island, killing the commanding officer and then surrendering to the enemy. Their motives had been similar to those in play on Cocos: the desire for political independence, the notion that Japan would help India get rid of the British Raj, the fear of Japanese reprisals in the event of their being captured and the growing antipathy to British officers.[3]

As many subsequently attested, Fernando never lost sight of the big picture. He spoke often of his vision of an independent Ceylon with its ethnically diverse communities living peacefully as one nation. Given time, the colonial masters would hand India and Ceylon the moral outrage to unite against the white man. But it could be a long wait, and the presence of the Japanese forces in the Indian Ocean presented an opportunity to hasten the process. Little did he imagine that independence could come soon after the war and without bloodshed.

Late one afternoon against the backdrop of an unforgettable sunset Fernando briefed his men. The key was to take control of the battery, which was inadequately guarded. Specific tasks were allocated. In another secret meeting with de Silva, Gauder and Anandappa, he announced that the password of the mutineers was to be 'Eggs'. The choice was inspired by a rotten poached egg that he had found on his breakfast plate that morning.

To understand the plan in more detail it will be necessary to have some notion of the set-up of the Ceylon Garrison Artillery. This had been under constant modification, and in many respects was no longer in accord with the recommendations of the

Australian army reconnaissance report of 1940.

Facing the sea on the western end of Horsburgh Island were two six-inch guns enclosed by a double-apron barbed-wire fence with a fifteen-foot-wide gate. Near the guns were ammunition pits holding about five hundred shells, trenches and an observation post. If the battery entrance was guarded by a conspirator armed with a machine gun, he would be in a good position to hold it. This was a vital part of Fernando's plan.

The observation post was at the top of a sixty-foot tower. At the base of the tower was a four-roomed building. Adjacent to each other were the duty officer's room (known as the Officers' War Shelter, where the officer on night roster would normally sleep) and a guardroom where the off-duty men slept; diagonally opposite the duty officer's room was another occupied by the guard commander and two assistant gunners. The fourth room was the artillery store, which was also where the relieving observation post man slept — though this may have been simply the personal preference of Gunner Thiakalingam Subramaniam, who was working shifts on the night of the mutiny. There were no interconnecting doors between the rooms, but there was a window in the wall separating the duty officer's room from the guardroom.

An initial part of the strategy was that all the off-duty guards were to be disarmed while they slept, and locked in, whereupon Fernando would climb to the observation post and seize the Tommy gun. Meanwhile other conspirators would be rendering inoperative the rifles lying beside the sleeping men in the barracks. Fernando would then confront Gardiner and Stephens. He was depending on seizing the commanding officer and demanding that he issue orders according to his (Fernando's) instructions. With control of the big guns, the mutineers could quell any opposition from the CLI by training them on Direction Island, where the infantrymen would be very conscious of the thousands of gallons of aviation fuel that were stored there.

Gauder was to remove rifles from the guardroom: it was anticipated there would be four or five men resting inside, and these had to be disarmed and locked in. Their rifles were then to be taken to the gun pit. There would be no problem about getting past the sentry, since Fernando would make sure that one of the conspirators was rostered for that duty. Anandappa was to hide in some bushes a little distance from the battery gate to back up Fernando in preventing any of the loyal troops from entering. A date for the uprising had to be chosen when moonrise would be no earlier than 2 a.m. so that the vital manoeuvres could be carried out in total darkness. Only dim torchlight and the password 'Eggs' would facilitate the action.

As the planning became more detailed, the vision of a bloodless mutiny began to fade somewhat, and serious attention was given to having adequate arms and ammunition on hand. Fernando's responsibilities allowed this to be a relatively straightforward matter. He was particularly concerned about having access himself to a machine gun.

From fairly early on, Fernando made it clear that the date of the mutiny was to be chosen so that the duty officer would be Lieutenant Stephens. He would thus be occupying the room next to the guardroom. Because there could be little doubt that, given the opportunity, Stephens' response to the mutiny would be a ruthless one, the question has since been raised as to why the second-in-command was to be rostered as duty officer and therefore present within the battery as the action took place. This was never fully clarified. Gerry Anandappa denied that it was because Gratien's aim was to pay off a score for Gauder, who hated Stephens, his old school boarding mate, with a bitterness he was to carry to the foot of the gallows. It is the case, however, that Gauder asked for a key position that would enable him to confront Stephens if the loyal men should be roused. It must be added that the release of the court martial files made available evidence that Fernando wanted Stephens inside the battery precinct so that he could be dealt with.

In a move that took his fellow mutineers by surprise, Fernando decided to have a rehearsal of the uprising and sound a false alarm. He saw it as a way of checking the resolve of those who had indicated that they would be involved. There was some cogency in that notion, but the risks were tremendous. It was well understood in the camp that any rifle fire was to be treated as an alarm, and all men would have to rush to their posts. The rehearsal was a crazy idea, and Anandappa was most unhappy about it.[4] Patterson, Porritt and de Silva also warned Fernando against embarking on such a course.

The subject of what would happen after the mutiny was discussed at a lonely spot near the southern end of the lagoon. As soon as Gardiner and Stephens were arrested, contact was to be made with the Japanese on Christmas Island. Porritt and Anandappa were to rush into the barracks and get a white bed sheet on which a red disk was to be painted to create a Japanese flag. This was to be hoisted on the observation tower as a sign for the Japanese to land on Cocos and take over the island.

Next an ultimatum was to be sent to Direction Island for the infantry to surrender. It was assumed that the Light Infantry would not know that Gardiner and Stephens were under arrest. Porritt told me that Gauder repeatedly warned Fernando that the infantrymen would thwart the revolt, but the bombardier would brush these cautions aside. In his mind the CLI would be neutralised by turning the six-inch guns on Direction Island. As he saw it, not only would the guns deter any attempt by a contingent of the infantry to come over to Horsburgh by boat, the presence of the aviation fuel store on Direction would make the infantrymen very cautious. 'Let's see how they'll come over here for a picnic,' Fernando would say.

Hamilton and another signaller were then to go to Direction Island and force the Cable and Wireless station to contact the Japanese commander on Christmas Island. Not surprisingly, this element of the plan struck some of the men as highly dubious. As Anandappa put it to Fernando, how could Hamilton's expedition hope to succeed when the infantry on Direction would not hesitate to use force to stop it? To the puzzlement of the other mutineers, Fernando was depending on nothing else but the challenge of the big guns. The only firing these guns had done on

Horsburgh was some target practice using dud shells. Despite such exercises, even Fernando, who had the rank of bombardier, was unfamiliar with the locking mechanisms on the cannon that Captain George Koch had installed when he was in charge.

The escape plan that was to be put into effect if the mutiny failed was thought over on one of the beaches. Fernando warned them not to back off: that would show them to be as gutless as the iguanas they had left behind in Ceylon. He assured them that, in the event of failure, he would use force to get hold of *The Wangle* to take himself and his men to Christmas Island. He had planned all the logistics of this operation, including the supply of petrol — and for good measure a Cocos girl or two.

The mutiny rehearsal was to take place on 28 April, and Fernando was to take on the crucial role of handling the Bren gun at the entrance to the battery. Ever since the mutiny this gun has been the subject of controversy among both the mutineers and the loyal troops. It was the gun with a hex.

According to Porritt and Anandappa, Fernando was not a qualified machine-gunner. He could take any firearm to pieces and assemble it with facility, but his experience in handling a Bren gun was very limited. Sergeant Peter Jayawardena of the CLI was in charge of training CGA personnel in the use of the Bren gun, and Porrit, Gauder and Anandappa had become competent.[5] They did not, however, press upon Gratien any suggestion that one of them should handle the machine-gun, because he had made it clear that he wanted to confront Gardiner and Stephens himself — to use the weapon on a men and a system that showed contempt for Asians and coloured people generally. While the Bren gun was to be used in the rehearsal, Fernando had in mind that for the real operation he would use the Tommy gun, which would be taken from the observation post.

The rehearsal did go ahead, even to the extent of firing a rifle as a false alarm.[6] They got away with it, but it was risky and by no means a reassuring success.

Fernando kept up the pressure on his followers by reminding

them of how Gardiner treated them. He recounted how the commander would have some of them pick up leaves in the blazing heat of the sun, and how he ridiculed the idea of an afternoon siesta. As for Stephens, he was 'a stooge, a Eurasian bastard who has forgotten his roots.'

The date set for the mutiny was the night of 8 May 1942. Gratien urged his men to be on full alert that day. De Silva was asked to shadow every movement of Stephens, while Gauder was to keep an eye on Gardiner. Peries, Hamilton and Diasz were to watch the battery enclosure so that they could be absolutely sure who was inside it: the concern was that at any moment Fernando's manipulated roster could be upset by non-mutineers exchanging shift allotments. Fernando remarked that he hoped Gardiner would be 'pissed' by evening — the captain had a reputation, how deserved it is difficult to say, for heavy drinking.

Anandappa and a few others had pitched tents outside the barracks proper and lived in them as a means of beating the unbearable heat that the season brought to Cocos, especially at night. Gardiner tried to clamp down on this concession, though it had started only after he took over the command. Had he gained his way, this would have denied the mutineers some flexibility in carrying out their program.

As zero hour approached there was a sense of premonition on Cocos, though events were to prove that neither Gardiner nor Stephens had any suspicions that an uprising was near. Camp talk was of a BBC radio news report about a battle that had just begun in the Coral Sea and appeared to be going against Nippon. It was not welcome news to the mutineers, who were depending on the success of Japanese forces for the ultimate triumph of their own venture.

On the night of 8 May 1942 on the Cocos Islands a mutiny was about to begin. An unusual breeze rustled the coconut palms as darkness fell on Island X.

9

Death Rattle on the Tower

It was an ill wind that blew from the Philippines on 6 May 1942. Between nine and ten thousand American and Philippine troops under Lieutenant General Wainwright surrendered to the Japanese at Corregidor. Then on the night of 8 May, at 10 p.m., while the Coral Sea Battle was raging fiercely, the CGA men on Cocos Keeling went to their barracks. At 11 p.m. the first stages of the mutiny began to unfold when Bombadier Gratien Fernando and three of his group — Kronemberg, Edema and Diasz — took over as members of the guard with the change of shift.[1]

At midnight gunners R S Hamilton and Ken Porritt lay awake in the barracks. Like the other soldiers lying there with them, they had their rifles and ammunition alongside their beds. Their immediate task was to disarm the others, which they were to do by removing the pins from the rifles. Of course they could not begin until all were asleep. This would be a difficult, risky manoeuvre, but the success of the mutiny partly depended on it. The operation was delayed when, a little past midnight, Hamilton observed that two of the men were still awake. Meanwhile Gunner Subramaniam, having finished his shift on the observation post, had retired into the artillery storeroom below.

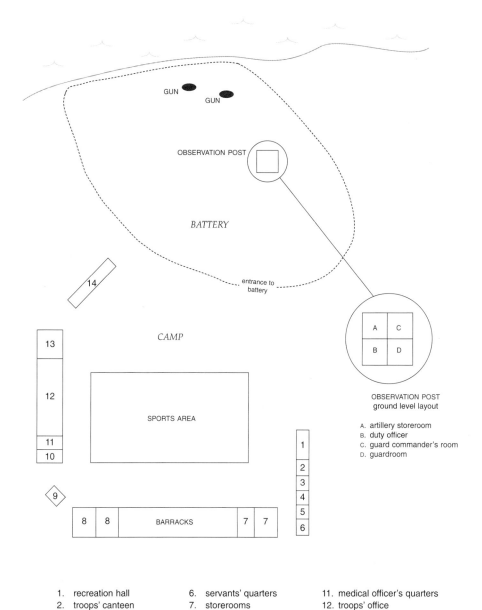

GUN

GUN

OBSERVATION POST

BATTERY

entrance to battery

14

CAMP

13

12

SPORTS AREA

11

10

9

8   8   BARRACKS   7   7

1

2

3

4

5

6

A   C

B   D

OBSERVATION POST
ground level layout

A. artillery storeroom
B. duty officer
C. guard commander's room
D. guardroom

1. recreation hall
2. troops' canteen
3. troops' mess
4. kitchen
5. cooks' quarters
6. servants' quarters
7. storerooms
8. NCOs' rooms
9. fuel store
10. medical room
11. medical officer's quarters
12. troops' office
13. BQMS quarters
14. officers' quarters

Layout of Horsborough camp and battery as recalled by Corporal Lucian Koch

Fernando anticipated no committed opposition from the twenty-five non-mutineers, who were nevertheless bound to challenge him when he announced that he was now in charge of the contingent at Rowe Battery. When they settled down he would order Gardiner to surrender his forces to the Japanese Imperial Command, specifically to its officers on Christmas Island.

Fernando had manipulated the roster so that he was free to place himself at the entrance to Rowe Battery. As the minutes ticked by he waited in vain for the flash of a torch to signify that all rifles in the barracks had been put out of action. After some time someone brought him the message that Hamilton had tampered with a mere seven rifles so far. This did not reassure Gratien, and he decided on a change of tactics: Hamilton and Porritt were to stop disabling the guns, and along with Diasz, take up positions near the barracks and hold the men under the threat of arms.

With the loyal troops in the barracks being held, it was time to get to work in the battery. The first move was to disarm the men in the guardroom. With all quiet and under control outside the battery, Fernando saw no need to take up his position at the entrance immediately, and he was present when the guardroom door was gently pushed open. To the mutineers' relief, all five men were asleep. One of the conspirators quietly approached the camp beds, took the rifles and handed them to Gauder; he in turn passed them on to Anandappa, who was standing outside. Fernando ordered his men to take the weapons to the trench. Gauder quietly shut the door of the guardroom and closed the latch, though the padlock was left open.

Some of the men now turned their attention to the artillery storeroom. Whoever it was that opened the door was startled to see that Subramaniam was still awake. Moving quickly, he kicked the rifle out of the sentry's reach and hit him with the butt of his own gun. Subramaniam slumped to the floor, dazed and bleeding. Gauder grabbed the rifle and flung it into the battery trench with the others.

Stephens was aroused shortly after this by someone tapping on the window that separated his room from the guardroom. It was Gunner R A V Perera, who didn't say much, but made it clear something was badly amiss. Grabbing his revolver, the officer came out immediately, unlatched the guardroom door and was told that all the rifles and ammunition had been taken. The gravity of the situation was instantly clear to Stephens, whose further questioning elicited the fact that one of the guards was sleeping in the storeroom. He set off in that direction with Gunner Callistus Seneviratne, ordering the others to lie low.

As he turned the corner he was confronted by Gauder, with his rifle raised. When Stephens challenged him, Gauder responded by firing a round that grazed the lieutenant's cheekbone. An exchange of fire followed, some ten rounds in all, with the two men standing about six feet apart. No serious injury was inflicted, though Stephens was also hit on the leg. With only one bullet left, Stephens limped away and found himself a well-protected place within the battery.[2] He lay very still with his heart pounding when, after some time, he heard Fernando calling to him to come out from hiding. A little later it was de Silva's voice: 'Stephens — where is that bastard Stephens?'

The mystery of why neither Stephens nor Gauder hit his target was never resolved. Stephens evaded the question when I asked him. As for Gauder, with all his embitterment against the excessive military discipline and the racist remarks from his commanding officers, and for all the personal animosity he bore towards Stephens, when it came to the point he just couldn't kill him. Patterson was convinced that, if either of them had been determined to kill the other, they could certainly have fired fatal shots.

Meanwhile Fernando climbed up to the observation post to get the Tommy gun, but found that he could not fix the magazine to it. He had to act quickly: he needed a machine gun to guard the entrance to the battery. The exchange of gunfire would surely have awakened the whole camp, and loyal troops could appear at any moment if Hamilton and the others were unsuccessful in

Gunner Samuel Jayasekera, killed on the observation post.

keeping them at bay. After a final attempt to attach the magazine, he covered it up again and ran down to retrieve the Bren gun, which he had hidden outside the battery entrance.[3] With him were Gauder and Anandappa with their rifles ready, and between them they had the battery reasonably well covered.

All the roster manipulation in the world would not have allowed Fernando to set up a situation in which he had only fellow conspirators with him in the battery compound. Apart from Stephens, Subramaniam and the other five guards mentioned there were a few others, including Gunner Samuel Jayasekera. Mahadura Samaris (Samuel) de Silva Jayasekera was a loyal soldier imbued with the highest traditions of his battery. He had been educated by the Jesuits at St Aloysius College in Galle, and left school after passing his eighth standard. The fourth son of the Registrar of Births and Marriages in Galle, he lived in Dadalla.[4] His elder brother had also volunteered for war service, and was in the Middle East.

The evidence is not quite consistent, but it appears that Jayasekera was on the ground when he heard the telephone at the observation post ringing incessantly, and, since the gunner on duty was not answering it, decided to ascend the staircase. As he approached the top of the tower he was confronted by de Silva, who challenged him twice and, receiving no answer, fired at point blank range. Jayasekera staggered back and fell. The single .303 soft-nosed bullet had entered just below his throat and then passed through the lumbar region of his spine. The body of the soldier slumped on the staircase and there was a brief death rattle.

Fernando cursed when he heard that Jayasekera had been killed, but he had to put that out of his mind. There was by now a lot of movement in the camp: Gardiner was awake, and so were the loyal troops. How they managed to brush aside Hamilton, Porritt and Diasz is not known, but a few of the more courageous were soon moving towards the battery. Fernando opened fire with the Bren gun. One man fell. The time was 4.30 a.m.

Many years later Corporal Lucian P Koch of the Medical Corps recounted to me how he had been asleep in his billet, which was attached to the Medical Inspection Room, when he was woken by gunfire. His first thought was that the Japanese Forces had at last landed.[5]

> At the sound of the rifle I slipped into khaki shorts and deck shoes, [grabbed] my first-aid kit — always ready — switched the light off and got out of the room. Within seconds a burst of machine-gun bullets skimmed across the cement tennis court a few yards in front of me. I was able to judge the line of fire of the tracer bullets and keep clear.
>
> I then sprang forward and leaned against a coconut tree. At that very moment I heard another report of a .303 coming from the direction of the observation post, a short distance from where I stood. I could get a clear view of Rowe Battery and the line of fire. I then saw three soldiers from our own crew walk from the direction of fire towards the observation post. I then rushed to the aid of the wounded Gunner B G de Zilwa and using the 'fireman's lift' method carried him to the Inspection Room.

Koch showed more than a measure of courage in getting at the injured man during the height of the mutiny. De Zilwa had been the first loyal soldier to get out at the alarm, and he had four of Fernando's Bren gun bullets embedded in the outer region of his chest on the right side. The Chief Medical Officer, Lieutenant S K Menon, was stationed on Direction Island, which meant that Koch would be on his own in dealing with this and any other emergency until well into the morning.

When the loyal troops responded to the alarm of gunfire, most of them grouped behind their quarters and then branched out in two directions. Some went to the beach on the right-hand side of the line of fire while the others took positions at the rear of the officers' quarters. Gardiner joined the left flank and took charge of that group. Fernando saw Gardiner creep behind a tree and fired at him, shouting to him to come out. The officer replied with a burst of shots from his rifle and called on the machine-gunner to surrender. While Fernando had been able to recognise the commander in the faint light, the latter was unable to see his opponent. He called to his men to find out who it was.

Gardiner had to meet the immediate challenge the mutineers were throwing at him, but he was also concerned for the safety of his men. There would be no reckless suicide charge. Gradually the loyal troops encircled the mutineers' position, but Fernando and his followers were still in a good position to hold them off. There was a stand-off. Then Fernando's voice echoed in the breaking dawn: 'Captain Gardiner to the battery.'

Gratien saw Gardiner advancing from the left flank. This was the moment. He would do it. He turned the Bren gun on his commanding officer and pulled the trigger. Then the unthinkable happened. The gun failed to respond. Fernando pushed the silent weapon aside and took his revolver, but the situation had changed in that instant. Thoughts jostled in his mind. The death of Jayasekera had blighted the situation, and last-minute defections had left him with a greatly weakened force. He turned and saw that a white sheet had been pulled over Jayasekera's body, and shook his head in disbelief. It was only a week before that he had sounded out Jayasekera and received no response.

In a desperate move that greatly puzzled de Silva, Gauder and Anandappa, Fernando ordered that the six-inch guns be turned on Direction Island. Whatever merit there might have been in such an action if they had had the upper hand, it was too late. Lieutenant Stephens had seen his moment and, together with Sergeant Pereira and Corporal Ferdinands, approached the observation post just as Captain Gardiner was nearing the enclosure. Soon the area was brought under control, with the mutineers in Rowe Battery finding about fourteen rifles and

Gardiner's revolver directed at them. With a suddenness that shattered his allies, Fernando walked to the corner of the battery and picked up a white towel. He fastened it to the end of his rifle and announced that he was going to surrender. The mutiny had failed, he told them, but his dream had not failed. This was small comfort to the men who had put their trust in him.

Fernando shouted to Gardiner that he wanted to surrender. The commanding officer demanded that all arms be thrown towards him. De Silva and Gauder were arrested by the injured Stephens and put under close guard. According to Koch, 'The mutineers were asked to put their hands up and come forward, which they did. They were placed under close arrest and marched into the camp. A bricked fuel store [with] barbed wire on top, … was cleared and the prisoners were kept under armed guard.' One of the guards was Lance Sergeant O M D W Perera, who would be subjected to heavy cross-examination by a number of the accused when he gave evidence at the Field General Court Martial.[6]

Gardiner doubted that he had detained all the mutineers, and this was soon confirmed. There was an appalling payback for real and imagined battery grievances when names were given to him. Torch in hand, Gardiner and Stephens began a march around the camp rounding up suspects. Gunner R S Hamilton was brought out from hiding with Lance Bombardier Kingsley Diasz. Gunners A J L Peiris, A B Edema, M A Hopman, F J Daniels and K R Porritt also fell into Gardiner's net and were arrested. Having declared that those found guilty would be executed at dawn, Gardiner sent a signal to Ceylon advising of the events and asking for reinforcements.

With the smoke settling on Cocos, there was a pall of sadness over the islands as preparations were made for a military funeral.

10

Grave-Digger of Cocos

The failure of the Bren gun at that crucial moment of the Cocos mutiny was the subject of much talk and speculation for a long time afterwards. It was some decades later that Sergeant Peter Jayawardena of the CLI, who had been a Bren gun instructor on Cocos, gave his story.

He had become aware of the intended mutiny, he said, and so during instruction sessions he gave incorrect information about the mechanics and use of the gun. He had also noticed Fernando showing an unusually keen interest in learning how to operate the Bren gun, which was one of the latest infantry weapons at the time. 'I had to think fast and do something. At the next instruction class, when the boys were given ten minutes for a smoke, I quietly loaded each magazine of the gun with the requisite number of ammunition rounds but introduced a dud round into each after the first three or four good firing rounds.'[1] The effect of this was that, when a dud round moved into the firing position, the gun jammed. The CGA men did not know how to remedy this, since he had deliberately given them incomplete instructions.

Lieutenant Henry de Sylva, who commanded the CLI on Cocos at the time, had a different explanation. He said that he and Jayawardena had taken turns in instructing the CGA personnel on the use of the Bren gun as an anti-aircraft weapon. When he (de Sylva) examined the gun after the mutiny, he did not find any dud bullets in it. According to him the gun stopped firing because of a gas stoppage. Henry Stephens later told me that he shared de Sylva's understanding: there was no dud bullet.

While the Bren gun inflicted injury on at least one soldier, it was a rifle shot that brought about the single fatality of the mutiny. The victim's body was taken to the sick room after the surrender, and at 8.30 a.m. the Chief Medical Officer, Lieutenant Menon, who had come across from Direction Island, examined it along with Corporal Koch. A death certificate was issued:[2]

Gunner Donald Patterson, grave-digger.

Rowe Battery
9-5-42

Death Certificate

I have examined Gnr M S de S Jayasekera No. 2189 and I certify that he died of bullet wound.

(Sgd.) S K Menon
Lieut. CMC
MO i/c Troops
8-30 hrs.   Contingent 'X'

In January 1993 in the suburb of Broadmeadows in Melbourne, Australia, I met Gunner Donald Patterson.[3] He had played a minor but significant part in the next phase of the drama.

Patterson had studied at St Joseph's College, Colombo, where he belonged to the same school cadet battalion as Stephens and Gauder. At the outbreak of World War Two he had been attached to the Ceylon 3rd Coast Searchlight Regiment. In the early 1990s he moved nervously about with the aid of a white stick: he was now totally blind. In September 1974, after a get-together with some of his wartime mates, he had lost control of his car, which hit a light pole. He suffered severe facial injuries and a complete loss of eyesight. His disability had not in the least, however, dimmed his memory of the uprising.

As young volunteers for a three-month stint at Cocos, they had looked forward to what was promised to be a romantic holiday in an exotic land of bare-breasted women. He was soon to discover the myth. 'If you were caught messing about with those well-endowed young Malay women you would get a harpoon into your guts,' he said. 'They could split an arecanut at twenty-five yards!'[4] Some of them took the risk, however.

Patterson grew nostalgic and, spoke of Gauder. 'That beggar was a harmless guy. He was an orphan who signed up to escape the drudgery of a home where he was like a servant boy. I know his only sister was devastated that he joined up. The poor devil couldn't kill a bug on a bed. I cannot understand how he got into the mess ...'

On the evening of 8 May 1942 the nineteen-year-old Patterson had won a fortune in cards playing the game of 'Asking-Hitting'. He was rather tired: along with a number of other soldiers he had been given fatigue drill after someone threw a brick into the officers' mess. The brick had been meant for Stephens, towards whom a number of the gunners now felt a deep animosity. According to Patterson, he collected his winnings and went to the barracks. While he adjusted his mosquito net he noticed that Gunner Noel Gunasekera was cleaning his gun. Then he turned in.

He was woken by a tap on the arm. It was Diasz. 'Pat, come and join us,' he whispered. 'We are going to start it.' This wasn't a complete surprise: earlier in the day Anandappa had said to him, as they came down from the observation post, 'It won't be too long.' Patterson's response to Diasz was that they had messed up the rehearsal so completely that they had no hope of pulling off a mutiny, and as far as he was concerned he was going to have a night's rest.

The next thing he remembered was being woken again, this time by a rifle shot. Then he heard a sergeant call out 'Alarm!' and soon the men were rushing out of the barracks. 'I ran to the cook's mess when someone shouted "The Japs have landed!" This is what we feared, as Bombardier Fernando had put the shits into us [over] what would happen if we fell into their hands.'

As Patterson ran towards the canteen there was a burst of machine-gun fire, and he fell flat on his face behind the 'medicine ball hut.' He knew that no bullet could get through that. 'I waited till dawn,' he said. 'I did not know what was happening. I could hear shouts from Captain Gardiner and Lieutenant Stephens and Sergeant I L Pereira.' It was only when Patterson emerged in the early hours of the morning that he knew for sure what had been going on. He also learned that Jayasekera had been killed.

A rollcall was conducted, after which Patterson was ordered by the battery quartermaster, A H Perera, to guard Jayasekera's body. 'It was one of the saddest things I ever had to do,' said Patterson. The body lay in state in the sick room awaiting the funeral, which was to take place with full military honours. A boxwood coffin had been ordered from Home Island.

At noon Patterson was relieved of his guard. It had been an ordeal for him to stand by the body of a comrade with whom he had had a long conversation just a few days earlier. Then at about 12.30 p.m. Patterson noticed Captain Gardiner in conversation with the quartermaster. They walked off some distance and marked a spot on the sand. Much to Patterson's puzzlement, they then walked towards him. Perera said to him, rather bluntly, 'Patterson, get two others and dig a grave six feet by four feet and do it quickly. We have marked the spot.'

Patterson chuckled to himself as he related his story: 'So I come all the bloody way to Cocos to be a gravedigger! Could have joined Barney Raymonds at Kanatta!'[5] It was a hot, sweaty job. 'I was lucky,' Patterson said to me, 'that I was not in the boots of Sergeant Ratnam.' Ratnam was later told to be ready to dig the graves that would be needed after a mass execution of the mutineers. He refused, however: 'I am a soldier, not a grave-digger.'

Patterson had been back from digging the grave barely half an hour when he saw Perera coming towards him once again. 'Gunner Patterson,' he shouted, 'you are under arrest.' This was a total shock. He pleaded with the quartermaster: 'This morning you got me to dig Jayaskera's grave, and now you are putting me under arrest. What the hell is all this about?' Tears welled in his eyes, and he began to fear that he had just dug his own grave. So this was what battery jealousies could do! He was led to the hut where the mutineers were sweating it out. They gave him a cold reception.

It was only when he was brought before the Field General Court Martial that he found out why he had been taken into custody. No doubt repeating something he had said earlier, one of the witnesses on oath said he had seen 'someone like Gunner G B de Silva or Patterson walking into the battery.' Patterson vehemently denied this. He said he was fast asleep and had an alibi, naming Gunner Noel Gunasekera, who was summoned. The latter confirmed that he had seen the accused going to bed when he was cleaning his gun, and was able to give the exact time. Patterson was later cleared of involvement: 'Gunner Patterson. Not guilty.' Very relieved, he sat down and asked for a glass of water. Fearing some sort of backlash from the mutineers, he persuaded Henry de Sylva to have him taken over to Direction Island the next day. On a later occasion he complained to Ivor Van Twest about the treatment of the Ceylonese soldiers and expressed the opinion that Gardiner should take most of the blame for what had happened.

But that is to jump ahead. A few days before he was killed, Jayasekera had written to his mother:

Cocos Keeling, Island X
May 3rd 1942

Dearest Mother,

When my term soon ends here in Cocos, I'll be back with you and the family. I know it gives you many hours and days of anxiety as my brother is in the Middle East and I am here in Cocos so far away from you. But don't worry. There is no danger here although the Japanese are prowling about. I am happy here. It's a nice place like the Bentota beach. After all, we have to serve the cause of our country in war and peace. Give Fr Gaspard and other priests at St Aloysius my kind regards. My thoughts are always with you, and I want you to be happy that I will be back soon.[6]

Sammy

The military funeral was to be held on the evening of 10 May. Captain Gardiner had given permission to some of the Home Islanders to attend the funeral following a request by Jayasekera's Malayan *sehebet*. This was the family friend who took care of a soldier, washing his linen and in a sense adopting him and entertaining him when he visited Home Island. It was the *sehebet* who made the simple coffin, besides preparing the body and helping with all the details that are part of a funeral director's work.

As Jayasekera's body lay in state, there was a tense mood throughout Rowe Battery. By now, of course, the Ceylon Light Infantry men on Direction Island had discovered what the overnight commotion on Horsburgh was all about, and their commander, Lieutenant Henry de Sylva, was to be present at the obsequies with a dozen troops specially selected to attend.

At 4 p.m. the coffin, draped in the Union Jack, was held high by six soldiers chosen by Captain Gardiner. They were Gunner Mervyn de Rooy, Sapper Corteling, Corporal Ferdinands, Sergeant I L Pereira, Gunner Sahadevan and Bombardier H L B Fernando. Gardiner wanted the funeral route to pass the temporary prison where the mutineers were held so that they could see the procession. This was his way of showing his contempt for the errant troops who had attempted to hand over Cocos to the enemy. He said as much to Stephens, who personally disliked the move.

In slow, measured steps the funeral march wended its way to the southern corner of Horsburgh near a cluster of palm trees where Patterson had dug the grave. The tread of army boots on the sand sounded a terrible warning of what was yet to come when the wheels of military justice would grind on Cocos Keeling. According to Stephens, the mood was depressing and tears came to the eyes of these young soldiers who were yet to face the realities of battle. 'There was a frustration,' he said, 'a sense of loss and of mistrust and betrayal.'

The froth of the ocean played on the coral and the rocks while the funeral cortege moved forward and the mutineers sat in the hot confines of their makeshift prison. The exhausted, crestfallen Fernando did not conceal his feelings from his guards. He saw clearly what was concrete and real: the magnitude of his failure and the price he would have to pay for it. Perhaps he thought of the lines he had written in his manuscript 'Island of Fate.'[7]

> Dreams used to come in the brutal nights,
> Dreams crowding and violent:
> Dreamt with body and soul
> Of going home, of loving, grieving and telling our story.
> The girls we loved in the shadows of a cadjan hut,
> Until quickly and quietly crept the morn:
> And the heart cracked in a bloodied quest.
> Now we have found our home again
> Our hunger is quenched as all the stories have been told,
> It is time soon we shall hear again the alien's command
> That you die at dawn ... and who cares to leave the fold?

The coffin was carried to the graveside to the commands of the battery quartermaster, A H Perera, whose voice echoed far into the sapadillas. As Jayasekera was a Buddhist, a broken column signifying that a young life had been cut short would not have been appropriate. That life would go on through the cycles of rebirth. Captain Gardiner gave a brief eulogy praising Gunner Jayasekera and extolling his courage and sacrifice. He then went on to speak at length on the meaning of mutiny, remarks that some found inappropriate and distasteful in the circumstances.

The *sehebet*'s family, who stood about a fifty yards away, did not conceal their grief. As Lieutenant Stephens nodded, a command was given and rifles were pointed to the sky. After a salute of gunfire that scattered the seagulls and reverberated throughout the islands, a shaky last post was sounded by a CLI bugler.

Placed on two crossbars, the coffin was lowered as officers gave a final salute of farewell. Then the *sehebet* family filled the grave with sand. And thus it was on 10 May 1942 that Gunner Mahadura Samaris de Silva Jayasekera was buried with full military honours.

In March 1958 a representative of the War Graves Registration Unit in Singapore, Warrant Officer Newman, visited Cocos Keeling to recover Jayasekera's remains from Horsburgh, which were taken by Bristol aircraft to Singapore. The headstone, however, remained in the West Island Cemetery. These details were discovered in some old papers in May 1979 by Robert J Linford, a one-time administrator of Cocos. I thought a follow-up would be appropriate, and in April 1999, at my request, a Singapore-based Sri Lankan, K C Selvadurai, visited the Kranji War Memorial, where a platoon of staff were maintaining the site well. He photographed Gunner Jayasekera's grave.

Today in Singapore's Kranji War Cemetery Gunner Samuel Jayasekera is buried in Plot 46, Row C, Grave 13. Adorned with the Ceylon Artillery Coat of Arms, the tombstone bears the wording:

> 2189 Gunner
> MAHADURA SAMARIS
> DE SILVA JAYASEKERA
> Ceylon Garrison Artillery
> 9th May 1942: Age 23

11

Field General Court Martial

Captain Gardiner decided to conduct a Field General Court Martial. This type of court martial was a makeshift dispensation of justice allowable in conditions of war in the face of the enemy. It was simpler and easier to convene than a regular court martial, and could be constituted by as few as three officers. If possible one of them had to be a major, but this was not mandatory. It was rare for a judge advocate to be appointed.

For a death penalty the decision had to be unanimous, and the area commander-in-chief had to confirm the sentence. The FGCM provisions that Gardiner was relying on allowed for the imposition of any sentence open to a General Court Martial or a District Court Martial. Unlike these two types of court martial, which could be held at any time anywhere, an FGCM could be constituted only in a situation of active service overseas.[1]

The military code of Great Britain, like those of the United States, France and many other countries, required a thorough and impartial investigation before an accused could be brought to trial by court martial. The uniform Code of Military Justice also provided that, after a conviction, the sentence had to be approved by a reviewing authority. This might be the commander who convened the court or some other commander authorised to convene a court martial of the type by which the accused had been convicted. The reviewing authority could quash findings of guilt in whole or in part.[2]

Gardiner asserted that, as he held a king's commission and was commander in that area of warfare, his court was in order. It was not a District or Garrison or Regimental Court Martial, in regard to which military law expressly stated that the court president could not be the commanding officer of the accused.

In World War One, 551 officers and soldiers had faced courts martial under section 417 of the Army Act, and 186 were condemned to death. In 18 cases (about 10 per cent) the sentences were carried out, while 168 cases were commuted to a lesser punishment. In a long search of archives held in Kew, I came across some interesting information relevant to the Cocos uprising, in particular File WO 93/40 on the death sentences carried out from 1941 to 1953 for offences committed during World War Two. This was the first breakthrough in my long quest for the court martial files of the Cocos mutiny, and the key record read as follows:

EXECUTIONS: August 1942

Bdr G H Fernando. 1 Coast Regiment. FGCM. Cocos Keeling Island Mutiny. 12–16th May 1942. Date of Confirmation: 22.7.42. Execution 5.8.42. (Causing or Conspiring with persons to cause a mutiny). Hanged.

Gnr G B de Silva. Executed 7.8.42. (Joining a mutiny). Hanged.

Gnr C A Gauder. (After coming to the knowledge of an intended mutiny failing to inform without delay the CO of the same.) Hanged 8.8.42.

The records show that, from 1941 to 1953, there were forty-four cases of murder, three of mutiny and one of desertion. All three mutinies occurred during World War Two. Thirty-three of those convicted for murder faced a firing squad and eleven were hanged. The three Cocos men were the only World War Two Commonwealth soldiers to be executed for mutiny. It is important to note that, with regard to individual cases of court martial that occurred before 1951, the Public Record Office records are closed for seventy-five years from the last recorded date of entry. But an exception had been made with regard to summary records for the death sentences carried out between 1914 and 1953.

The freedom of information debate in the United Kingdom resulted in the media compelling the release of more complete records, for example of the British 8th Army mutiny at Salerno in southern Italy during 1943, and I was eventually successful in seeing the full Cocos mutiny file (WO/71/741) 'under Section SS4.'

According to the file, Captain Gardiner had to make a quick decision, and his decisive step was to issue this document:

> On Active Service this 12th day of May 1942, whereas it appears to me the undersigned, an Officer in Command of Ceylon Defence Force Contingent 'X' on active service that the persons named in the annexed schedule being subject to Military Law have committed the offences in the said schedule mentioned;
>
> And whereas I am of opinion that it is not practicable that such offences should be tried by an Ordinary General Court Martial (and that it is not practicable to delay the trial for reference to a Superior Qualified Officer);
>
> I hereby convene a Field General Court Martial to try the said persons and to consist of the Officers hereunder named:
>
> PRESIDENT:
> Capt. George Gardiner (1st Coast Regiment Ceylon Garrison Artillery)
> MEMBERS:
> Lt de Sylva Henry (Ceylon Light Infantry)
> Lt Menon Sivasankaram Kumaran (Ceylon Medical Corps)
>
> (Sgd) G Gardiner, Capt. CGA
> Commanding CDF Contingent 'X'
> Convening Officer

To establish an Ordinary General Court Martial, Gardiner would have needed to find three officers with more than a year's service in addition to a president. There were only four officers on Cocos, one of whom (Stephens) was a witness and therefore could not be a member. Apart from the numbers being insufficient, Menon had been commissioned for less than a year. It would be argued that there was no need to establish a court martial so quickly or in that location. Gardiner's response was that he feared a Japanese landing and could no longer be sure of the loyalty of his troops.

Gratien Fernando had his own objections to the proceedings. He maintained that when he surrendered to Gardiner he asked to be sent to Ceylon for trial, and it was on this condition that he raised the white flag. He also disputed that Cocos was a front-line situation such as would warrant setting up an FGCM, a standpoint somewhat at variance with one of the arguments he had used to win recruits to his mutiny.

Gardiner denied any undertaking about Fernando being tried in Ceylon — in the height of the gun battle Gardiner had wanted surrender without any qualification — and insisted that, bearing in mind the Japanese takeover of Christmas Island, the military forces on Cocos faced Japanese invasion at any moment and in that sense were in the thick of battle. There was, needless to say, plenty of room for military historians and lawyers to dispute this in the future.

Despite his claim that his surrender had been conditional, and despite having raised a hue and cry to the effect that he and his followers would not receive a fair trial, when the court was convened Fernando did not challenge its authority.

A room in the administrative block on Horsburgh Island was turned into a courtroom and the Field General Court Martial went into its first session there on 12 May. A revolver on the table faced the mutineers as they were brought in in batches by the guards. The details are set out in army form A2 on yellow paper now ravaged by age. The court martial was conducted between 12 and 16 May 1942, its purpose being to try fifteen members of the regiment, 'mobilized soldiers of the Ceylon Defence Force, doing duty with His Majesty's Regular Forces Overseas.' They were subject to military law by virtue of Section 19(2) of the Ceylon Defence Force Ordinance 1910.

The fifteen men named were:

No. 1712 Bdr Fernando G H
No. 2002 Gnr Gauder C A
No. 1989 Gnr de Silva G B
No. 2028 Gnr Hamilton R S
No. 1766 Gnr Anandappa G D
No. 1971 L/Bdr Diasz K W J
No. 2190 Gnr Peries A J L
No. 1727 Gnr de Zilwa L B
No. 2152 Gnr Edema A B
No. 2154 Gnr Kronemberg T B
No. 2022 Gnr Hopman M A
No. 2147 Gnr Patterson D A
No. 2139 Gnr Daniels F J
No. 1996 Gnr Porritt K R
No. 2055 Gnr de Zilwa S H

The offences alleged to have been committed at Rowe Battery 'on or before 9.5.1942' were:

1. Causing a mutiny in His Majesty's Military Forces or conspiring with other persons to cause a mutiny in His Majesty's Military Forces.
2. Joining a mutiny in Forces belonging to His Majesty's Military Forces.
3. After coming to the knowledge of an intended mutiny in Forces belonging to His Majesty's Military Forces failing to inform without delay their Commanding Officer of the same.

The charges were read to the accused, and they were asked if there were any objections to being tried by the members of that court. As there were no objections, the court was sworn in. There were eighteen witnesses for the prosecution, all of whom had submitted signed statements.

The court was to hear the cross-examination of the witnesses for the prosecution by the accused. The statements of the accused in their own defence and those of the witnesses for the accused would also be heard.

Bombardier Gratien H Fernando (No. 1712), the leader of the mutiny, told the court on oath:[3]

> I wish to say that I was quite sane at the time. The whole thing was planned with a purpose. Capt. Gardiner was just an obstacle. I just wanted to break away from the White people. I am not so much anti-British as anti-White. I have felt this for a long time. I was not doing it for my own sake.
>
> I had not the least grudge against Capt. Gardiner personally. I would have done the same to any White man. I felt that if I succeeded I might do things that would revolutionise the war effort in the East. I wanted to try and get Japanese help. I firmly believe in Asia for the Asiatics. I am in sympathy with Japanese war aims. I came to Cocos because I wanted to get out of the Galle Face Battery.

Here Fernando is being consistent with the sentiments he expressed to his colleagues, though the last sentence is perhaps a surprise. He went on to say:

> I had Gnr Anandappa and Gnr Gauder in my confidence. They knew my plans. My plan was to disarm the Guard. I ordered my Sentry to shoot the Night Officer on duty. I went up the OP [observation post]. I fired a shot. Someone ran up. I shot at him. I tried to get the Tommy Gun. Could not fix the magazine — so put it under cover.
>
> I doubled to the Bren Gun, which I had already put near the Battery gate outside. I wanted to pick off the men as they got bunched coming into the gate. I thought when I fired the first burst of the Bren Gun I had got Capt. Gardiner.

> I meant to send the alarm to Direction by the Secret Code.
> They would have sent an SOS. I have studied the Direction
> Island defences and felt I could have overcome them.

None of the other evidence offers any support to the notion
that Fernando fired a shot at someone who was climbing up to
the observation post. Perhaps he was trying to protect Benny de
Silva by suggesting the possibility that he (Fernando) fired the
fatal shot — there was, after all, little doubt but that the instigator
of the mutiny would be convicted.

Fernando went on to explain that he could have sent a
message to Direction Island in the morning as if from the
commanding officer asking for say ten men to come over, and
could have dealt with them. 'With about eight men from
Horsburgh I could have [then] overcome the remaining CLI on
Direction Island.' Perhaps he devised this strategy after his
original plans for dealing with the infantry unit received such a
dubious response from his allies. It may not be entirely
convincing, but it appears to be much more plausible.

After stating that he had had no intention of killing the staff of
Cable and Wireless and the Radio Naval Direction Finding
station, but only of disarming them and destroying the two
stations, he went on:

> I once casually explained my feelings to Weber and Edema. I
> don't think they understood what I really meant, nor did S H
> de Zilva and Patterson. They all told me not to be mad. If I
> was successful I might have been helped by L/Bdr Diasz,
> Gnr Peries, Daniels, Hamilton, G B de Silva, Hopman. I don't
> think Daniels knew anything about it. I forgot he was the OP
> Lookout. I don't think Gnr L B de Zilva would have been
> any use to me, nor Edema nor Kronemberg. I had no faith in
> them. Patterson is a coward and would not have helped me.
> He is very fickle.

The statements about Daniels are puzzling. There is first the
contradiction of naming him as one of his main allies and then in

effect denying it immediately. More bewildering is his claim that he had forgotten Daniels was on observation post duty — it is hard to imagine he could overlook something as central to his strategy as who was to be on the tower. Wouldn't he be very happy that one of his core supporters was there?

If Fernando was lying, why? Was he trying to protect Daniels? Or was he, on the other hand, attempting to account for the failure of his strategy by attributing it to a lapse of memory rather than inadequate planning or clumsy implementation? Patterson told me that he believed the leader of the mutiny did not tell the full story of the vital moments when he failed to synchronise the strategy.

In a separate statement, in which he acknowledged that he had been cautioned that his words might be used as evidence against him — as were all the accused — Fernando covered some of the same ground and then took the story further:

> On the night of 8th/9th May 1942 I ordered my sentry Gnr C A Gauder to shoot Lt Stephens. Before that I had disarmed four guards, who were the relieving guard, locked them up in the Guard Room, and went up to the OP. Gnr Daniels was the OP Lookout at the time. I fired a round in the air from the observation post, and while coming down I shot someone, I don't know whom, who was climbing up the stairs. He was on about the third landing. I wanted to take the Tommy Gun but failing to fit the magazine I put it somewhere under cover. I came running to the Bren Gun on the other side of the OP, and took post outside the battery in the bushes.
>
> I manned the Bren Gun from there and fired at anyone who approached the battery. After about two hours I removed the barrel of the Bren Gun and entered the battery. I found the Guard Room open and searched for the guards who were not there. I met Gnr Subramaniam giving water to Gnr Daniels who was wounded in the Weapon Pit.
>
> I searched for Lieut. Stephens and his sentry. I came out and shouted 'Captain Gardiner!', who advanced. I surrendered myself and explained everything. I went round

with him first to Lieut. Stephens' room. He was not there. I entered the Guard Room in his company and we found Gnr Wijesekera behind the door. I shouted for Gnr R A V Perera and he came out of the camouflage.

Capt. Gardiner flashed a torch and found him wounded on the eye. Capt. Gardiner went up the OP. While going up the OP he was confronted by Gnr Seneviratne who was crying. Capt. Gardiner went up the OP and found Gnr Jayasekera dead.

Fernando added: 'The events that took place that night were just a conflagration that had been smouldering for years in me.'

It will have been noted that Fernando twice told the court that he had ordered Gauder to shoot Stephens. This was confirmed by two other depositions, which indicated as well that he had first asked Hamilton to do so. If it had been part of his plan to kill Stephens — so much for a bloodless mutiny — this would unequivocally explain his decision to make sure the lieutenant would be on duty. If only Gauder had been given the task, it might be possible to imagine it was a spur-of-the-moment decision prompted by the sudden appearance of Stephens on the scene. But the evidence suggests there was very little time between Stephens's emergence and his confrontation with Gauder — not nearly enough for Hamilton to be given the order, spend some time considering it (according to Gauder's version) and ultimately refuse before Fernando turned to Gauder.

The Court in its afternoon session summoned Lance Sergeant O M D W Perera. He was a well-known Ceylonese boxer who, in meets conducted by the YMCA and other local groups, had shown prowess in this activity. All these years he has been the stormy petrel of the Cocos story, as will become clear. Fernando denied many of the statements that Perera attributed to him. Perera began by saying:[4]

Since the time the mutiny ended Bdr G H Fernando told me that the following were involved in the plot: L/Bdr Diasz, Gnrs A J L Peries, Hopman, Daniels, Anandappa, Gauder, G

B de Silva and Hamilton. He said that the rest of the accused were also involved except Gnr S H de Zilva, who he said was definitely innocent. He told me he had torn up a paper with some names after the mutiny. He said he had instructed some men not to go into the battery if there was an alarm that night, but gave no names.

He was then subjected to vigorous cross-examination by a number of the accused, the aim probably being to cast doubt on his claim that Fernando had, with the one exception, confirmed that the accused were participants in the mutiny and otherwise to undermine his integrity as a witness. The record is incomplete in the respect that only some of the questions are reproduced.

Fernando: 'When did I tell you this?'

Perera: 'You told me this on the way to the shed.'

Perera in reply to Anandappa: 'It was on or about the second day after your arrest that Bdr G H Fernando told me this.'

Perera in reply to Fernando: 'You did not mention L/Bdr B G de Zilva's name nor that of any other man, other than the accused in the battery.'

Perera in reply to Anandappa again: 'He stated that the rest of the accused were in it. Bdr Fernando asked me in the evening of the day of the mutiny who the accused were. The next day he told me that all the accused except Gnr S H de Zilva were in the plot, and gave the names I have stated above.'

Perera in reply to Porritt: 'You were already in arrest when Bdr G H Fernando asked who the accused were.'

Perera in reply to Hopman: 'I gave Bdr G H Fernando the names of the accused when I was guard over the prisoners. I have no witnesses who heard Bdr G H Fernando make this statement about the accused.'

The court then became involved in the tale of a piece of paper that might have had damning evidence as to who took part in the mutiny. Perera is not quite convincing in his further reply to Hopman:

I thought it of no use to attempt to pick up the torn up pieces of paper after I had been told that it contained certain names. I have not reported this until now as I wanted to give that information in my statement. Bdr G H Fernando's very words were 'They are in it, the arrested, except for Gnr S H de Zilva.'

Gunner Peries then cross-examined Perera, who replied:

I took Bdr G H Fernando to the hut to change his clothes at his request. He took out some books, which I took, and a piece of paper which he tore up before I could stop him. It was useless to try to pick up the torn bits of paper.

Perera had a firm response when Gunner Ken Porritt suggested to him that he had conceded that he (Porritt) was not involved:

Two days after your arrest I told you that I knew your parents and your brothers as well. I told you that I never expected to see you under arrest. I did not say I was sorry to see you there. I did not tell you that you were put under arrest for keeping bad company. I did not tell you not to worry as you had not become involved in it so far.

It was Hamilton's turn to question Perera, who replied: 'When Bdr Fernando opened his trunk, I was standing near him.' The focus on Fernando's box, which a complete transcript no doubt would illuminate, continued in Perera's reply to Kronemberg: '… I did not know that books and dangerous instruments were removed from the boxes of the accused.' Hamilton pressed with a further question along these lines, but the Lance Sergeant remained unflappable:

I did not have reasons or suspicions for searching Bdr G H Fernando's box after he had finished changing and I had taken him back to prison. I did not think there was anything suspicious in the box, after the other books had been taken and the paper torn up outside the barrack room.

Fernando then challenged Perera. His main complaint was that he had not said things he had been quoted as saying:

> I burned the piece of paper [that] he says I tore up and threw outside. There were several people — I cannot say who — who saw me burn the paper. I burned it with two film negatives. All this information was volunteered and I said to Sgt O M D W Perera that the paper contained the names of everybody in the Battery and that if Capt. Gardiner got it he would not know what to make of it.
>
> I did not mention any of the names stated by ... Perera as implied by him in connection with this. I mentioned these names just casually. He told me that the others involved were cowards. But I made no remarks or statements to any effect. I also mentioned that Gnr S H de Zilva, Edema, Patterson as far as I know were quite innocent, although all the names of the accused were mentioned to me. I was definitely very cautious about Gnr S H de Zilva, Patterson and Edema.

Some doubletalk over the mention of names will be noted here, as will the fact that, by selecting out de Zilva, Patterson and Edema, he was implicating all the other accused. At this distance it is difficult to see the significance of burning papers as opposed to tearing them up, but it was clearly a major point of contention. Fernando got a heated response from Perera:

> You tore up two Post Office Savings Bank books. I do not remember you burning anything. I asked you why you tore the paper. You said it contained names. You did not say it contained the names of every person in the battery. You did not tell me that there were crosses against certain names. You did not tell me that the paper would not have made any sense to Capt. Gardiner. I did not ask you why you had a

paper containing names of all the battery. At the time I did not know whether the paper was important or not.

For some reason Hopman decided to pursue the matter of the bank books, prompting this reply from Perera:

> The savings books were the usual size. I did not know if there were papers in the books or not. I thought they were merely Savings Bank books, and allowed him [Fernando] to tear them up, although I was not certain whether there were any papers in them or not. He tore up the papers and afterwards the books were torn. The papers were torn inside the trunk and thrown outside the barrack room.

Former Lance Sergeant O M D W Perera died in Melbourne on 29 November 1999. He was cremated at a Buddhist ceremony in Springvale Cemetery after a funeral oration given by war veteran Clarence Corera.

In Cocos Keeling on 12 May 1942 it was a long and hard day for both witnesses and the accused. The latter were less than impressed by the performance of Henry de Sylva, who interrupted them frequently. Yet Fernando remained forthright. Gardiner was determined that all the procedures of military law were observed in conducting the case.

In the corner of the court, Gunner Carlo Augustus Gauder was waiting his turn in the drama.

12

Vendetta Against Lieutenant Stephens

Lieutenant Henry Stephens was a handsome young officer whose role in the Cocos mutiny was both ambiguous and tragic. His demeanour was confident and stylish, and he always played by the book. Though himself a Eurasian, Stephens was a racist of the deepest dye, prone to affirming in very forthright terms the elevated role of the white man in Asia. Indeed some of his off-the-cuff remarks in the Cocos canteen made it clear that he believed Hitler was justified in culling the non-Aryan races.

It was Gunner Carlo Augustus Gauder, Stephens's Josephian boarding mate, who was detailed to carry out the final vendetta against him during the mutiny. In his evidence on oath at the Field General Court Martial, Gauder, now obviously rattled at the turn of events, decided to come clean:[1]

> I knew everything that was going on about two weeks before the mutiny. Bdr G H Fernando told me about the plot. He said it was to break off the differences between the Europeans and the Ceylonese. He told me what part I was to take in the mutiny, and I agreed. I said I thought it was useless as there was only one European and apart from him we would be killing our own blood the Ceylonese. Hamilton insisted that it should be done. I did not know what I was

doing when I agreed. I admit that I was just foolish.

He went on to describe to the court how on the night of the mutiny he was on guard when Hamilton came up and told him he was going to shoot Stephens, and then went inside the battery. In his statement Gauder clarified the part he played:

> I heard one round fired from the Bren gun, which had been taken outside of the battery. Gnr Hamilton came back and told me that he could not shoot Mr Stephens. Bdr G H Fernando told me then to shoot Mr Stephens. I went to the Guard Room and saw Mr Stephens in front of it. I fired at him three times and went to the sandbag emplacement. I don't know why I fired at Mr Stephens. I have no grievance against him, nor Capt. Gardiner, nor anybody here.
>
> I think the following are involved in the mutiny: Gnrs Hamilton, G B de Silva, A J L Peries, Daniels, L/Bdr K W J Diasz.

At this stage the court adjourned, with the accused led away by the guards under the supervision of Perera. At resumption the next day Gauder submitted another sworn statement to the court, which began: 'I wish to say nothing further in my defence. I wish to call no witnesses in my defence. I took part in the mutiny.' He went on to say that that the men he had mentioned — Hamilton, de Silva, Peries, Daniels and Diasz — were present when the plot was discussed and all expressed willingness to participate.

> I did not know that the mutiny was going to take place that night, but when I heard the firing I realised what it was. Bdr G H Fernando told me that night 'Don't break down.' I thought there was going to be some trouble.

Gauder expressed the opinion that S H de Zilva, Edema and Patterson were innocent, though he added that this was what Fernando had told him while they were in the shed under arrest.

He went on: 'Gnr Hopman said that he was against the mutiny. He said so to Bdr G H Fernando.'

Captain Gardiner, as president of the court, then summoned Lieutenant Henry F Stephens, who was a witness for the prosecution. Having taken the oath, Stephens stated that on the night of 8/9 May he was in the Officers' War Shelter at Rowe Battery as duty officer.[2] After he fell asleep he was roused by Gunner R A V Perera. 'He spoke to me through the window in the wall between the Guard Room and the Officers' War Shelter,' said Stephens.

> He told me that ... all the guards were locked in the Guard Room. So I went to the entrance of the Guard Room. It was latched from outside, the padlock being open. I opened the door and asked what the trouble was. The Guard Room was in darkness. They all said that the rifles and SAA [small arms ammunition] had been removed. I was told that someone was asleep in the artillery store with a rifle and ammunition. I left the Guard Room with one of the guards Gnr Seneviratne.

Stephens explained to the Court that as he turned the corner he saw somebody coming towards him.

> It was Gnr Gauder coming towards me with his rifle under his arm pointing in my direction. He was about two yards away when I spoke to him. I called his name. He fired a round at me. One bullet grazed my right cheekbone just below my eye. I fired my revolver where the flash came from. He fired another round at me. I fired back. I think Gauder fired four or five rounds at me.
>
> As I had only one round left, I took cover in the camouflage by the OP. There was a man in the OP trench and one or two outside it. I went to No. 1 Magazine and took cover in the space between the magazine wall and the splinter proof wall. I heard two bursts of Bren Gun fire. After some time I heard the voice of Bdr G H Fernando calling out

[to me]. I also heard him shout several times: 'Capt. Gardiner to the battery.'

From my cover I saw Bdr G H Fernando come into the magazine and look for me. He then went away. Before the first burst of Bren gun fire I heard a row on the top of the OP and shots. I heard somebody shouting and there seemed to be a lot of confusion.

Continuing his evidence, Stephens stated that he stayed under cover till daylight. When he heard the voices of Corporal Ferdinands and Sergeant Pereira he decided to come out of cover, and he met Gardiner at the magazine entrance. He told Gardiner that Gauder had fired at him. In a footnote to his evidence he said that, just after Fernando had called to him to come out from hiding, he had heard de Silva's voice calling 'Stephens — where is that bastard Stephens?' He was absolutely certain it was Gauder who had fired at him.

Benny de Silva then cross-examined Stephens, asking whether the officer had actually seen him. Stephens replied: 'I heard your voice but did not see you. Your voice came from the direction of the OP. I heard it after the shots in the OP, and after I heard Bdr G H Fernando's voice and the groaning and shouting in the OP.'

In reply to Fernando he said: 'I cannot say at what particular time I heard your voice.' To a question by Hamilton his answer was: 'After the first shot was fired I did not shout for anybody.'

It was now Gunner R S Hamilton's turn to give evidence. In doing so he presented the prosecution with what it wanted to hear,[3] for it seemed he was determined to tell all. He did not allow his original commitment to Fernando's plan to concern him, and what he had to say was in a real sense a betrayal of his mutineer friends. He began:

Bdr G H Fernando was the main cause of all the trouble. He had said that he was anti-British although he was in the army. He prejudiced me and some of the other men. He said that Capt. Gardiner and the officer must be shot, and in other ways spoke abusively of Capt. Gardiner.

On the night of 9 May 1942 Gnr G B de Silva came to my bed at about 11.30 or 12 and told me I was wanted in the Guard Room. When I was entering the battery with him I saw Bdr G H Fernando coming out of the battery with the Bren. He told me not to get out as I would be shot. Gnr G B de Silva came to me with a revolver and asked me to kill Lieut. Stephens. I told him I could not. Then he told me to get into the sand bag pit, giving me a rifle and 40 rounds. Gnr Gauder was in the sand bag pit when I entered it. Gnr G B de Silva told me that I must shoot anybody coming into the battery. Gnrs Gauder and G B de Silva ran to the Guard Room. I then heard the first shots being fired. I left the rifle that was given to me and ran to the recreation room, crawling through the barbed wire by the beach.

Retracing his steps a little, Hamilton said that Diasz was with him in the pit after Gauder left, and that he had a rifle. When Diasz heard a burst of fire from the Bren gun, he left Hamilton and ran away.

I then went and hid in the shed where the hay is kept. At about two o'clock when the firing had stopped I went to the recreation hut and slept there, and Bdr H L B Fernando came in the morning with a rifle and said that I was the cause of all this.

I saw Gnr Gauder shoot Lieut. Stephens. I saw Gnr Daniels shoot Gnr Wijeysekera. I saw Gnr G B de Silva shoot Gnr R A V Perera.

He went on to report that he had heard Fernando say, presumably on a previous occasion, that they should take the battery by killing both officers and all the sergeants, but that they should spare as many of the men as possible. He wanted all the staff of Cable and Wireless on Direction Island to be killed, 'and then send a message to the Japs asking them to come and destroy this place.'

We must then go to Home Island to kill the Governor and his Secretary and take all the boats and go to Christmas Island. He did not tell me any plans.

During this night Bdr G H Fernando wanted to signal to Direction to get the Machine Gunners and Lewis Gunners over as if the CO wanted them, telling us to take post by the jetty under cover, and as soon as they approach to shoot them. He said that if after this all happened an English vessel came here we could say that there had been a Japanese attack. He wanted to shoot at any such ship.

Hamilton continued with three disconnected statements:

On that night Bdr G H Fernando told me that if I did not shoot anybody who came into the battery, I would be shot myself when everything was over.

About a month before, I heard Bdr G H Fernando, L/Bdr Diasz, Gnr Edema and Gnr G B de Silva talking about this plan.

I am quite innocent of this and had been told that if I got out of the battery I would be shot.

Gnr Hamilton then spoke of two pistols that had been buried close to the beach 'near the shed where the hay is kept.' Ammunition was also buried there.

I saw L/Bdr Diasz and Bdr G H Fernando, Gnr Hopman and Gnr Edema coming from that direction about three weeks before the mutiny. About four days before the mutiny, Gnr A J L Peries told me that these things were buried there.

On the day of the mutiny Gnr A J L Peries told me that if there was an alarm to run to the recreation hut and not to the battery. When I asked him why he said he would tell me later. When Gnr A J L Peries fell down from the OP when on guard a few days before the mutiny, it was done on purpose so that he could visit the [Medical Inspection] Room ... and take rifles and ammunition from the BQMS Store.

Hamilton later said that he did not wish to make any statement in his defence. He named those whom he said were prejudiced by Fernando in favour of mutinying as Diasz, Daniels, Edema, Hopman, L B de Zilva, G B de Silva and Porritt.

> [Fernando] discussed the idea of a mutiny with those men and me about a month before the mutiny in the Barrack room.
>
> Gnr A J L Peries was trying to improve on the plan and make suggestions. So was L/Bdr Diasz. Gnr Hopman was against mutinying, as he said he had only six months here. He said it was useless. Bdr G H Fernando said he would attempt the mutiny on a day when he was on guard.

Hamilton's evidence was obviously giving weight to the prosecution case. He added: 'I did not shoot at anybody on the night of the mutiny. I found L/Bdr Diasz standing at the corner of the Sergeants' Mess at the On Guard position. When the Bren gun first fired, he fired a round and then climbed up a tree.'

Hamilton recalled Hopman saying to Fernando: 'If you want to do anything like this, why don't you do it by yourself instead of dragging poor people in.'

Hamilton told the court that Porritt and Edema just listened to the discussions about the mutiny without saying anything. He added that it was de Silva who suggested taking the Clunies-Ross boats and going to Christmas Island.

The Field General Court Martial adjourned after its third day of hearings, leaving the mutineers probably more worried than they were at its beginning. It was Gunner Mark Hopman's turn to testify, and he would add another nail to the coffin.[4] With the opening of the next day's proceedings Hopman was cautioned and then began his story:

> On the night of the mutiny I was awoken by a burst of machine-gun fire. When I awoke there was nobody else in the hut. I took my rifle and equipment and as I ran out I bumped into Gnr Kronemberg who told me that they were

firing on people running into the battery. We both went out through the back door of the barrack room.

Hopman recounted how they reached 'the building behind the kitchen,' where they met gunners C Wijenayake and L B de Zilva, who did not know what the trouble was except that Captain Gardiner had given orders that they should keep under cover. He did not load his rifle, as he understood that the orders were not to load. After a time Diasz came up and repeated the message that they were to keep under cover. Then he went off.

After some time Hopman, Wijenayake, Kronemberg and L B de Zilva decided to try and get to a place where some of the other men were gathered. When they got to a tent where the observation post staff slept, Hopman found that only Wijenayake had followed him. After a time Porritt came in and told them that the men had gone into the barracks, so they went there.

With regard to the build-up to the mutiny, Hopman told the court:

> About a month before the mutiny I heard Gnr G B de Silva and Hamilton talk about something of this sort, but did not attach any deep motive to it. One night Gnr G B de Silva woke me up — about this time — and said that if there was an alarm not to go out. I asked why. He asked me to come out and meet some other people.
>
> I went out and found Gnr Anandappa and Gauder. They told me that everything was prepared and they were going to capture the battery. They said that the other people in this were in No.2 Magazine. I went there and found Bdr G H Fernando, Gnrs Patterson, Edema and Hamilton. They said they were going to capture the battery. I told them they would never be able to do it and would be shot. Everybody went to bed and I thought that was the end of it.

To a question from Lieutenant Menon, Hopman answered: 'Gnrs Donald Patterson and Alfred Edema did not seem to like it. About three or four days before the mutiny Gnr Anandappa, who was a good friend of mine, did not speak to me.' Hopman felt that something suspicious was going on, but he did not think much of it. He said:

I attached no importance to it until the night of the mutiny. Bdr Diasz came and told me 'We will settle our accounts today' or something of that sort. After dinner Hamilton suggested going to the Guard Room to have some tea. As he told me that Bdr G H Fernando was guard commander that night, I thought I would take the opportunity of asking him about what Bdr Diasz had said.

We went to the Guard Room, Hamilton and I. On the way we were joined by L/Bdr Diasz and Edema. Bdr Diasz again began to talk saying 'I'll do some good shooting today' and so on. I told him not to be a fool. Gauder came up about this time. I told them that they talked big, but would not do anything, and that I was not going to stand for seeing my own friends shot.

They then went into the guardroom and drank some tea. There were quite a lot of them there, and Hopman could not remember who they all were. He remembered Daniels, Edema and G B de Silva. After they had had their tea a number of them went away. Hopman then told the court of his final session with Bdr Fernando:

Bdr Fernando came in. I asked him if they were starting trouble again. He said it was all right and that I could go to sleep. I went back to bed. Gnr Edema and A J L Peries came back with me. I did not know whether to tell Mr Stephens or not, but did not think they would really mutiny, and so I did nothing further.

In an attached statement in the Field General Court Martial file, submitted as part of the proceedings of the court martial, Hopman stated:

I wish to say that referring to that part of my voluntary statement in which I said that L/Bdr Diasz had talked about doing some good shooting, he said this in Sinhalese and in a flippant manner and I did not attach any importance to it at the time. It was only after the trouble began that I realised its significance.

I wish to make no further statement in my defence.

I do not wish to call any witnesses in my defence.

When I went to the magazine about a month before the mutiny, the men there were Gnrs G B de Silva, Anandappa, Gauder, Patterson, Edema L/Bdr Diasz and Bdr G H Fernando. They definitely stated that they would sound the alarm and force those who came in to surrender, and they would seize the battery. I told them that this was nonsense and everybody went off. I did not think of taking it seriously.

Although Hopman had closed his case, he yet decided to approach the court again to make a further statement to justify his position. Incidentally Captain Gardiner was at pains to attest that 'the statement was made before the findings of the FGCM.'

Re the affair of a month ago I must mention that when I went over to the magazine, I noticed that not a single man had brought any arms or ammunition with him. This just proves what I thought, that all this was just idiotic folly and I really did not give the matter a second thought.

The reason why I did not report this is that I would not have had a shred of proof, and if action was taken, all that would have happened would have been a counter charge by Bdr G H Fernando against me for bringing a false charge.

The reason why I did not tell Lt Stephens 'unofficially' is that when nothing happened I would have been just a sneak who tried to set up an officer against a comrade.

Hopman expressed the hope that the court would see his position, as he could 'boldly' state that he had done nothing crooked or against what he thought absolutely correct. As regards the actual mutiny, all he had heard was the remark of Diasz, which he felt might very well have been just a bit of flippant bravado.

> Just for a fraction of a second I thought that there might be something behind it, but when Bdr G H Fernando said that nothing was further from his mind, I went to bed without a further thought about it.

Hopman assured the court that, had he heard anything further, he would most certainly have told Stephens about it, 'but of course this statement will cut no ice now after the fact.' He felt that the chief disadvantage of his case was that two of his friends were involved in it, and so it seemed likely that he also might have been in it.

> I can give a reason why I was not told, but can furnish no proof unless the Court makes Bdr G H Fernando coincide with it by refreshing his memory.

Hopman then went on to say:

> I recall a conversation of long ago, now that I know the reason for this mutiny. Bdr Fernando asked me casually 'Hopman, if the Japs were to attack this place, would you give your life in fighting against them?' I was positively astonished and exclaimed, 'Of course, what a question to ask?' He said 'But why? What wrong have the Japs done you.' I said 'That's not the point. We have *volunteered* to fight for the British, and our Corps, Ceylon and the Government have chosen us to hold this outpost for them. If we don't, we will be abusing their trust and letting them all down. If you feel you must side with the Japs, you have first to get back to Ceylon, leave the army and then join them. Don't you think so?' He thought for a minute, then said, 'Yes that's true. It's strange it never struck me like that.'

Lieutenant Henry de Sylva, CLI Commander on Direction Island, member of the Field General Court Martial.

The conversation, he said, took place a long time ago, but Fernando might remember it.

Hopman was critical of the procedure followed during the court martial investigations and hearings. One of his complaints was that he was not allowed to make notes to help him to conduct his defence. He was among those who took strong exception to de Sylva's frequent interruptions on matters that were hardly relevant to the case.[5]

As dusk came to Cocos Keeling, there were others who knew they had still to face the court. Some were the hangers-on; others were fighting their own rearguard actions to save themselves from the supreme penalty.

13

Silent Hangers-on

On the outskirts of Colombo in the suburb of Nugegoda I met Gunner Alfred Edema in July 1992. The visit came as an unwelcome surprise to a soldier who played a tenuous part as one of the hangers-on in the Cocos mutiny. But like all those who claim to be silent listeners, Edema was to pay a price. His daughter Gwen said that her father had wanted to write his story for the Readers Digest, but she realised that he had only scanty information to base it on. He was unwilling to speak with me at first, but later relented.

Edema's opinion of Gardiner did not coincide with the one most of his former colleagues expressed. He kept insisting that the captain was not a hardened racist, nor a martinet, but simply an officer who enforced a high standard of discipline. He was inclined to blame the BQMS, A H Perera, for a large part of the grievances on Horsburgh. Fernando, Edema said, had very compelling powers of persuasion. 'G H had a way of asking us why we were fighting the war. Wasn't Asia for the Asians?' Nonetheless he gave me the impression that he had allowed himself to be brought into the inner circle through a sense of Galle Face comradeship more than anything else. In the end he paid a heavy price.

At the Cocos atoll in May 1942 Edema faced the Field General Court Martial as one of the accused in the mutiny.[1] He began:

On the night of the mutiny I was awoken by the sound of a shot. I took my arms and equipment. As I crossed the tennis court I heard the Bren Gun being fired. I saw some men coming back and I turned back.

He described to the court how he had met up with Peries and Patterson near the servants' quarters, and then saw the Bren gun being fired again. They waited for some time before going to the entrance of the recreation hut. All of them loaded their magazines with five rounds, he said, and as they waited they saw some men were going to the barracks. Gardiner came and took them back to the battery at about 5.30 or 6 a.m.

Edema did not want to call any witnesses. He went on:

I have never heard anybody talking about a mutiny. I heard Gnr Peries telling the servants not to go out. I did not think it unusual and I was dazed by the firing. Bdr G H Fernando was a very good friend of mine, but he never told me anything about an anti-white feeling.

His evidence did not differ widely from that of Gunner A J L Peries, who said:[2]

I was asleep in the barrack room when I heard the first firing, I thought it was an alarm and took my equipment. As I was going out Bdr E A Fernando spoke to me and asked me what I was looking for. I said my helmet is missing. Bdr B G de Zilva asked me what the trouble was. I told him there was an alarm. I found I had not taken my respirator, and I came back for it and followed Bdr B G de Zilva out of the barrack room.

He went on to relate that at the foot of the steps of the barrack room they both loaded their rifles.

At the corner of the tennis court I saw the Bren gun firing in my direction and men taking cover. I ran back and hid in the servants' quarters. Gnr Patterson and Edema were there with me. We waited there for about two hours and then we all went into the recreation room. We came out and went into the barrack room. Gnr Patterson met me in the barrack room. Capt. Gardiner then came in with a torch and unloaded the magazines of our rifles [and told us to go to the battery]. When we had got into the battery, Gnr Patterson was already there.

Patterson's remarkable agility may be remarked upon in passing. Peries then gave a brief account of his movements early in the evening. He had been in the guardroom at about 8.15 p.m., after which he went back to the barracks. The lights were already out, so he took S W Perera's torch in order to arrange his bunk. Perera then 'lit the lamp.'

Gunner Peries refused to make any further statement and expressed the wish to call as witness Lance Bombardier Perera, who had given him the torch.

In response to questions from Lieutenant Menon, Peries said that he did not remember meeting anybody on the pier on any evening, nor had he ever met anybody in the battery for a chat. He thought the alarm was enemy action and, because he heard voices, he went to the servants' quarters.

> I have never gone into the servants' quarters on an alarm before. I saw other men running in all directions. (I went into the Guardroom that night at about 7.45 p.m.)
> Anybody who says that I am involved in this mutiny is telling a deliberate lie.

Peries then elaborated on some of his earlier evidence. He had turned back after hearing four or five shots coming from the direction of the battery and before the Bren gun firing began. He had heard the first burst while he was running.

> I sat in the servants' quarters and saw the second burst when I was there. Other men were going back too, so I went back

also. I heard an order to take cover. Although on other alarms in the form of rifle shots from the battery men have always advanced to their positions in action, in this case they were coming back. It did not strike me as strange although it has never happened before. I thought it was enemy action, and went to the servants' quarters and told them not to come out. I told them casually. I would not have shot the servants if they had tried to go out because I had no reason to.

Peries now found himself in a net of conflicting evidence. Questioned by the court, he replied:

I cannot say why in my voluntary statement I saw the Bren gun firing from the corner of the tennis court, when I have told the Court that I first saw tracer bullets going past when I was in the servants' hut.

In reply to another question he said, 'The time between the first and the second burst was not more than five minutes. It may have been less.' An annotation to the transcript in Gardiner's hand reads: 'It was 5–10 seconds.'

Gnr Peries concluded his evidence:

I remained in the servants' hut until the firing was over. Later Capt. Gardiner found me and Edema in the barrack room, and unloaded our magazines and told us to go to the battery and report to the BQMS.

In a trellised house that was part of a sub post office close to the Dehiwela Bridge in a Colombo suburb, I met Gunner Gerry Anandappa. At first he was reluctant to give me any details of the part he played in the Cocos mutiny, but gentle persuasion was rewarded.

A soft-spoken, candid man, he loved the dance floor. There, as he and his dancing partners measured the steps of a waltz, he would tell them, in a rather cryptic way, that he nearly faced a firing squad in World War Two. Anandappa struck me as a man of his word who believed that loyalty in comradeship could never be bartered.[3] His testimony to the Field General Court Martial was enthralling:[4]

> I knew about the plot about 2 or 3 weeks before the time of the mutiny, but I never for a moment thought that it would materialise. It was in just common talk I agreed. I did not know the day on which it was planned to take place. I did not release a single round from any kind of weapon. Bdr G H Fernando told me about the plot. He told me nothing in detail about the plot and in common talk I gave him my word. He told me about the feeling he had which was something to the effect of 'East for the East.'

When I met him, Anandappa spoke of Fernando's extensive knowledge of the progress of the Japanese in the war, their war aims and their endeavour to put an end to the white man's regime. Continuing his testimony, he said, '[Fernando] asked me if I would back him up if he did something. I thought it was just a wild hope and said I would back him up.' Anandappa agreed to back him up, rather than not do so, because he 'trusted him too much.' When the actual mutiny took place he was bewildered. Because he had given his word, he could not actually sneak out of it when it was happening.

> I do not want anyone to think that I was out for murder, as I did not want to fire a single shot. I had only two rounds that I picked up and shared with Gnr Subramaniam, who said he had no ammunition.

He did not call any witnesses. He admitted to the court, on being cross-examined by Captain Gardiner, that he could have stopped Fernando firing his Bren gun, but did not do so because he had given him his word to stand by him. Then he came out with an amazing statement:

> The only thing I thought of doing, which I suggested to Bdr

G H Fernando, was that I should shoot him first and then myself. We disagreed on that and I walked into the battery hoping to be riddled by bullets. I shared my two rounds with Gnr Subramaniam in the hope of being shot by him.

At this point the court changed tack and began to hear evidence from the loyal troops. First it was the turn of Sergeant I L Pereira,[5] who began as follows:

On the night of the mutiny I was able to get into the battery, with Cpl Ferdinands, Sapper Corteling, Bdr H L B Fernando and Gnr Sahadevan. They got in before me.

Questioned about the influence of Gratien Fernando, Pereira replied:

Since the mutiny has ended, Bdr G H Fernando has told me that he was anti-British. He said he was more anti-British after being in the *Kelantan*.

He said his intention was to get Capt. Gardiner and Lt Stephens and all those who were against him. He told me that men had been placed in certain positions in the battery to pick off the men who filtered in. He said there were also men detailed to take up positions outside the battery. One place mentioned was No. 2 Magazine. He said that he mistook Cpl Ferdinands for Capt. Gardiner and opened fire.

On being cross-examined by Fernando concerning the identity of the men involved, Pereira answered:

You told me that there were certain men who were definitely innocent of all you had done. I cannot remember your telling me that they were cowards and of no use to you. You mentioned as such men Gunners S B de Zilva, Patterson, Weber, Kronemberg and Edema.

It was in December 1986 that I interviewed Gunner Mervyn C J W De Rooy of Perth, Australia, who was on Cocos from 3 March until 30 August 1942. De Rooy surfaced at a time when Lance Sergeant O M D W Perera was telling the Ceylon Artillery Association in Australia a tendentious story in which he presented himself as the saviour of Cocos.[6]

De Rooy had no recollection whatever of Perera playing a part in bringing the mutiny under control, much less doing anything that would qualify him as the hero of Rowe Battery. 'That was pure fantasy,' said De Rooy. He maintained that it was a man with an almost identical name — Pereira — who played the most important role in bringing the mutiny to an end. 'Sergeant I L Pereira was the orderly of the day. It was he who relieved me of my guard duty, and then Gunner Samuel Jayasekera took over.' De Rooy noted at the time that Gratien Fernando seemed displeased when Jayasekera appeared on the scene.

> It was Pereira who, during all the firing that was taking place, managed to creep under the battery barbed wire and at rifle point get Bdr G H Fernando to surrender and called out for Capt. Gardiner to proceed to the battery.

According to De Rooy, 'Captain Gardiner was a disciplinarian … but by no means a martinet. Those who thought he was an unbearable officer brought it upon themselves; [he] had every reason to enforce law and order.'

Speaking of the unrest on Horsburgh prior to the mutiny, he recalled one incident in which stones were thrown at and damage done to the sergeants' quarters. There were frequent complaints about the meals, but the situation was unavoidable: shipping and supplies were delayed owing to the Japanese presence in the Indian Ocean.

Mervyn De Rooy said that there had been discontent among some of the senior gunners such as Gauder, Benny de Silva and Diasz. They had assumed that, having served in Seychelles, they would have been considered for promotion, and since being overlooked they were somewhat disgruntled. Then he spoke of Fernando:

> [He] at no time had anything good to say about the British regime. In fact when he was seen off at the jetty by his friend Bombardier T N Ousmand, he said he was 'going to create history.' On one occasion he approached me and wanted my opinion on the way we were being treated. I told him that we volunteered to go to Cocos, and under war conditions one has to expect a certain amount of discomfort, or the other alternative was not to have volunteered at all.
>
> G H Fernando for me was a 'Walter Mitty' character. It was foolhardiness on the part of the rest of the crew to have blindly followed him because no good came out of it.

He insisted that in no way was anyone ill-treated. 'We were under war conditions,' he said, 'and our sole purpose was to be ready to defend to the best of our ability. That is why we volunteered to do what was requested of us.' He regretted very much the involvement of some of the Burgher boys.

> I am the son of a Boer former prisoner of war. My mother was the daughter of Charles Strantinberg, Crown Proctor of Jaffna. I was educated at St Patrick's College, Jaffna, and always maintained the College motto 'Faith and Labour'.[7]

Some felt that De Rooy was over-inclined to highlight his European ancestry. The deep traditions of colonialism and the culture of the British Commonwealth were hard to dispel.

His praise of the efforts of Sergeant I L Pereira is at odds with the finding, at a later stage of the legal process, of the Judge Advocate General, who asked that 'action be taken against this officer for not doing anything to control the situation.'

In the Cocos prison Gunner G B de Silva awaited his turn to face the court. He had been in the 'inner sanctum' of the mutiny, and his evidence would erode some of the statements of the hangers-on.

14

Gunner Benny's Odyssey

Every year on 7 August in Edmonton, Alberta, Canada, a well-attended Requiem Mass is said for the repose of the soul of Gunner G Benny de Silva. The memories are kept alive by one of his cousin, Dr J T L C Fernando, a noted medical practitioner in that city, whose parents tried desperately to save the soldier from execution.

The story begins in the Colombo suburb of Moratuwa. Benny was born on 24 February 1919; two years later a sister followed, but the difficult confinement took the life of the mother. Their father having died also, the two young children were raised by Dr Fernando's grandmother Mrs Robertina Mendis de Silva and her husband, Gabriel Benedict de Silva, headmaster of St Sebastian's primary school, run by the De La Salle Christian Brothers. Benny's father, Edward Francis de Silva, had been a well-known and beloved teacher at the secondary school. When Benny was eighteen, he and his sister Mildred came under the tutelage of Dr Fernando's parents, Joseph and Bridget Fernando, both of them also dedicated teachers.[1] Then, while still a teenager, Benny left St Sebastian's, deserted home and went on the road.

Dressed in a sarong and unshaven, he would sometimes sit begging outside the Maradana Railway Station in the bustling city of Colombo, where well-dressed middle-class former school mates would greet 'Gal Bola', as he had been known in school.

Gunner Benny de Silva, hanged on 7 August 1942.

Contemporaries Vernon Forbes and Solomon Perera would remember the bright Benny de Silva who passed the Junior Certificate Examination in the First Division. Drop-out though he had become, they could not believe it when they later heard that he had been involved in a wartime mutiny

Mildred became a nun in a Diocesan Order of St Francis at Bolawalana under the tutelage of its foundress, Mother Marie Solange. Mildred de Silva (now Sister Benedicti) agonised over her brother, not least when he suddenly decided to volunteer for overseas service upon the outbreak of World War Two. His foster parents tried their best to dissuade him. 'Benny was anxious to go,' said Dr Fernando. 'Whether it was the extra income or a desire to prove himself I do not know. When he got into trouble during the mutiny my parents took care of legal bills and did their very best for him.'

Sister Benedicti has maintained silence about her brother's fate, refusing all interviews. A teacher by profession, she worked in adult education after her retirement. She spent some time in Hong Kong doing missionary work and later moved to Thailand. Now back in Ceylon, Sister Benedicti, who in 1998 celebrated fifty years as a nun, still maintains a reserve regarding her brother's part in the Cocos mutiny. This is understandable, and one can only reflect on the suffering she must have experienced over this matter.

As the Field General Court Martial continued, Lieutenant Henry de Sylva went on irritating witnesses with his barrages of questions and sundry interruptions. Many of the accused were upset also because they wrongly believed they were entitled to defence counsel, not realising that at the height of tension after a mutiny these legal aids were dispensed with.

Gunner G B de Silva began his testimony thus:[2]

> A little more than three weeks ago Bdr G H Fernando, Gnr A J
> L Peries, Gnr Hamilton, L/Bdr Diasz were having a
> conversation between the junior NCOs' mess and the canteen.
> When I got close to them they stopped talking. I asked them
> why they had stopped talking. They said that a little later on
> they wanted me to meet them in the recreation hut.
>   At 7 p.m. I met them at the pier. I heard Bdr G H
> Fernando telling the others that we must finish up the
> battery pretty soon. The same men were talking. I asked
> them what battery. Peries winked at Bdr G H Fernando.
> They stopped the conversation and said it was just for fun.
> Gnr Hamilton said that things like that should not be said in
> fun as I might take it seriously and tell Captain Gardiner. I
> thought it was a joke and forgot all about it.

He went on to give his version of the events of 8/9 May, when
(as he claimed) he was duty signaller. He had been in the
guardroom looking for a blue flag, which he had lost a few days
before, until about the time that one of the soldiers, Gunner I L
Pereira, came in. Then he told Fernando that he was 'going up [to
the observation post] to sleep.' He was woken some time later by
Fernando and asked if he would do a small favour.

> [Fernando] then said that Captain Gardiner had sent a
> message asking for his revolver in the OP. I took the
> revolver, which was loaded. When I asked why it was
> loaded, he said that it was normally kept loaded at night. I
> took it and came down. Bdr Fernando stayed up in the OP.
> As I was on my way to the officers' mess I met Gnr Hamilton
> by No. 1 magazine. He asked if Bdr Fernando had given any
> message. I told him where I was going and why. He said
> that he was the man who had brought the message. He took
> the revolver and went away.
>   I went up the OP again and met Bdr G H Fernando
> coming down. He then told me to come down as he wanted
> to tell me something. He asked if I were duty signaller and,

as I was, he told me to go up again, and if there were an alarm and I came down again I would know the consequences. I went up again and went to sleep, as I did not take him very seriously.

According to de Silva what happened next was that he was woken by three rifle shots.

I then heard shots that sounded like a machine-gun. I loaded a rifle. Just afterwards I heard a shot fired at the front of the staircase. I cocked the rifle and got under cover. I heard footsteps coming up the OP. I challenged and somebody challenged back, asking who was firing. I challenged again. As the man was on the last step I pressed the trigger. The man fell down. I recocked the rifle and somebody jumped on me saying 'I am Subramaniam' and he took the rifle from me.

The accused said that the reason he cocked and fired the rifle was that he had been warned that he would 'have to take the consequences' if he went down from the observation post. Subramaniam brought him down and told Gunner A M Jinadasa that Benny de Silva had 'shot at' Jayasekera. Jinadasa took him to the nearest trench. 'Later on,' de Silva said, 'when Capt. Gardiner had come into the battery, I told him that I had fired a shot.'

When some other men … and I were placed under arrest, we were put into a trench. Bdr G H Fernando said to me 'You would not have been in this trench now if the people who went back had worked with me.' I asked what he meant. He said 'You would have been in your own homes after a few days' imprisonment.'
He told me the plan, and said he was sorry he could not tell me before this. He asked if I had given the revolver to Hamilton, [and] I said I had, as he had asked me to. He told me it was he [Fernando] who had manned the Bren gun. He told me that the lookout who was missing from the top of the OP when I went up there on the sound of the first shot was at the foot of the OP. The missing lookout was Daniels. He said

that more than three-fourths of his converts had let him down.

A contradiction will have been noted in regard to de Silva's presence in the observation post. In the earlier part of his testimony he affirms more than once that he was the 'duty signaller.' In combination with his claim that he went to sleep, this amounts to a protestation of innocence, but he undermines it later by letting slip that he had actually replaced Daniels, who had gone missing. The court would probably have reasoned that only someone in on the plot would have been permitted to take over the observation post.

The references to Gardiner's revolver are also interesting, though I find them somewhat mystifying. Any order from the CO would of course be obeyed without hesitation, but the way Daniels tells the story Fernando is completely unruffled by the captain asking for his gun late at night just as a mutiny is about to start. Wouldn't it have occurred to the bombardier that Gardiner might be preparing himself for an uprising? Or issuing some sort of warning? Apparently not, and as it turned out he was quite right not to be bothered.

De Silva next stated that, while he was sitting in the trench under arrest, three men passed him and said that he was responsible for shooting their friend, and that they would 'make use of this.' Then, he said, Fernando told him that Daniels had fired at and missed the man he (de Silva) had shot, that is,. Jayasekera. The various references to Daniels add up to a remarkable story. First, he leaves his post (why?), then he shoots Wijeysekera (why?), next he fires at, but misses, Jayasekera (why?) and finally he ends up wounded in the weapon pit (how?) with Subramaniam ministering to his needs. If there had been a statement by Daniels in the mutiny files it could have made for interesting reading, but I could not find one.

After a recess the court assembled and heard a further statement. 'I was the man who shot Gnr Jayasekera and nobody else,' said de Silva. Then he went on to describe how, when he was stationed at Seychelles, Major Spurrier had asked him and

Gunner Keegel to make a plan of the whole battery and buildings for the purpose of putting up light shades. He made two copies. He gave one to Major Spurrier and the other he kept in his own service register along with some photographs. In the absence of the full transcript, the relevance of this discourse about a Sechelles map is rather baffling. It might be surmised that the prosecution's thinking ran along the lines that only a soldier intent on mischief would possess a plan of his camp, and so he would have to be a suspect when he was in another camp where an uprising took place. He went on:

> This morning I was allowed by the Guard to go to my trunk to get a towel and these snaps, and I found the plan missing. I suspect that certain things which might convict me were put into my suitcase. I want to say that I am innocent, and that even on my days of duty, I always did extra work in the battery.

The next day de Silva sought permission to make a further statement. In part this was a response to Stephens's evidence that he had called out 'Where is that bastard Stephens?'

> I wish to say that Mr Stephens could not have heard my voice calling for him as he states, because after Subramaniam brought me down from the OP I remained in the trench with Jinadasa. For the same reason neither R A V Perera nor Seneviratne could have heard me.

It is apparent here that R A V Perera and Seneviratne had supported Stephens's evidence that it was de Silva who had been searching for him. In the next part of this new statement there was a retraction:

> I do not wish to call any witnesses in my defence. My guilt is apparent only. In the discussions on the pier to which I refer in my statement, nobody made any suggestions on the subject. When G H Fernando said 'This battery must be

finished up' I knew he must mean this battery. I thought it was a joke and did not bother to report it.

He added that he was 'shocked' when he knew that the likes of Hopman, S H de Zilva, Porritt, Kronemberg and Edema had been arrested. They were usually very quiet, he said. With regard to the plan of Seychelles, it did not strike him as being a serious matter. He had kept the plan as a souvenir. He did not realise he had it with him when he left Seychelles

Benny de Silva felt the pangs of conscience. He looked back to his school days with the De La Salle Brothers in Moratuwa and his practice of the Roman Catholic faith. He remembered recounting to Patterson, as they sat by the lagoon one day, how the students would all stand up every hour at the ringing of a bell and say: 'Let us remind ourselves that we are in the presence of God.'

He decided to make yet another statement to the court. Much of it was retraction of his previous submissions. At one point in the new deposition he said: 'For my conscience' sake I wish my former statement to be torn up,' and at another: 'I am making this further statement because I swore on the Bible and my conscience is against me.' The first section of it offered an interesting variation on his account of the events leading up to the shooting of Jayasekera:

> When I was in the OP I saw two figures coming up the OP steps. When they asked who I was I replied 'duty signaller.' When they challenged again I fired ... Bdr G H Fernando [had] asked me to go to the top, and to stop anybody by force if necessary. When these two men came up I could not stop them by force and I was forced to fire. After firing, Subramaniam took me down and gave me to Jinadasa in the OP trench.
>
> I did not use the alleged words calling to Lt Stephens ...
>
> About an hour before the mutiny I was given my instructions by Bdr G H Fernando.

Benny de Silva watched as the court tore up his first statement, in which he had said that he was not aware of the plan of the mutiny. Then he said: 'I am sure as far as my knowledge goes that the following are innocent of this: Hopman, S H de Zilva, Porritt, Kronemberg, Edema.' He then admitted for the first time that he had been in on the planning of the mutiny, and in doing so he pointed a finger at others who had been involved:

> The following had a discussion with me and knew the plan. This was about three weeks ago: Bdr G H Fernando, L/Bdr Diasz, A J L Peries, Daniels, Anandappa, Gauder and Hamilton. I consider the ringleaders were Bdr G H Fernando, Gnr Peries and L/Bdr Diasz. The rest were merely tools. We discussed this in the battery at about 9.30 at night or on the beach.

Two unrelated statements completed the deposition:

> The Seychelles plan being with me was a bona fide mistake. The plan was definitely made for putting in light shades by another gunner whom I helped.
> I do not wish to be put down as a murderer. I did not wish to murder.

Gunner G B de Silva's confusions and contradictions did not impress the court. What did stick was the fact that he knew the plan and was an active participant in the execution of it.

As the Field General Court Martial heard the evidence of other witnesses for the prosecution, there was growing anxiety about the legality of the proceedings. These misgivings came too late to provide any support for Fernando's protests. And they did not wash with the president of the court, Captain Gardiner, nor with Lieutenant Henry de Sylva, who gave the impression that the mutineers would all hang.

PART THREE

DESTINY

15

Verdict at Eventide

Late in the evening of 16 May 1942 the president of the Field General Court Martial, Captain George Gardiner, delivered its verdict and the court passed sentence. Seven men were found guilty on all three charges: firstly, of causing a mutiny or conspiring with other persons to cause a mutiny in His Majesty's Forces; secondly, of joining a mutiny; and, thirdly, of not conveying knowledge of an intended mutiny to the commanding officer.

Guilty on charges 1, 2 and 3:
No. 1712 Bdr Fernando, G H: Death
No. 2002 Gnr Gauder, C: Death
No. 1989 Gnr de Silva, G B: Death
No. 2028 Gnr Hamilton, R S: Death
No. 1765 Gnr Anandappa, G D: Death
No. 1971 L/Bdr Diasz, K W J: Death
No. 2190 Gnr Peries, A J L: Death

Guilty on charges 1 and 3:
No. 2152 Gnr Edema, A B: Imprisonment for one year without hard labour.

Guilty on charge 3:
No. 2022 Gnr Hopman, M A: Penal servitude for three years.
No. 2139 Gnr Daniels, F J: Penal servitude for seven years.

No. 1996 Gnr Porritt, K R: Imprisonment for one year with hard labour.

The condemned men were uncertain of Gardiner's next move. There was a suggestion abroad that the executions would take place at dawn by firing squad as he had promised, this being the more believable because of an added detail — that they would be conducted near Rowe Battery.

After the decisions of the court martial were wired to the headquarters of the Ceylon Army Command, confirmation did not come as quickly as expected. Stephens told me that Gardiner became worried about the delay: the commander was keen on having the execution at dawn, yet the death sentences needed confirmation from a superior officer.

Lieutenant Henry de Sylva claimed some expertise in military law, and he assured Captain Gardiner that his Field General Court Martial was in order and so were the sentences. Nevertheless the delay caused the latter some anxiety; perhaps there was something they had overlooked.

Hand in hand with the question of legality went the matter of jurisdiction. General Sir Archibald Wavell and Admiral Sir Geoffrey Layton reaffirmed the position formerly declared by General William Slim: that Captain Gardiner was an operational commander under the Asian Command, which was an Allied Command. Where there did appear to be some room for doubt was in the matter of the mode of execution, a point that Fernando had already raised. If the decision were taken that the men were to be executed by hanging, they would have to be sent to Ceylon.

Some military commentators whom I consulted were of the opinion that, if Gardiner had stood by the belief that he was supreme commander on Cocos, he could have executed the men without any reference to General Wavell, Admiral Layton or the Ceylon Army Command — which seems at odds with the stated requirement for death penalties to be confirmed by a higher source. Whatever the resolution of that particular riddle, it is quite clear that Gardiner was unwilling to go ahead without confirmation.

Peter Hastings, a former Research Fellow in the Strategic and Defence Centre of the Australian National University, felt that Gardiner had been too hasty in convening a Field General Court Martial, even though he was facing a serious problem. He also found fault with the way it was conducted, especially in the respect that the accused were not given a reasonable opportunity to prepare their defence. Lieutenant Colonel Lyn Wickramasuriya thought Gardiner was on very shaky ground in convening an FGCM with himself as president, even though this was technically permissible.

The wartime censorship and control of news were observed by all the Ceylon newspapers apart from the Communist press, and that was closed under defence regulations. Admiral Layton insisted that no news of the mutiny was to be released to the general public in Ceylon or elsewhere, and similar injunctions came from the Command at New Delhi. Apart from this being a normal wartime precaution, such news could have further eroded the flagging war morale in Asia. It might also have deterred men from volunteering for overseas service in the armed forces.

In spite of all attempts to enforce this policy, the parents and relations of the men on trial soon found out enough to cause them alarm. Fernando's family and John Gauder, stepbrother of Carlo Gauder, cabled Cocos and succeeded in receiving replies. The Galle Face Battery in Colombo was stormed by relatives of all the volunteers on Cocos, and Major Mervyn Joseph became quite concerned. Sir Geoffrey Layton was approached by the Roman Catholic parish priest of Holy Cross Church in Kalutara, the Rev. Fr E A Chaulieu, who wanted information about the fate of the men.[1] Layton assured the priest, and through him the parents, that there would be no miscarriage of justice on Cocos, although he already knew what the findings were.

Meanwhile Fernando had succeeded in getting messages to Colombo even while he was in custody. This remarkable achievement probably had a lot to do with the fact that he had befriended many of the Australian Cable and Wireless staff on

Direction Island, where, interestingly, the mutiny leader enjoyed a substantial measure of support within the CLI. He sent cables to Major Mervyn Joseph and to a friend in Galle Face Battery, Gnr T N Ousmand. The cable to Ousmand was despatched two days after the mutiny and before the court martial proceedings began. It read:

> May 11th 1942
> Bdr Ossman [*sic*] Galle Face Battery Col. You are more than ever in my thoughts at this time. Fondest wishes from all of us. Keep smiling.
>
> Gratien Fernando

Apart from requesting confirmation of the court martial's findings and sentences, Gardiner asked Layton for immediate relief, to which the admiral's reply was that he 'did not wish to waste British ammunition on Asian bastards who had betrayed their mission.' It was at this time that the admiral had a visit from the British services chaplain, a bespectacled, burly Scotsman named Fr John Gardiner — no relation to the commander at Cocos. When he approached Layton for news on the Cocos events he got the reply: 'I don't know what the hell your namesake is up to in Cocos!'

General Wavell and Admiral Layton were not slow to see the political implications of executing Ceylonese volunteers for mutiny. Sir Oliver Goonetilleke, the Ceylon Defence Commissioner, and leftist politicians like Dr N M Perera and Dr Colvin R de Silva wanted the mutineers brought back to Ceylon. The Manual of Military Law stated that persons found guilty of mutiny were to be shot or hanged. If Gardiner wanted the execution at dawn, since there was no gallows on Cocos, the alternative was a firing squad. But were there hesitations about this back at Command?

In the makeshift prison on Cocos the mutineers facing death affected indifference. Some passed on the addresses of their families so that any souvenirs or final messages could be conveyed to them. Benny de Silva was more sanguine. He told Hopman: 'We shall not die, because I have made the nine First Fridays in College at St Sebastian's under the guidance of Brother Anthony. It means that I will have a priest near me at my death.' There was a sad irony in this. Anandappa said that he was ready to go at any moment, and had no fears of what the future might bring.

Late in the evening, when news of the verdict was the talking point in the camp, Gardiner went to Rowe Battery with Stephens and R A V Perera and ordered three men to pile sandbags at the left of the observation post. This action alarmed the mutineers under sentence of death. The commander was indeed making preparations — but he still had no confirmation of the death sentences.

Sergeant Ratnam somehow got hold of the news that Captain Gardiner had been sent two ciphered messages from Army Command in Ceylon, and that the first of them said that relief was coming. Ratnam was not able to find out what the second cable contained — but Fernando managed it! His Cable and Wireless contacts got the message through to him that all the mutineers were to return to Ceylon, including those sentenced to death. There they would have to await a review of the findings of the Field General Court Martial by the Judge Advocate General (JAG) in New Delhi.

On 7 June the Assistant Judge Advocate General (AJAG), Major J B Harrison, wrote to the headquarters of Army Command in Ceylon regarding the Field General Court Martial.[2] He sent a 'memorandum' on the court martial by the Judge Advocate General and his own 'report' elucidating and expanding on it. There was a misconception, which has remained through the years, that the mutineers were to get a fresh trial at the Supreme Court. Nothing of the sort happened, nor could it have happened. The Supreme Court had no jurisdiction on a military offence committed in the field of battle.

In 1712 the British Mutiny Act had been revised. Formerly it had not applied to overseas territories, and the Articles of War were applicable only on active service. Now the courts martial could try soldiers for misbehaviour or neglect of duty and await sentences of corporal punishment. The Crown was also given statutory power to make articles of war and hold courts martial anywhere abroad both in war and peace. In 1718 the Military Act was extended to cover overseas offices.

The AJAG's report nearly opened a new can of worms. It stated quite categorically:

> Many weaknesses are apparent in the proceedings, but most were due to circumstances existing in the place of offence. It is to meet such circumstances that the Army Act provides for trial by a Field General Court Martial, in which type of court martial most of the ordinary rules of procedure may be dispensed with, e.g. it is not necessary to appoint a defending officer.

The confirmation of this last point by the Judge Advocate General would have helped Gardiner in meeting the criticism from the condemned men that they had been wrongly denied this type of support. The report went on to state that two decisions by the JAG would affect the Cocos findings and sentences. The first of these was that 'the convictions on the first charge [that the mutineers had caused a mutiny in His Majesty's Military Forces or conspired with other persons to cause a mutiny] should be set aside.' On face value it looked as if the backbone of the prosecution case had been broken.

The second decision was that 'the sworn and signed statements by the accused, which were attached to the evidence given by them at the trial, are inadmissible.' The AJAG pointed out that 'many of the accused gave evidence which implicated other accused,' and he went on to explain that:

> In strict law the evidence of one accomplice, without any corroborating evidence, is sufficient to convict an accused person, but it is now held that it is the duty of the judge to warn the jury of the danger of convicting upon the uncorrob-

orated evidence of an accomplice and that if he does not do so the conviction must be quashed.

The Assistant Judge Advocate General clarified this point further:

The reasons for this caution with regard to such evidence are two: first, that if a person is an accomplice in an alleged offence then he is presumably a man of bad character and as such his evidence is suspect; and, second, that an accomplice may give false evidence against a co-accused, or exaggerate the part played by him, in an attempt to exculpate himself or to minimise his own part. At a court martial, the court combines the function of judge and jury and therefore should consider carefully before convicting on the uncorroborated testimony of an accomplice.

The report continued with a statement that, where there is a judge advocate, it is essential that he should warn the court on this point.

In this case there was, of necessity, no judge advocate and therefore it is important that the confirming officer should realise the danger. He should be quite satisfied before confirming a conviction based on the uncorroborated testimony of any of the accused against other accused. It must be clear that the testimony can be relied upon, and was not given with the object of minimising the guilt of the witness at the expense of the person he implicates.

The Assistant Judge Advocate General continued by observing that in his opinion there was no evidence except that of accomplices to implicate Diasz, Peries, Edema, Daniels and Porritt. He added that corroboration by another accomplice, or even by several accomplices, does not suffice, and went on to clarify the three types of admissible evidence that had to be considered against each accused:

Each man's own evidence given before the court. This is the most satisfactory testimony upon which to base a conviction because voluntary statements on oath made against self-interest are more likely to be true than any other.

Evidence of prosecution witnesses.

Evidence of accomplices [subject to the conditions outlined above].

Taking into consideration the Judge Advocate General's rulings, the AJAG amended the findings and sentences in regard to each of the accused:

Bdr G H FERNANDO

The Chief Ringleader and undoubtedly the man who caused the mutiny, but the conviction on this charge (causing or conspiring with others to cause [a mutiny]) must be set aside. His own evidence at the trial, however, is quite sufficient to convict him on the other two charges without his attached statement. In fact his evidence goes much further than his statement and the admission of the latter in no way prejudiced him.

I suggest confirmation of the conviction in the second and third charges and of the sentence of death.

Gnr G B de SILVA

In his evidence he admits shooting at some person in the observation post. Gnr Subramaniam states that he saw this accused shooting at Gnr Jayasekera, who was killed. This, with the other points in the accused's own evidence, is sufficient to convict him of joining in the mutiny and of having had previous knowledge of it and not reporting it.

I suggest confirmation of the convictions on the second and third charges and, because he actually killed a man, that the sentence of death also be confirmed.

Gnr C A GAUDER

In his evidence this accused says 'I took part in the mutiny.' Lt Stephens says definitely that Gauder fired four or five shots at him from a range of about two yards after he had spoken to him. One bullet grazed Lt Stephens' face and another wounded him in the leg. It appears certain that Gauder meant to kill Lt Stephens. Other evidence e.g. [from] Gauder himself and G B de Silva makes it clear that Gauder had previous knowledge of the intended mutiny.

I suggest that the convictions on the second and third charges be confirmed and, because of this accused's deliberate attempt to shoot his officer, that the sentence of death also be confirmed.

Gnr R S HAMILTON

Convicted of all three charges and sentenced to death. The first charge must be set aside. There is no admissible evidence to support the conviction on the second charge. The accused's own evidence corroborated by Gauder and G B de Silva shows that he knew of Fernando's plan weeks beforehand.

Suggest confirmation of conviction on third charge only and commutation of sentence to penal servitude (3 years).

Gnr G D ANANDAPPA

Convicted on all three charges and sentenced to death. Conviction on first charge to be set aside. Admits taking part in mutiny and that he could have stopped Fernando firing the Bren gun but did not. Therefore conviction on second charge sustainable, although he does not appear to have fired his rifle. G B de Silva in his evidence says that Anandappa knew of plan beforehand, and this is implied in his own evidence in which he says that he had given Fernando his word to stand by him. Appears to have been greatly under the influence of Fernando.

Suggest confirmation of convictions on second and third charges and commutation of sentence to penal servitude (3 years).

L/Bdr K W J DIASZ

Convicted on all charges and sentenced to death. Conviction on first charge must be set aside. Denies any part in, or previous knowledge of, the mutiny, and there is no evidence to show that he actually joined in the mutiny. On the other hand [other evidence] corroborates his own statement that he spent most of the time after the first alarm up a tree outside the battery enclosure.

Gauder, Hamilton and G B de Silva all say that he knew of the plan and took an active part in the preliminary discussions. Fernando says that he hoped for help from him. Hopman also says that Diasz was in the plot beforehand.

Suggest confirmation of the conviction on the third charge only and commutation of sentence to penal servitude (4 years).

Gnr A J L PERIES

Acquitted on second charge only and sentenced to death. Conviction on first charge should not be confirmed. Denies all knowledge of intended mutiny, but Fernando says that he hoped for his help. Gauder says that he was present when plot was discussed. Hamilton says he made suggestions to improve the plan and de Silva says he was a ringleader.

Suggest confirmation of conviction on third charge and commutation of sentence to penal servitude (4 years).

Gnr A B EDEMA

Convicted on third charge only and sentenced to imprisonment without hard labour for one year. Fernando says he was definitely very cautious about him. That may mean that he approached him. Hamilton and Hopman say that this accused was present on different occasions when the mutiny was discussed. Gauder and de Silva say that they think he is innocent. The court probably felt that he was a mere hanger-on who knew that some trouble was intended but did not report it, hence the light sentence.

I suggest confirmation of finding and sentences.

Gunner Mark Hopman, in 1995.

Gnr M A HOPMAN

Admits in his evidence that he heard talk about a mutiny about a month before the event. He says, however, that he told the conspirators that it was all nonsense and that he left them. Fernando says he hoped for help from him. That he tried to dissuade the others is confirmed by Gauder and Hamilton. It is apparent that he must have heard talk of the mutiny on more than one occasion; nevertheless he did not report it and I suggest confirmation of the finding.

Whether the sentence should be commuted to a lesser one in view of his apparent disagreement with the plan is a matter for the confirming officer.

Gnr F J DANIELS

Was convicted on the first and third charges and acquitted on the second charge and sentenced to seven years penal servitude. The conviction on the first charge should not be confirmed. The acquittal on the second charge is difficult to reconcile with the evidence [that he was seen] firing at Jayasekera. Gauder, Hamilton and G B de Silva say in their evidence that Daniels knew of the plan.

I suggest confirmation of the conviction on the third charge and a reduction of the sentence to one appropriate to this offence only.

Gnr K R PORRITT

Convicted on third charge only and sentenced to one year's imprisonment with hard labour.

The only prejudicial mention of this man in the whole case is by Hamilton, who says that he was present at one discussion on the mutiny about a month beforehand, but that he said nothing. There is no evidence that he was present at any other discussion nor that he was with the other accused on the evening of the mutiny.

The conviction however is sustainable, and I suggest confirmation and reduction of the sentence to a few months imprisonment with hard labour. Even if he had heard one discussion it was his duty to report it.

'These remarks,' said the AJAG, 'are based entirely on admissible evidence, and the inadmissible statements by the accused have been ignored. Although these statements were before the court, in my opinion, none of the accused was prejudiced by them. I have also ignored the passages of hearsay in [certain of] the evidence.'

The Assistant Judge Advocate General then made a rather startling statement: 'I suggest for your consideration that some further inquiry be made as to the conduct of certain senior NCOs and others on the night of the mutiny. No. 1691 L/Sgt Perera and No. 1429 Sgt I L Pereira apparently got into the battery enclosure at the first alarm, yet there is no evidence to show that from their favourable position they took any action during the succeeding hours to restore order.'[3]

The Ceylon Army Command made all preparations to get the mutineers to Ceylon from Cocos, and to see that the sentences were duly carried out.

16

A Secret Mission

Lieutenant Ivor D M Van Twest of the Ceylon Garrison Artillery volunteered to go to the Cocos (Keeling) Islands on what the army called a 'secret mission.' A voyage in rough seas aboard the Indian warship *Sutleg* duly brought him there, whereupon, with little delay, Fernando, de Silva, Gauder, Hopman, Porritt, Hamilton, Peries, Anandappa and the remaining accused were taken on board under heavy guard.

The mood of the mutineers on the journey was one of despondency, but Van Twest did his best to keep morale at a reasonable pitch while he made as much speed as he could. After a rather hazardous and eventful voyage, during which the *Sutleg* was always 'on alarm' because of the presence of prowling Japanese submarines, it docked at the old Colombo harbour and British officers boarded while a strong British guard armed with Tommy guns stood by. The mutineers were handcuffed and taken ashore. The lieutenant was given an escort as he delivered the reports and files of the court martial that had been handed to him by Captain Gardiner.

When I spoke to him in Colombo on 21 September 1970, Van Twest was highly critical of the conditions on Cocos in 1942 and of Gardiner's handling of affairs. He was baffled at the poor lines of communication between the officers and men, and felt that the mutiny would never have come about if such a high level of provocation had not been engaged in by Gardiner and Stephens. 'A mutiny was bound to occur at any moment,' he said. Certainly Fernando had exploited the latent anti-colonial sentiments that were starting to bubble to the surface, but these were not the driving forces of the revolt. Van Twest found Gardiner's temperament quite disturbing — cool, composed and in a sense calculating, while under the surface there was seething anger. He was rigid to the point of believing that military law could never be an ass.

Lieutenant Ivor Van Twest, who brought the mutineers back to Ceylon.

The former lieutenant also criticised some aspects of the Field General Court Martial, especially what he referred to as the denial of natural justice. He thought de Sylva had wielded an unhealthy influence on the court procedure, not least by taking upon himself some of the duties of the president. He was in no doubt that Gardiner had been hell bent on proceeding with the execution of the seven men at dawn, anticipating that New Delhi would send him immediate confirmation.

Brigadier Swinton was quite impressed with the success of Van Twest's mission, and invited him to join the next contingent that was to go to Cocos six months later. Apart from Lieutenant Van Twest, the officers in this batch would be Major Williams of the Ceylon Royal Artillery and Lieutenant Owen Wambeek of the Ceylon Light Infantry.[1]

When they arrived in Ceylon the mutineers were marched under heavy guard at night through Colombo's Gordon Gardens and down to the military prison in Flagstaff Street. Fernando was placed in a separate cell, as were Gauder, de Silva, Anandappa and Peries. Hopman and Porritt shared a cell. More facilities were given to the mutineers than had been the case in Cocos, and a Sergeant Muller helped them send out letters to relatives. Major

Mervyn Joseph tried desperately to save the men of his Galle Face Battery, and played no small part in helping the condemned to draft their petitions for commutation of the death sentence or for a lessening of their long terms of penal servitude.

Benny de Silva became desperate for a reprieve. On 17 June, helped by legal opinion secured by his relations Joseph and Bridget Fernando, he wrote to the adjutant of the CGA 1st Coast Regiment. The letter read as follows:[2]

> I beg to unfold to you in writing some of my bona fide feelings though in a fettered state, for a crime [of which] I am apparently guilty. I joined the army of my own free will because I loved and longed to be in it. It was with huge influx of patriotic pride that I left Ceylon in the first Ceylon's Contingent.
>
> I served overseas for 13 months and returned home. After a month I volunteered again and went out with another contingent. Today I am here with a bad name earned, founded on the brutal and inhuman treatment received at the hands of some [of] my comrades when I was under custody, and a detail of which was given to you Sir in my letter dated 3rd June.[3]
>
> To convince the world with material proof of my above statement, I with my own free will place myself at the disposal of the military authorities to make me as an instrument to do any risky thing in any part of the British Empire where the war is raging at its highest, in the infantry or in the artillery as I had a training in both units.
>
> I appeal to you Sir that I wish not to die a death for a crime I am not guilty [of]. I might be apparently guilty but not really. I beg of you Sir that copies of this letter and my former one be submitted to the proper authorities inquiring into this case.
>
>
> Thanking you Sir
> I remain
> Your Obedient Servant
> Gnr G B de Silva
> 1st Coast Regiment
> Ceylon Garrison Artillery
>

Six days later, on 23 June, de Silva presented yet another petition, hoping once more to bolster his case. Little did he know that the die had already been cast.

> I state that I am not guilty. On the night of the incident I was on duty at the observation post and was asleep as I was allowed to. I was then awakened by the sound of rifle shots. I thought there was an attack. I picked up one of the rifles in the observation post and loaded it and waited at my post on the OP.
>
> I was alone. I heard machine-gun firing and then footsteps coming up to the OP. I did not leave my post. The OP as usual was in total darkness. Some bullets came into the OP. I saw figures coming up the steps and I challenged. Someone asked who is that. I replied I am the duty signaller. I challenged again and there was no answer and I fired. Then one of those coming up came to me, held my rifle and shouted, 'I am Subramaniam, don't fire.' I let go my rifle and Subramaniam took it.
>
> I then went down to the foot of the OP and Gnr Jinadasa who was there took me to a trench. About two hours after I heard Capt. Gardiner calling all to the Battery. I went up to Capt. Gardiner and told him that I fired a shot. I was then taken into custody.

So far the story is by and large consistent with his court martial evidence. But this was followed by a totally new scenario and an elaborate justification of his failure to reveal it earlier:

> The next night I was taken into a jungle by the BQMS and two sergeants and assaulted. I was asked to make a statement as instructed by them, that I knew there was a plan to shoot Capt. G. They asked me to implicate others whose names they gave. They warned me that if I did not do this I would be shot then and there.
>
> A loaded rifle was levelled at me and I was told that Capt. G. had ordered them to shoot at the slightest movement …

On the following morning I was taken before Capt. G. to make a statement and the sergeant who assaulted me stood behind me. On the way to Capt. G. this sergeant said, 'Now remember last night's decision.' I made a statement to Capt. G. part of which was not true, through fear of being shot. In the statement I said that I knew there was a plan — that was not true.

I was assaulted daily from then till the Court Martial sat, and warned not to cross-examine witnesses. In spite of that I cross-examined the first day, and the same day I was assaulted by one of the witnesses who was also one of my guards. At the end of the 3rd day of sitting I made a statement similar to what I told Capt. G. The court was about to adjourn and I signed my statement. The court sergeant, who was one of those who had assaulted me, tied my hands and said, 'I will shoot you tonight if you don't make a fresh statement as we told you.' I got frightened and called out 'Sir, I want to make another statement.' I then made a statement as I had been instructed. That statement was not true and was made through fear.

After sentence was passed on me the BQMS, A H Perera, told me, 'You would have been alright if you had originally stuck to the statement I told you to make. Capt. Gardiner is an old BC of mine and I could have saved you, as I saved all my Battenburg Battery boys. He will never disregard my word.'

De Silva concluded his petition: 'There was a conspiracy against me because I was the only man who killed anybody. I swear that I fired in good faith because I thought there was an attack. The deceased and I were good friends and belonged to the same Battery in Ceylon. I actually asked him to volunteer for Cocos and go with me there.'

If de Silva was having his last fling in attempting to avoid execution, there were other mutineers who sought the crumbs that fell from the court martial table. On 25 June 1942 Gunner Kenneth R Porritt appealed against his conviction on the third charge and the sentence of a year's hard labour.

In 1971 I met Porritt in a Pettah eating-house opposite Colombo's Fort Main Railway Station. The interview was arranged when he rang Independent Newspapers offering more information on the mutiny. Soft-spoken and seemingly mellowed by his experiences, he showed no embitterment beyond giving voice to a scathing appraisal of Captain Gardiner's tenure as commanding officer. He willingly provided a group photograph he had of his mates before they left for their overseas posting. 'I don't need this any more,' he said. 'The photo brings sad memories of Cocos — it reminds me of Gratien and his fatal dream.'[4]

In his petition Porritt referred to the full statement he made at the Field General Court Martial on Cocos, in which he detailed his whereabouts and actions on the night of 8 May 1942. He emphasised that he was among those outside the battery who were 'held up by the firing across the gate.' He was in fact a few yards from Gardiner and heard his order to take cover. He pointed to the fact that Gardiner himself had posted him as a sentry at the barrack room door.

> The NCO in charge there relieved me as I was ill, having reported sick the night before. I went to my tent having also reported myself to the NCO in command of the Op Staff. I fell asleep on my bunk and slept till morning. *This explains why I failed to answer the roll call later*. This was supported at the Court Martial by the NCO in charge of OP staff, who said he *answered for me at the roll call*.[5]

He went on to say that no direct evidence was given against him at the court martial, except that of Gunner A M Jinadasa, who stated that he saw him and the others flashing messages to each other in the OP tent, which they stopped doing as Jinadasa entered. Porritt explained that it was quite a common practice for the signallers to send messages to each other for the purpose of improving their signalling. Jinadasa himself had admitted this, and also that he had indulged in the practice himself.

I have every reason to think that the only grounds for my conviction are a suspicion drawn from the above facts and from a statement alleged by Lt Sylva, one of the members of the Court, to have been made against me at the proceedings in my absence. I submit that the Court had no right to entertain or even listen to such a statement in the absence of an accused. At any rate, if such a statement had been made I should have been given an opportunity of cross-examining the person who made the statement. The failure to do so has prejudiced me in my defence.

I asked the Court who had made the statement — which was that [I] was lying on a bed nearby while the plot was being discussed. Lt Sylva's reply to this was 'Do you think anyone is going to lie after taking an oath?' I submit that this was an entirely wrong attitude for a court to take up and showed prejudice against the accused. I should like to be allowed to say, though I do so with great reluctance, that Lt Sylva cross-examined me in such a manner that it was apparent to me that he was trying to muddle me.

Porritt insisted in his petition that he was 'prejudiced by' de Sylva in another respect also. Speaking for the court, the latter had refused to allow him to call Kronemberg, whom he (Porritt) said could have proved that a statement made in cross-examination by Perera was false.

Lt Sylva refused my request on the grounds that Gnr Kronemberg was one of the accused. The President of the Court gave no ruling and was silent. I submit I was entitled to call Gnr Kronemberg even though he was an accused.

I believe I failed to point out in my statement that my rifle had been examined and found clean and my ammunition checked and found correct soon after the incident.[6]

Major Mervyn Joseph received detailed briefings from Lieutenant Van Twest. On a balance of probabilities his appraisal of the Cocos situation seemed plausible, though there were many who felt that his strictures on Gardiner and Stephens were too severe or indeed unwarranted. Be that as it may, the lawyers who were acting on behalf of the convicted soldiers were perturbed that his report was buried, believing that there might have been in it some grounds for establishing that there were mitigating circumstances. The lawyers also sought information from officers who had been on Cocos, and Lyn Wickramasuriya, for one, expressed to them the view that the mutineers had been badly handled in a very provocative situation.

Every effort I made at the Public Record Office to access Van Twest's report failed. Eventually I was able to conclude that there was a simple reason for this: the Ceylon Army Command did not include it in the official papers sent to the War Office. Van Twest was far from happy about the handling of his report, and told me that, while it was more than scathing, he felt that Army Command had been obliged to table it.

The relatives of de Silva and Gauder desperately sought out expert legal opinion with the aim of formulating last-ditch petitions of appeal against their sentences. Eventually Joseph and Bridget Fernando, who looked after the interests of Benny de Silva, were officially informed that the decisions of the Field General Court Martial regarding the executions were final and that they should not entertain any hope of a reprieve. There was categorically no further avenue of appeal, and the sentences would be carried out shortly by hanging.

In contrast to the exertions on behalf of de Silva and Gauder, Fernando doggedly accepted his fate. The other side of this particular coin was that he was offering no help to the two comrades who wished to avoid theirs. Some felt that he was nursing a grievance that his closest associates had let him down, and that there was an element of petulance in his unwavering resolve to pay the full penalty. But there was also defiance: he would not have a bar of what he called 'the White man's clemency.'

Meanwhile N M Perera was arguing with Army Command and the Ceylon Defence Commissioner that to execute Ceylonese volunteers for participation in the mutiny at Cocos would be political dynamite. Van Twest told me that other leftists, including an angry Colvin de Silva and Philip Gunewardena, were making impassioned statements about British imperialism using Ceylonese volunteers as pawns in their game.

It was on 27 July 1942 that the headquarters of the Ceylon Command confirmed the sentences of death passed on the three mutineers with the approval of the Judge Advocate General in New Delhi and the AJAG in Colombo. There was a sense of desperation among the immediate relatives of those who were to be hanged. They were not the only ones to be disturbed: two well-known Buddhist political figures, H W Amarasuriya and Susantha de Fonseka, approached the governor, Sir Andrew Caldecott, and Admiral Geoffrey Layton with pleas for clemency, but the authorities remained unmoved.

The final word had been given, but an air of uncertainty prevailed while Army Command refused to divulge any further information. Two chaplains, Fr Brennan and Fr Claude Moffat Lawrence, were allowed to see to the spiritual needs of the prisoners, but even they were not informed as to when the executions would take place.

17

Footsteps to the Gallows

On 27 July 1942, after confirmation of Gratien Fernando's death sentence, a pall of sadness hung over the home in Gampaha where his parents, Daniel and Margaret, resided. The mood altered when Carlo Gauder's stepbrother John made contact with them, suggesting that they pool resources in order to launch a last-minute effort to stay the executions. Once again an all-out attempt was made to approach Admiral Layton and General Wavell in New Delhi, this time through the good offices of the civil defence commissioner, Sir Oliver Goonetilleke. Sir Oliver, whose relationship with Admiral Layton was not of the best, did not succeed in his mission.

Fernando's brothers (Hector, Gordon and Patrick) and two of his sisters (Eva and Lena) were at last able to see Gratien on 4 April. Helen, the youngest, did not join them. They had not been told the execution was to take place on the following day, though they were advised of this before they left the prison. In 1970 Eva Fernando told me of that farewell visit. She said she was surprised at her brother's calmness — though from time to time he would give vent to a sudden angry outburst. Another thing she noted was his repeated references to 'the cause'. She had a clear recollection of him saying something very close to the following:

I'll never ask pardon from the British: that would disgrace the cause. Many years hence the world may hear my story. It won't die with me. I bear no grudge against Captain Gardiner or Lieutenant Stephens; I only hate their philosophy — that Asian soldiers were to be used like cattle. Gardiner never stopped calling us 'sons of bitches' and 'black bastards.' He was a racist all right, and so was his sidekick Stephens. Funny that a Eurasian like Stephens could treat his countrymen like that.

Much later, in May 1999, I managed to interview Helen Fernando, Gratien's youngest sister and by then the only one surviving, in Colombo. She gave me some background:

My father was a superintendent at the Central Telegraph Office when Mr J P Appleby was Postmaster General ... Gratien was brought up as a Buddhist, though he attended St Thomas College at Mount Lavinia. He was converted to Roman Catholicism by Fr Brennan of St Philip Neri's in Pettah.

He had no broken love affair before he left for Cocos, as one British author has alleged. He joined because he wanted to serve King and Queen. Also many friends were joining; he was caught up in the enlistment wave of the time. He also said there was no point wearing a British uniform and remaining in Ceylon — he wanted to go abroad to face the enemy.

Asked about her father petitioning the army authorities to commute the death penalty, Helen gave a new slant to the story: 'My father ... asked his good friend Sir Oliver Goonetilleke to try to save Gratien. Sir Oliver met Admiral Layton, who decided to interview Gratien before he acted on the petition. At the interview Gratien was adamant that he did not want a reprieve or pardon.' The family was deeply troubled by this turn of events. She recalled some of the things her brothers and sisters told her when they came back from Colombo:

Gratien talked to them in his calm manner and he had no final requests. He had lost weight. He said he was glad that mother and father had not come. He noticed that his married sister, Lena, was expecting a child, and was sorry that he would not be there to see the new arrival.

Speaking of her mother, Helen said she was extremely upset, and the family decided not to keep her informed of what was happening. This was taken to the extreme of not telling her that the execution was about to take place. 'I remember that day very well,' she said.

> It was 5 August 1942 when my brother was to hang at Welikade. We all got up early and were crying and mourning silently, wondering why this had to happen to a family who had sent their son to war. Then late in the morning some cousins arrived, and they were dressed in white. My mother asked why they were in white and what made them come. She then realised the truth and began to cry. She became almost inconsolable.[1]

Gratien's parents were devastated by the execution, and hardly spoke afterwards. His mother became paralysed; both were dead within two months.

But that was still in the future when Gratien Fernando sat writing his farewell letters in his cell. He sent one on Sunday 2 August to his friend Bombardier T N Ousmand of the Galle Face Battery.[2]

2.8.1942

> Dear Ossy,
> This is just to wish you the best of everything on Earth before I die. On Wednesday I am to swing high. I am not in the least worried about it. I attempted something great, but I failed for the present, but certainly I have not lost. The cause shall live and I know soon my ideals will materialise. When I think of the days at Face with you, I can smile at all the fun we had. Happy were those days and happy am I when I

think of them. I hope you will rise high in your ranks. How about being BQMS? How about the rice we landed with butter? Fine wasn't it. I am sure your little son is keeping fine: same eyes, hair and that happy Tahitian smile of yours. I can imagine the little fellow.

So Cheerio Ossy, my best pal. Best wishes for you and your family.

God bless you all,

Gratien

On 4 August 1942 Fernando was taken by prison van from the Hulftsdorf Gaol to Welikade Prison, where he was taken to death row. It was the eve of execution, and the prisoner went through the routine of being weighed for the hangman so that he could adjust the death drop. Fr Claude Lawrence and Fr Brennan were on hand to attend to Gratien's spiritual needs.

Fr Claude Lawrence, OMI, chaplain at the execution of the three mutineers.

R J N Jordan, a retired deputy commissioner of prisons, recalled the details of the execution in a letter to the Ceylon *Sunday Times*, published on 8 August 1992, which he wrote in response to my articles on the mutiny:

> The bizarre story of the Cocos Island Mutiny by Noel Crusz underlines the importance of proper relationships between superior and subordinate.
>
> Having been in the Prison service in 1942 and having had much contact with [the] mutineers Joe Peries, Anandappa and Kingsley Diasz, all of whom served long prison terms at Welikade Prison, I would say the one motivating factor for the revolt was the discriminatory treatment accorded to these servicemen.
>
> All the subsequent upheavals in this country could be traced to unfair or indifferent attitudes to one section or another. If I could add a few embellishments to Noel Crusz's narrative, the prisoners after sentence were held at the Hulftsdorf Prison (a Military detention barracks then) and now the site of the Superior Courts Complex, and one by one each day were transported at or around 7.45 a.m. to death row at Welikade Prison to be executed.
>
> A Major Whitelow was the Provost Marshal, who supervised the hangings whilst Prison executives looked on and provided the hangman's service. The words spoken by Gratien Fernando and his indomitable courage on the way to

the gallows were on everybody's lips for weeks to come, both amongst prisoners and staff.

I have been a witness to scores of executions but never did experience a disposition of such a nature.

Fernando was an angry man right to the end. If he had one last wish it 'would be to give Captain Gardiner a dose of what he gave us: a "racist bullet." Give me a revolver and I will do it now. The white man doesn't deserve to have his day.' This he said to Fr Brennan. But he would soon cool down and come out with something quite contradictory: 'I have no grudge against Gardiner. In fact I liked him. Quite a decent chap!' After this, a gem of his wisdom: 'Loyalty to a country under the heel of a white man is disloyalty.'

On the morning of 5 August 1942 Fernando took his final steps, led by Fr Brennan and Fr Claude Lawrence reciting prayers. He remained silent beyond saying a few words to a prison official. He nodded at Provost Whitelow and looked at Jordan with a face that betrayed both a sense of achievement and resignation. His courage baffled the onlookers.[3] Fr Brennan was forbidden under oath to reveal the location of the grave site at Kanatta. There was no identification at all to mark the place.

Correspondent Hector Cooray, from Kurunegala in the central west of Ceylon, wrote in the *Sunday Times* of 9 August 1992 :

> Gratien Fernando's ideal that he and others fought for did materialise, and was achieved by others in quite a different way much earlier than expected. To the band of soldiers fighting with the gun to achieve their objectives, [this] was what they thought was just, right and correct.
>
> This might seem wrong to others, for different men think differently. They did what Weera Puran Appu, Keppittipola Disawa, the Ven Wariyapola Sumangala, Gonagalegoda Banda and such other national heroes of an earlier period did in pursuit of this very same objective: liberating the Nation.

On 7 August 1942 Gunner G Benny de Silva awoke for his day of destiny. Holy Mass was said by Fr Brennan, assisted by Fr Claude Lawrence, opposite his cell; then he was escorted to the gallows, where he stood, resigned, as the noose was put round his neck. He uttered a prayer, and the trapdoor was released. The prison doctor confirmed death and permitted Fr Brennan to go down the scaffold and give the single anointing on the executed man's forehead.

One of de Silva's relatives, Marcus Fernando of Birmingham, England,[4] remembered the death of the former gunner in an article published in the May 1998 edition of the British publication *After the Battle*:

> Benny, G H Fernando and C Gauder were executed, but my grandparents (Joe and Bridget Fernando) succeeded in getting special dispensation to have Benny's body buried in the civilian cemetery. For years it lay unmarked, but in 1992 a stone was erected in his honour.[5]

It was Gunner Carlo Gauder's turn the following day, just seven days after his twenty-first birthday, which he celebrated alone. Brennan was assisted in his ministrations on this occasion by Fr Emmanuel Alles, a philosophy professor at St Bernard's Seminary and an assistant to the prison chaplains.

Gauder showed neither stoicism nor bravado on the way from death row to the scaffold. Fr Alles recalled the frightened, pale face of a schoolboy unwillingly dragged to the death chamber.[6] 'Oh God I don't deserve this,' he said, with tears coursing down his face. As the sickening thud of the released trapdoor reverberated

Gunner Carlo Gauder with his sister Totsy and niece Marlene prior to leaving for Cocos. Gauder was hanged on 8 August 1942.

throughout Welikade, outside its gates Carlo's stepbrother John kept a lone vigil. He had somehow come to know of the date of the execution, but his efforts to gain possession of the body were not rewarded.

In an interview on 9 September 1977 in the Sydney suburb of Croydon, Totsy Gauder, the gunner's sister, and her husband, Reg Collinson, retold the story of those harrowing days. 'Carlo was in the first batch to go to Seychelles,' she said. 'Later he volunteered for Cocos. I knew so many of his friends like John Elders of the CLI. Carlo was my only brother; I was born in 1920 and Carlo in 1921. My parents died when we were quite young. I have stepbrothers and stepsisters … The day before he was hanged he wrote a letter to me saying that he was not guilty, and wanted me to look after myself, and knew he was going to a better place.'

As Collinson saw it, 'Carlo was a foolish chap. He was one in a crowd, a simpleton led like a lamb to the slaughter. I am not biased against the British in this particular case. I don't find fault with them. But I find fault with the soldiers who fell into a trap. However trying and difficult the situation was, they forgot that there was a world war on. They should have realised the dangers in inviting the enemy.' He acknowledged that he had had a lot of trouble with officers himself when he was in the Indian army. 'I had to use a certain amount of patience. I feel that Carlo was innocent: he hardly realised the implications of what he was getting himself into.'

Totsy Gauder spoke with much emotion and many tears: 'I was twenty-two years old when he died. I was brought up in the Convent of Our Lady of Victories in Moratuwa, and Carlo was a boarder at St Joseph's College, Maradana, where Henry Stephens was also a boarder.' When asked of attempts to get a reprieve for her brother, she said: 'We did everything possible — wrote petition after petition to the army officials. John, my stepbrother, did this.'

She recounted how they got the first news of Carlo Gauder's involvement. 'I did not know anything. Naturally they did not want to upset me. My stepbrother was a well-known businessman, and he was at a dinner at the Galle Face Hotel when he was called out and given the news that the death sentence had been imposed on Carlo for taking part in the mutiny.' It was only later that day that a cousin accidentally divulged the news to Totsy, thereby compelling John to tell her everything. 'I began to cry. Carlo was my only brother. John promised to take me to see him. He said [the condemned men] had been brought in under escort late the previous night.'

Totsy and John's daughter Marlene (Carlo's niece) went with them to the Hulftsdorf Gaol.

> Carlo was brought handcuffed with two guards beside him, and under strict regulations we were forbidden to talk on any subject about Cocos or the mutiny. I just broke down, but he said: 'Totsy, I am innocent. Don't worry.' After that visit we went regularly to see Carlo on certain allotted days. It was at this time that John was trying very hard to get the death sentence commuted to life imprisonment. He got me to write petitions to Admiral Layton and all the big officers, and even to Sir Oliver Goonetilleke. But we knew what the army had already told us: that there was no chance of a reprieve.

She then described how they got an urgent message to visit Carlo, although they were not told that it was the day before his execution. They knew it was coming, as they had heard that Fernando and de Silva had already been hanged.

> John got permission from the prison authorities for me to take Carlo some milk toffee, which he relished. John and all my stepsisters and I went to the prison at Hulftsdorf. Carlo was brought out again with two guards. In fact he did not show any fear and he was quite calm. Each one was sent one by one to meet him for a few minutes, since all were not allowed to go together.
> I was sent last, after John and the rest warned me not to

break down and make it harder for Carlo. How can you blame me? We are ordinary people not used to visiting prisons to see our own flesh and blood about to be hanged. As I saw him I began to cry and I could not talk much. I kissed him and he said: 'Don't worry Totsy. Everything will be all right. Only look after yourself. That's all I want. I told you before I am going to a better place.'

The next morning Carlo Augustus Gauder posted a letter to his sister, once again pleading his innocence and remarking that he didn't deserve to die. 'I burnt all his letters before I migrated to Australia,' said Totsy. They were too painful to keep as memories to be cherished. I had to get on with my life … Carlo had written regularly from Cocos and sent me half his pay.'

On the day of the execution, 8 August 1942, John Gauder had set off early in the morning. He was distraught and spoke little. He was told by the prison chaplains that Carlo had had to be helped to the scaffold. In a surprising relaxation of execution ritual, John was permitted to view his stepbrother's body after execution. The limp body in prison clothes was wrapped in a torn blanket and placed in an ordinary boxwood black coffin. Totsy continued the story:

> When John came home he asked all of us to get ready, and we went to the general cemetery in Kanatta. I was in a state of shock and could hardly cry. At the cemetery we were taken to a plot of unmarked graves in unconsecrated ground, where the earth was fresh. There were two fresh graves side by side and Carlo had been buried in a third. We knelt and said some prayers and I lit two candles, which I placed on the grave with a wreath that John had bought. Then the tears came.

For the young woman the war had taken its toll. She felt it was a heavy price to pay for the Asian dream. She confessed that her brother joined the army to escape from a humdrum life at home: gardening, housework, running errands. 'It was only after he had joined that he told us,' said Totsy. 'He said that it was the best thing, as he was not happy at home. Carlo was a very shy boy, very backward, and did not like to be in company too much. He often spoke of our parents, who died within a year of each other. Carlo was only eight years old when my parents died.'

Totsy and Reg regretted the fact that the army did not send them any official notification of the sentence or the execution. 'They were Gunner Gauder's guardians,' said Collinson. 'If you die in action your relations are immediately informed. But if you are executed, nothing is officially conveyed to the next of kin. I suppose this is war.' It was a surprising statement, and one that eluded any checking: mutinies are few and far between. John Gauder had got his sister to send innumerable petitions asking for clemency, as she was the only surviving relative of the condemned man. One wonders if the letters ever reached the authorities to whom they were written.

Reg Collinson has since died. Totsy Gauder, now retired and living with her daughter in Queensland, admits that memories of the Cocos tragedy are still with her. 'I think of Carlo often. But my children and grandchildren keep me busy ... After the execution I was sent to a friend's place to try and make me forget. But there are some things in life and death that you can't forget. It makes me sad to think that he was buried in unconsecrated ground. I suppose it does not matter. St Monica, the mother of St Augustine, used to say: "Bury me wherever you wish, for nowhere is far from God."'[7]

As for the executed mutineers, none of them has been commemorated by the Commonwealth War Graves Commission. This was not the case when British servicemen were executed.[8]

During the month following the executions, a special parade was held in Colombo under the command of Lieutenant Colonel McLeod Carey and Adjutant Toby Kane[9] at which Quartermaster Sergeant A H Perera was dishonoured and drummed off.[10]

Thus did the curtain come down on the final act of the Cocos mutiny story. All that remained were the bitter aftermath, the myths and the legends, and finally the truth of it all. There were the scapegoats and the villains, even some who with the passage of time exploited the fate of their comrades to seek the limelight. It is for the historian to assess the significance of the events. Lord Macaulay said, 'The most frightful of all spectacles was the strength of civilisation without its mercy,' but who would condone mutiny?

18

Telling the Story

After the war, news of the Cocos mutiny gradually began to emerge. Its ultimate source appears to have been the relatives of the convicted men — certainly not the Ceylon Garrison Artillery, which did not want the prestige of the Galle Face and Battenburg batteries sullied in any way. An equivalent code of silence was maintained by the Rowe Battery officers.

It took a long time for many of the wounds to heal. In the meantime there was a spawning of factions not only within the services and the postwar associations of wartime comrades, but also among the media men who wrote about the mutiny — despite the best efforts of some, it was not long before the subject found its way into the Ceylonese newspapers. Indeed, two of the leading papers, the *Times of Ceylon* and the *Sunday Observer*, introduced the saga to a wider public. The impact of these articles was all the heavier in view of the fact that three Ceylonese men had been executed. This gave a sharp edge to the issues of racialism, colonialism and justice implicated in the story.

Needless to say, more specific matters also figured in the coverage. Did the circumstances warrant the meting out of summary military justice on the Cocos atoll? Was it appropriate for the very commanding officer against whom the mutiny was directed to be president of his own court martial? Such questions as these have dominated discussions ever since.

According to the late Peter Hastings, former research fellow in the Strategic and Defence Centre at the Australian National University and foreign affairs editor of the *Sydney Morning Herald*, Captain Gardiner acted with unusual haste in setting up the court martial. As to the causes of the mutiny, he told me that he felt Gardiner and Stephens gave Fernando, de Silva, Gauder and the others enough provocation to produce some kind of explosion. It was while Hastings was at the *Sydney Morning Herald* that its features editor, Ian Hicks, invited me to write an article on the Cocos story for the newspaper's 'Good Weekend' supplement (eventually published 31 May 1980). He asked Hastings, who was known for his meticulous checking, to provide some oversight, and the latter spent considerable time contacting military lawyers and Defence Department personnel to clarify and discuss all aspects of Gardiner's Field General Court Martial.

Of course at that time Hastings and other commentators were not in possession of all the Field General Court Martial records, and their appraisals were therefore in a sense provisional, but even in the light of these records I have found little to disagree with in his comments. He supported the view that the mutineers did not get a fair trial at Cocos, and he gave Fernando credit for requesting a military trial in Ceylon. Behind the reasons Gardiner offered for conducting an immediate court martial, and in the process giving himself virtually unlimited powers, Hastings saw excuses for not paying regard to the spirit of military law, according to which the proceedings of a court should not be prejudicial to the accused.

The Cocos mutiny raised large questions about Asian loyalty, but it was not the only World War Two incident in that region to do so. Two-thirds of the Sikh Squadron of the 'Central Indian Horse' refused to obey orders, in spite of the entreaties of their officers, when they were delayed in Bombay during 1940 prior to going overseas. After facing a court martial, they were sent to the

Andaman Islands, where they were captured by the Japanese in March 1942.[1] Their new situation sharply raised the stakes in the matter of loyalty.

The 60,000 Indians among the 85,000 prisoners taken by the Japanese in the Malayan campaign had been subjected to Nippon's ceaseless indoctrination. They were promised better treatment if they cooperated with the Greater East Asia Co-Prosperity Sphere, but in typical fashion the Japanese went a lot further: the Indians were threatened with disastrous consequences if they failed to cooperate. They inflicted corporal punishment of absolute brutality, and the threat of the Bidari concentration camp was often enough to have unwilling Indian soldiers helping the enemy. Thousands of prisoners were shipped to Japanese labour gangs in the South Pacific, and many signed a new oath to a provisional Indian government in exile based in Singapore, the head of which was Subas Chandra Bose.

Despite the intense pressures, many Indian soldiers refused to cooperate with the enemy, and not a single Gurkha went over. The 3rd Cavalry was loyal owing to the leadership of two commissioned officers, Captain Hari Badhwar and Captain Dhargalkar. They remained with their men and refused to give in to Japanese demands, with the result that they were kept in an iron cage for weeks.

The main option offered by the Japanese to the Indian soldiers was that they become members of the so-called Indian National Army, though some joined voluntarily. This military group had been started by Mohan Singh, who became disillusioned when he realised the Japanese would not treat him as an independent ally. The first Indian National Army division, which fought with the Japanese in a battle at Imphal, comprised 6000 men, of whom 715 deserted, 800 surrendered and 400 were killed. The rest — around 4000 — died of disease and starvation.[2] Bose had believed that their love for Mother India would make up for the mutinous troops' inadequate training, leadership and equipment. After that debacle the Japanese were prepared to use Bose's men as infiltrators and spies, but they had no faith in their military usefulness.

Cambridge-educated Bose held the deep conviction that India would secure her freedom only by force. As Hugh Toye, Bose's 1959 biographer, explained: 'Bose's theme was Nationalism and the Motherland. It was heady emotional stuff: he poured scorn and contempt on those who were toadies of the British and in any case the British were everywhere defeated.' That last point was decidedly making an impact. And memories came back. The 1919 Nationalist massacre of 379 Indians by the British at Amritsar in the Punjab state of north India, and the 'crawling' order,[3] were blights on British rule in India that were close enough in recollection to fuel any notions about a switch in loyalty.

The Indian National Army was held in contempt by loyal troops of the Indian army, and British officers voiced sentiments like those of Captain Gardiner: 'The Indian National Army deserters should have been court martialled and dealt with on the spot. All the INA men had waged war against the King Emperor and this was punishable with death.'[4]

But in the field of battle it is not easy to implement decisions that logically follow upon a mutiny or desertion or an act of cowardice. The letter of the Manual of Military Law begged the question of how the spirit of the law could be brought to bear in upholding natural justice and securing a fair trial. A responsible British officer could not readily order the execution of hundreds of troops for desertion and cooperation with the enemy. Nor was referring the decision up the line any solution: General Slim was too busy with matters of the battlefront to sort out the destinies of the Indian National Army mutineers.

The causes of mutiny can be complex. The British military historian Lawrence James gives an excellent background to the unrest on Cocos.[5] He outlines the expansion of Asian popular anti-colonial movements, inspired by educated elites who wanted responsible government, and traces the effects of the Japanese thrust southwards and its blow to British power and prestige.

Of course 'Asia for the Asians' was not a new by-product of Japan's co-prosperity vision. The sentiment had long been present in the simmering feelings of Asian people, who wanted to be released from the worst aspects of imperialism and colonialism. In my school days I heard the taunt: 'The sun never sets on the British Empire because you cannot trust an Englishman in the dark!' This was bettered by someone James quotes: 'One black American soldier suggested that his epitaph might read "Here lies a black man, killed fighting a yellow man for the protection of a white man."' It was not just black soldiers who saw their position as equivocal: the author points to Americans who wanted to know whether they were at war with Japan just to restore the European colonies in the East.

Lawrence James shows how the Western reaction to the new forces in Asia was fumbling and dismissive: a mixture of concession and moderate repression. Condescension continued also, epitomised in the belief that Japan's accurate bombing of Hong Kong in 1941 could only have been explained by the use of German pilots. But, as events in Asia unfolded, Europe began to reappraise its disregard of the Japanese as mentally, industrially and militarily incapable of shaking European hegemony in Asia. Alfred Duff Cooper put it this way in a 1941 report: 'We are now faced by vast populations of industrious, intelligent and brave Asians, who are unwilling to acknowledge the superiority of Europeans or their rights to special privileges in Asia.'[6]

James can be criticised in matters of detail. The Cocos contingent was not entirely Sinhalese, as he makes out: many were Burghers and Eurasians. He accurately portrays Fernando's anti-British and anti-colonial sentiments, but the causes did not come from living in Malaya: Fernando never resided there. And it is surely wide of the mark to point to 'the pent up fury of one man' as the cause of the Cocos mutiny.

If a major criticism is to be offered, it is of his description of the Cocos mutiny as 'a small affair'. This is a strange assessment, bearing in mind the causes and repercussions. That three soldiers were hanged — the only executions for mutiny in World War Two — speaks for itself. But there is a more serious point to be made. The evidence from my interviews with the surviving mutineers suggests that the revolt had every chance of success. Furthermore, whereas James says the islands themselves (as well as the mutiny) were 'of very slight significance,' it must be emphasised again that a successful mutiny would have delivered into the hands of the Japanese a vital Allied communications link. Lieutenant Henry de Sylva's opinion was that Fernando's revolt could have resulted in a serious change to the Japanese plans, since it would have given them a new platform and haven from which to pursue their war aims

It is fascinating to see how down the years the Cocos mutiny has spawned myths and legends and even preposterous claims, not only from the rank and file but also from certain officers. Time can lend an easy camouflage to both the belittling and the exaggeration of individual behaviour at the height of battle. But in the dog-eared folders of the Public Record Office in London the documents lay stacked for over half a century, ready to unfold their remarkable disclosures.

The Cocos mutiny was not the only one to occur in World War Two. We have noted the mutiny of the Indian troops on Christmas Island, and files in the Imperial War Museum at Lambeth reveal details of other uprisings. A yellow 43-page manuscript by A R Evans tells the story of a mutiny in the port of Cape Town in January 1942, when British troops made a serious attempt to sabotage the war effort. An important memoir by Sergeant J C E Prentice of the Royal Corps of Signals tells of a naval mutiny in July 1944. During the passage of HMS *Lothian* from Britain to the Pacific for service with the United States navy as a communications ship, the crew mutinied at Balboa in Panama in protest at the living conditions, and Prentice's section was required to compel the ringleaders to return on board. His document emphasises the veil of secrecy with which the events were surrounded at the time. Yet another wartime mutiny took place at Madras harbour in January 1942. A war service motor transport driver, L E Rawson, gives a fascinating account of this uprising in a 138-page manuscript.[7] The Cocos mutiny of 8 May 1942 stands way ahead of any of these in terms of both planning and execution.

Many of those then present have since spoken. Lynette Ramsay Silver in *Sandakan (A Conspiracy of Silence)* issued an apt caution to those who would tell their stories: 'Five decades have passed, and time can play strange tricks with the memory — minimising or magnifying events and telescoping one into another.' The court martial files provide a stable criterion against which to check the oral evidence of the survivors. Not all the Public Record Office files of courts martial could be accessed — some of individual cases are closed until 2019! — but enough was available from File WO/213 (1909–1963) to provide sufficient a check.

Lance Sergeant 1735 O M D W Perera has consistently maintained in the media and the post-mutiny world that he was the real saviour of Cocos. Reference has been made to his claims already, but they merit thorough investigation, not least because all who have dared to mention the Cocos mutiny have been pounced on by this man with all his guns firing. The fact that the media in Britain and Australia have seen fit to publicise his claims has led to heartache among surviving officers and men and the relatives of those who were involved.

A student of the Jesuit-run St Aloysius College in Galle, O M D W Perera was among the first batch of volunteers to go to Cocos and was also involved in a second tour of duty. He was one of the guards detailed by Captain George Gardiner to take care of the arrested mutineers after the events of 8–9 May 1942. By the time of his demobilisation he had been promoted to sergeant.

The president of the Ceylon Artillery Association (Australia Branch), Lieutenant Colonel Cecil F Fernando, who was adjutant of the 1st Coast Battery during the war, says that he cannot remember any special report in which O M D W Perera was mentioned. Along with other evidence, this observation runs counter to what Perera assiduously claims to be the true facts of the mutiny. In the British press a story was run under the headline 'War Hero's Quest,' with a picture of Perera and the caption 'Vincent Perera searching for the man whose life he saved.' The item went on:

An ex-serviceman's world wide quest to find the man whose life he saved in 1941 during the 'Great Mutiny' [sic] has finally led him to Richmond. Sri Lankan born Vincent Perera aged 59 of Lower Richmond Road, Richmond has heard that his General officer [sic] and two other officers are living in this area.

During the Second World War he volunteered for a Secret Mission to the Virgin Island. It was whilst he was on the ship SS *Kalantan* [sic] that 14 volunteer gunmen who had boarded the ship in Colombo tried to commandeer the vessel.[8] Moments before the office of the General George Gardiner was blasted in a hail of gunfire and he shouted at the General to get out.

Mr Perera also saved the life of Capt Stephens who had been shot three times in the leg. 'I saw his green eyes in the dark and his revolver pointing out through sandbags,' said Mr Perera. 'He was half unconscious and I put him on my back and carried him to the Medical centre.' Mr Perera has appealed to anybody who may know General George Gardiner's whereabouts.

In 1988, while on a visit to Australia, Perera told the same story to the media. Diana Gordon of the *West Australian* ran it on 11 February. The former sergeant's quest this time was in Perth.

A World War Two serviceman is in Perth looking for the officers and a Sergeant whose lives he saved as a boy in 1941 during what became known as the Great Mutiny. Sri Lankan born Vincent Perera (58) of London said he wanted to hold a reunion with the three men who he believed were living in West Australia. During World War Two Mr Perera volunteered for a secret mission to the Virgin Islands, past Japanese patrols on an unseaworthy ship called SS *Kalantan*.

During the voyage ill-feeling erupted among the 14 volunteer gunners, who joined them from Seychelles. The gunners were disciplined by a British Army General for getting drunk while on shore. They tried to commandeer the ship in the middle of the night amid fierce gunfire.

Perera went on to repeat the story of yelling to Gardiner to get out and carrying Stephens on his back. Diana Gordon's report went on: 'Mr Perera is looking for I L Pereira whom he rescued from the mutineers.'

On 21 October 1992 Toni Lea in the Melbourne suburban paper *Oakleigh Springvale Times* wrote:

> Mr O M D W Perera emigrated to Australia four years ago after living in England for 22 years. He left his home country Sri Lanka in 1960 for political reasons. He has marched in every Anzac parade since moving to Australia.
>
> Mr Perera has written to Queen Elizabeth appealing for recognition for himself and four fellow veterans who never received field decorations for quashing a mutiny in 1941. At the time the Ceylon Garrison Artillery guarded the most important cable station, between Australia, New Zealand, Ceylon, India and England [*sic*].
>
> Fourteen members from within the Artillery unit started the mutiny, but quick action by Mr Perera and his fellow soldiers prevented disaster. But the report on the matter was misplaced by the Commander in charge.

These stories caused concern among the men who had been on Cocos at the time. In a letter to me Henry Stephens dismissed Perera's claims as 'pure fantasy.' None of the available documents at the Public Record Office in Kew and the Imperial War Museum at Lambeth, nor the recollections of others present on Cocos at the time, offers anything to substantiate Perera's stories.

Matters came to a head when O M D W Perera became secretary of the Melbourne-based Ceylon Artillery Association (Australian Branch), succeeding the genial war veteran Clarence Corera. In a newsletter edited and written by Perera himself there came these observations, reproduced exactly as they appeared:

> About the Mutiny at Cocos, where I lead the fight against the 14 mutineers and made it possible the arrest of all 14.

Only three were hung out of the 14, when they arrived in Ceylon. General Farndale in his address to the Members of the RA Association UK categorically states that he appealed to all those who had done hard soldiering with absolute loyalty, must endeavour their best to ensure the correct records of such soldiering goes into the record book for recognition. I could not agree more concerning the concocted stories by journalist cum evangelist Noel Crusz who's story about the mutiny has been published not once, but twice including what appeared at Sydney.

The witness to my leadership in the arrest of mutineers at Cocos and who helped covering me up until I rescued the GOC and Capt Stephens from death, and witness to the surrender to me by Bdr Gratien Fernando and the Second in Command Anandappa at 03.30 hours are the only two who followed me into the area showered with automatic fire at 03.30 hours are Sgt I L Perera [sic], Sgt M E S Perera. These two are still living and are hale and hearty here in Australia.

I have found out that Capt Stephens and Sgt I L Perera are in Perth not forgetting Gunner Hoffman [sic] who was with Gnr Carlo Gauder, when Gauder shot and wounded Capt Stephens and left him presuming that he was dead.

I witnessed Hoffman and Carlo Gauder running from behind the look out post on the beach towards the canteen past the short pier, a few minutes before Bombardier Gratien Fernando and Gunner Anandappa surrendered to me at 05.30 hrs. I did not shoot at the two of them as they were running minus their firearms, and to my knowledge I was sure that Carlo Gauder a harmless fellow would have been under threat to kill Capt Stephens that day.

As for Hoffman he was capable, which fact I had informed the GOC and put down in my report, which Sgt Major M V P Perera was handed as required by the GOC. But obviously not handed to the GOC George Gardiner but Capt [sic] Silva of the CLI.

It was Carlo Gauder who told me during my interrogation while under my guard in a cell, where I could find his plans to that mutiny. I found it under the bunk bed of Bdr Gratien Fernando glued to the woodwork, with the presumption that the mutiny will be successful.

It has been agreed between the 14, it read to the effect that Gratien was to be the Officer Commanding, Gnr Anandappa was to be Second in Command and Chicago Dias was to be the BSM. Gnr Karunaratna was to be Sgt Major, Gnr G.B. de Silva was to be the Quartermaster Sergeant. This was the recommendation that was to be handed over to the Japanese, once they arrived after they have been informed of their success in the mutiny.

Hopefully this brief will please comrades and clear concocted stories. Consider I now ask all of you whether this bit of news is a private matter of mine or of military importance?

Please also be informed that I protested in writing while resident in UK when it was published to the effect that Prime Minister Mrs Thatcher had flown 10,000 miles to Faulkand Islands to place a wreath on the grave of an Argentinian pilot, who had flown over to bomb the British troops, but ignore a loyal gunner of Her Majesty who was shot dead while in the performance of his duty attempting to arrest a mutineer. I have the acknowledgement not only for that letter, but all correspondence on the mutiny to Her Majesty the Queen, and all Prime Ministers of the UK including the present Hon. John Major.

I was offered a Commission by the GOC whilst at the top of the look out post 60 feet above sea level when Gunner G B de Silva was arrested by both the GOC and Sgt O M D V Perera. But I refused to accept, until the 14 faced the firing squad arranged by me on orders of the GOC. It was after the FGCM that our GOC came up to me and expressed his appreciation considering the reason I gave him for my refusal to accept that Commission. He then showed me the cable sent to the Commanding Officer CGA recommending that Commission on my arrival in Ceylon. The Major who saw it that I did not get my Commission on arrival I do not want to mention until the investigation into their false story about this mutiny is concluded. May I now quote 'An ounce of loyalty is worth a pound of cleverness.'[9]

The Association was acutely embarrassed by all this, and prompt in distancing itself from Perera's claims. The secretary was duly cautioned about hijacking the newsletter to propagate his personal fantasies about the events at Cocos. In October 1992, at the Annual General Meeting of the Artillery Association, Perera was ousted as secretary by fifteen votes to five. He was quick to seek out other paths of involvement: in the *Oakleigh Springvale Times* of 21 October Toni Lea, in a story headlined 'Sri Lankan Gunner Keen to Form Group,' wrote:

> A Noble Park resident and former Army Sergeant wants to form an Association for those who served in the Ceylon Defence Force. L/Sgt Perera said: 'The whole purpose is to promote the togetherness of the veterans, to communicate with all parts of the world and to help those in need.'

She went on to repeat some of Perera's earlier claims: 'Mr Perera has written to Queen Elizabeth appealing for recognition for himself and four fellow veterans who never received field decorations for quashing a mutiny in 1941 [*sic*]. Quick action by Mr Perera and his fellow soldiers prevented disaster. But the report on the matter was misplaced by the Commander in charge.'

In all Perera's accounts of his involvement there was one grain of truth — Gardiner did use Perera as a guard for the mutineers. But that was a routine duty he shared with others. The rest of his claims could not be corroborated either from documents or from oral evidence, and they did indeed border on what Stephens described as fantasy.

In a long audiotaped interview with Perera in Melbourne, I was at the receiving end of the same wild claims that had appeared in the press, though I found myself face to face with a disarmingly friendly man. The Lance Sergeant's loyalty was in no way to be questioned. He had been deeply committed to his volunteer service in the war, and now took a keen interest in the social welfare of ex-servicemen. On the other hand he made good use of his phone to abuse critics who exposed his exaggerations, and I received my own share of his invective.

Perera's claims that he was offered a commission on the observation post by Gardiner was rejected by Stephens, who said it was also news to him that Perera had seen 'his green eyes in the dark' and carried him piggyback to the 'Medical centre.' Apart from that, the idea of the tiny Perera carrying the hefty Stephens on his back does challenge the imagination.

In the Melbourne interview, which took place on 22 October 1992, Perera said that the 'Cocos mutiny really started … [when] the ship [was] in the Colombo Harbour.' It was all about fourteen troublemakers from Seychelles who were now on their way to Cocos bound together in an established comradeship. There was an element of truth in this.

The former sergeant commended Captain Gardiner 'as a true gentleman and not the martinet and racist he was made out to be. One of the causes of the uprising was liquor: It was a boozing mutiny.' Nothing I heard from anyone else offered much support for that contention. Perera felt that Gauder was an innocent victim of Fernando's powerful ways of persuasion, and that he did not deserve to die. Here at least, there could be a good deal of truth.

But some of his statements were in an altogether different category. 'It was the first time in the history of the British army that a sergeant ordered a general out to the bush. I had to call him back to save him.' The documents and the evidence of other eyewitnesses belie this claim and many others that Perera has made. Lieutenant Colonel Lyn Wickramasuriya observed to me that 'if a sergeant orders a general, the bold sergeant deserves to face a court martial!'

19

Night of the Officers

The men at the helm on the Cocos (Keeling) Islands played important roles when mutiny came to the atoll. Their stories add interesting angles to the saga. I would have been especially interested to hear the story of Captain George Gardiner, the main character in this drama, but all my efforts to make contact with him failed. Henry Stephens told me that he also made unsuccessful attempts to find him. The War Office will supply no information about former officers unless the request comes from relatives, so that line of enquiry led nowhere. It is known that he remained with his battery in Ceylon for the duration of the war after returning from Cocos, that he returned to England, and that he blocked efforts to have the loyal troops of the Cocos garrison awarded the 1939–1945 Star and the Pacific Star,[1] but practically nothing beyond that. Stephens believed that he had passed on.

But Lieutenant Henry de Sylva, who was in charge of the Ceylon Light Infantry on Direction Island at the time of the mutiny, did not remain silent. Through the years since the war he has added his own controversial page to the Cocos story. A former schoolteacher from Kandy known for his strict discipline, he obtained his commission at the outbreak of the war. On the morning after the mutiny, he said, he received a signal from Captain Gardiner to come over to Horsburgh Island, but there was no mention of mutiny. According to de Sylva, when he learnt the facts after his arrival there he 'placed the mutineers under arrest.'[2] Anyone who has read this story so far will see this as a preposterous claim. He went on to say that he examined the Bren gun used by Fernando, found no dud bullets in it and formed the opinion that it had jammed due to a gas stoppage.

It will be recalled that the 'dud bullet' story had come from Lieutenant Peter Jayawardena, who in turn contradicted part of de Sylva's story by saying that, when the latter received Gardiner's message, which referred to 'a little internal trouble',[3] he did not go over to Horsburgh himself but delegated Jayawardena to do so, in company with some other CLI personnel. Jayawardena examined the Bren gun on Gardiner's orders, in the mean time telling the commanding officer that he knew what was wrong with the weapon as he had been responsible for setting it up. Jayawardena claims he learnt of the impending mutiny from one of his best friends in the Ceylon Garrison Artillery, Gunner Mark Hopman.

Hopman had persuaded Jayawardena to swear 'by all the saints' that he would never divulge the information to anyone, least of all de Sylva or Gardiner. The lieutenant recalled that this put him between the devil and the deep blue sea: his promise to Hopman and his loyalty to his officers and men. So his only alternative was to sabotage the whole operation on his own. Jayawardena claimed that he not only got the gun back into working order while he was on Horsburgh, but used it to flush out some of the mutineers who were still hiding in a cluster of trees nearby. None of the other evidence supports this last scenario, although such a startling intervention could not have failed to attract the attention of everyone on the island.

Lieutenant Henry Stephens confirmed that Jayawardena had been assigned the task of training some of the CGA men in the use of the Bren, and that there was every possibility he was aware of the mutiny. This state of affairs would have implicated him insofar as he did not inform the commanding officer about it. This point had been ignored in the investigation, however. But

Stephens doubted Jayawardena's story about loading the magazine with dud bullets. If it had been true, Jayawardena would have had to know the exact date of the uprising. Stephens supported de Sylva's conclusion that the failure of the Bren gun was due to a gas stoppage.

In my discussions with the officers there arose the subject of jurisdiction and priority of command. This was a matter of which de Sylva was acutely conscious, and he had always claimed that, as head of the CLI on Direction Island he had the status of commanding officer. Stephens asserted that de Sylva had most certainly not been in command on Cocos: Gardiner was the commander of the entire garrison, both the CLI and the CGA; it was only to him that the official cables came, and only to him were the secret codes entrusted. Gardiner was, however, happy to leave the CLI garrison entirely under de Sylva's control, and did not interfere.

This might have encouraged the lieutenant's authoritarian stance, which came to the fore during the Field General Court Martial. His overbearing interference when witnesses were examined was deeply resented by the mutineers. De Sylva's propensity to grandstand emerged also with his consistent claims after the war that he was 'the only person in Ceylon who knew the true facts of the mutiny.' In a letter to me he set out another claim:

> It was I who convened and conducted the Court Martial, as the two CGA officers were involved in the incident. I had to act as Prosecuting officer, as the other two officers of the Court had no previous Court Martial experience. It was my responsibility to hand those found guilty to the Indian warship that came there to remove them.

That these contentions are unfounded can be seen in the official War Office Court Martial Files (WO/71/741), where Captain George Gardiner is unequivocally stated to be the Convening Officer and President of the Court.

De Sylva also elaborated on his claim to special knowledge: 'Neither Stephens nor any of those involved in the mutiny can tell you the reason for the uprising. At that time it was very confidential.' He emphatically denied that anyone else could have had access to the relevant confidential documents; these, he said, he had handed over personally to the commander-in-chief, Admiral Layton. Sworn to secrecy, only he knew the true story of both the mutiny and the court martial.[4] He still had in his possession some important papers and notes, but these would be released only in return for payment.

All these claims reeked of the military piffle that typified the Cocos mutiny story. When, as editor of the evening daily, the *Star*, published by Independent Newspapers Ltd, I ran 'The Cocos Island Mutiny', the seventeen-part serial by Marie Tirzah, de Sylva indulged in virulent correspondence, threatening not only to sue the newspaper but also to write to Her Majesty the Queen about his grievances. He seemed to be overlooking the fact that it had been clearly pointed out in the first episode that the serial was a fiction based on the facts of the mutiny, and that liberties would be taken in fleshing out the story. When D B Dhanapala, the doyen of Ceylonese journalism and editor-in-chief of Independent Newspapers, received de Sylva's threats, he was amused: 'Let him sue,' he beamed. 'It would add more spice!'[5]

At around this time Pauline Bunce, an Australian research scholar from the University of Western Australia who had worked in the Cocos (Keeling) Islands, came to Ceylon chasing the mutiny story. She examined my unpublished University of New South Wales Master's thesis on the mutiny,[6] and traced de Sylva to his home in the Kandy hills. She said that he insisted on one thing, which was that his name be spelt 'Sylva' and not 'Silva'! Beyond that he was reticent and wary of making any comment on the part he played at Cocos. Perhaps it would have been different if she had offered him payment.

Eventually curiosity prompted me to pay the fee de Sylva had stipulated, and in due course I received photostats of what were purported to be important documents. What I got was an account of the building of the airstrip at West Island and other trivial details that had nothing to do with the mutiny.

At the Field General Court Martial, not only did de Sylva interrupt witnesses who were giving evidence, there was a complaint in the files at the Public Record Office that the interruptions were interspersed with his own interpretations, which were sometimes wrong. There were several heated moments when Fernando, who was well aware of his rights and had a good grasp of military law, objected to the bias that was creeping into the proceedings. De Sylva remained unconcerned, however, even ignoring an obviously valid objection raised by Diasz: that some of the witnesses at the court martial were also guards, and had heard evidence of the other witnesses before they themselves gave evidence.

By 1985 de Sylva had mellowed, and I met him once again in the salubrious hill country of Kandy, though he was seriously ill. During that visit he told me that he had had no difficulty in agreeing with Gardiner and Menon about imposing the death penalty, a decision that had to be unanimous. The former military man still stood by his claim that only he knew 'what the great secret was about the Cocos events.'

Henry de Sylva died on 27 August 1986 in Kandy, and was buried at the local cemetery in Mahaiyawa. He took with him what he continued to claim were the secrets of Cocos.

In 1950, during the years of my priestly ministry, I was summoned to a bedside in Colombo's Durdans Hospital to anoint Lieutenant Henry Stephens who was thought to be dying of pneumonia. In his semi-comatose condition, he was raving about the war. But around-the-clock care by Dr Douglas Flamer-Caldera and Sister Megan Chapman saved the patient's life.

Henry Stephens resumed his planting career at Sorana Estate, Horana, where he and his brother Alick (Jumbo) were popular figures, often referred to as the 'European Stephens.' The Cocos second officer remained a flamboyant, charming character, but he was not inclined to speak about his tour of duty on Cocos —

though he would occasionally show the scars he received in his gun encounter with Carlo Gauder.

Like many of the Cocos participants, Stephens migrated to Australia. In an interview in Adelaide in December 1982 he said:

> George Gardiner was not a martinet nor a racist and held no animosity towards the Ceylonese, nor was he a heavy drinker and was not drunk on the night of the mutiny. Carlo Gauder was a boarding mate of mine at St Joseph's in the time of Fr Le Jeune. Carlo was quiet by nature, not a particular friend of mine and therefore [there were] no scores to settle. Bdr Gratien Fernando was as a person a hell of a nice guy, but a misguided fool at best ...
>
> I did meet the senior Clunies-Ross on a couple of occasions, a very colourless personality. He was an old man then and perhaps a bit senile. As for Lieutenant Henry de Sylva, he had a big chip on his shoulder — yes, a king-size one — and for a person of his intelligence it was pathetic.

Stephens added that he had lost touch with Gardiner after the latter returned to England. Nearly two years later he wrote to me from Fairview Park in South Australia. I had asked him to comment on certain aspects of his involvement in the mutiny, and of the embittered feelings that many of the Cocos troops had towards him. He replied: 'There are two schools of thought on the Cocos mutiny. George Gardiner and I are accused of maltreating the troops, which I know is the biggest load of bulldust.' He went on to suggest that the troops enjoyed a tropical island holiday for all the time they were there.

> George Gardiner was most considerate, devoid of all colour prejudice and a true gentleman. Matter of fact Lyn Wicks was a damn side more difficult to get on with. I am sick of trying to give people who hold the opposite view the facts as they were. At Fr Le Jeune's funeral in July 1957, which I attended, I felt the first impact.[7]
>
> My College mates gave me the dead cut, every one of

them, which brought me to realise the distorted view that some sections carried. When that happens, you try to avoid explaining yourself over and over again by steering clear of the controversy.

Stephens was emphatic in challenging the accounts that O M D W Perera had given in the newsletter of the Ceylon Artillery Association.

The Lance Sergeant is suffering from a serious case of amnesia. Very few of the facts he relates are correct. He was an NCO and held no position of consequence, nor did he hold any position of authority. He refers to George Gardiner as a General, when Gardiner was a mere captain and CO of the Combined Artillery and Infantry Force stationed in the Cocos Keeling Islands. I was his Second in Command and a mere Lieutenant. L/Sgt Perera speaks of the mutiny taking place on a ship. This is the first time I ever heard that version. I was wounded by two bullets and not three, thankfully not seriously, and was able to resume my normal duties shortly after. The person who fired the bullets was Gauder and not Diasz. Talking of fantasy, this one must be the limit.[8]

Stephens was only nineteen when he got his commission. When he was in control he did not shirk his duties as second in command. The strikingly handsome young officer was outspoken and carried himself with a military gait that betrayed colonial arrogance. For this he was hated, but a part of the hatred was born of jealousy. Many felt that it was his lofty style that eroded communication with the troops on Cocos. Fernando would have his joke that 'Stephens feels he is still on an estate and we poor devils are the rubber collectors or tea pluckers! No wonder he loves to give us pack drill.'

Before enlisting, Henry Stephens married the beautiful Eileen Phillips, and in later years had two equally charming daughters, Kay and Patricia. When he migrated to Australia in the 1950s he did consultancy work in accounting and administration at the University of Adelaide, residing in the beautiful hills of Fairview Park. He found time to play competitive bridge in addition to indulging in extensive spells of swimming. He made no excuses for vaunting his British ancestry and was inclined to look down on those who belittled the Mother Country.

Henry Stephens spent his final years in isolation, affected by a terrible loneliness and an inability to come to terms with what was a silent and heavy halter: his part in a mutiny that sent three men to the gallows. He told me that the Cocos experience haunted him all his days. He was, essentially, a big-hearted man, ready to forgive but at times unpredictable and enigmatic. He remained vibrant to the end.

On 25 June 1995 I receivedf a message that Henry had died suddenly at the age of seventy-four. He had suffered a heart attack in his garden at Fairview Park, where he had just completed building a rock garden. Police were called when neighbours missed seeing the handsome, genial army officer and uncollected mail and newspapers piled up at his doorstep. It was only then that his body, which had lain unnoticed for two days, was discovered. He was laid to rest on 7 July at a Roman Catholic requiem service in South Australia. I had sent over the following elegy, which was read at the ceremony:

> *You hear the sounds of war neath the wailing waves*
> *On Cocos Keeling sands where time is born ...*
> *Young bloods destined for unknown graves*
> *Rebellious ... still waiting for another dawn ...*
> *Dreams of swaying palms ... the crabs ashore ...*
> *Bare breasted belles in the twilight moon ...*
> *The winds of war breathe forth once more*
> *When love glistens in a night of doom.*
> *Your tryst is over in God's chosen time*
> *The final days of loneliness that glow*
> *The call so sudden in a breath divine*
> *The bugle silent for you ever more.*

20

Journey's End

Writing to me in 1989, a research officer at the Army Historical Branch of the British Ministry of Defence presented the disappointing news that 'little material on the subject of Cocos survived in former War Office Archives of the Second World War.' The reason given was that 'the event did not receive much publicity. Not surprisingly little is known about it.' He confirmed that in May 1942 the CGA had two officers and thirty-seven men on Horsburgh Island, there was one platoon of CLI with thirty-two personnel on Cocos, and there were fifteen hundred local citizens.

Somewhat reassuring was a note as to the significance of the location: 'The Cocos Islands were strategically important as being the Cable Station on the Trans Indian Ocean route to Australia, a refuelling base for flying boats, and the only alighting place on the Ocean route from India to Australia.' And, yes, there was a little about the mutiny: 'On 10th May 1942 the Commander-in-Chief of the East Indies reported that the previous day, part of the garrison had attempted an armed mutiny.' The report went on to note the casualties as one British officer and three Ceylonese other ranks wounded, but no casualties among the mutineers. Strangely, there was no mention that a soldier had been killed.

After the revolt, he continued, some twenty of the gunners

were relieved of duty, while HMIS *Sutlej* was sent to the islands with relief, supplies and reinforcements. The Ministry of Defence felt that:

> the mutiny was probably caused by the fact that part of the garrison had been on the island for some time without relief and was extremely apprehensive of a Japanese attack. Moreover there were few amenities for troops on the islands. It is believed that these men had also racialist undertones [*sic*], with anti-European sentiments expressed by one of the ringleaders. As a result of the mutiny, it was decided that reliefs of officers and other ranks on Cocos should be carried out automatically every three months instead of four as previously.

According to the research officer, the commander-in-chief in Ceylon reported in September 1942 that HMIS *Somawathie* had visited the islands and found the garrison and population well supplied with food and other stores, and in good heart. The island experienced no further military action until 1944, when the Japanese mounted a brief bombing raid in which an islander and a Royal Navy seaman were killed. After January of that year it had become necessary for India to furnish the garrison, as Ceylon was no longer able to find volunteers for the task.

It was in 1944 also that the RAF built the temporary 7500-foot airfield on West Island. As mentioned earlier, the rapid end to the war meant that the airstrip had only a limited role. The air force abandoned it in 1946, and it remained a derelict reminder of World War Two until 1951, when Australia purchased 368 acres on West Island from John Clunies-Ross for a permanent aerodrome. After removal of the steel matting that had served as the original airstrip, a new 10,000-foot runway was built, and completed by July of the following year.[1] Its immediate importance was as a refuelling station for commercial air services between Australia and South Africa, though it was not many years before it became strategically important as an aerial surveillance base when the Russian navy became active in the Indian Ocean.

To many observers in the postwar period, the little Cocos community began to stand out as an anachronistic bastion of feudalism while the process of decolonisation went on elsewhere. Others, among whom I counted myself, saw it as preserving in a valid way some of the gentle values of traditional Asian societies — the tranquil, non-competitive way of life, the closeness to nature — while former European colonies to its north and east became more and more ruthless and consumerist.

Many were thinking about the atoll's future, and Britain was quite happy to cede sovereignty to Australia. For its part, Australia was happy to accept; what was to happen with the Clunies-Ross regime was a matter for the future. So it was that in November 1955 the islands were detached from the colony of Singapore and accepted by the Commonwealth of Australia as a Territory, to be known thenceforth as the Territory of Cocos (Keeling) Islands. Australian currency replaced the plastic tokens that had served for money under the Clunies-Ross regime.

The Australian Cocos (Keeling) Islands Act of 1955 established administrative, legislative and judicial systems, an administrator appointed by the governor-general being responsible for law and order. At the federal level the Cocos (Keeling) Islands became an electoral district of the Commonwealth Division of the Northern Territory. A local government system based on that of Western Australia would be introduced in 1992, and the first seven-member shire council elected in 1993.

The 'Tuan' himself was not relinquishing sovereignty, however. He owned the islands and was deferred to by the locals as their ruler; as far as he was concerned whatever little deals England and Australia did with each other hardly made a scrap of difference. Thus there was something of a stand-off for a number of years, with the Australian press at one stage noisily expressing outrage at the persistence of the feudal regime but later coming around to the view that it would be churlish to disturb the islanders' idyllic lifestyle. Meanwhile the United

Nations would berate Australia from time to time for allowing the 'terrible situation' on Cocos to continue.

In 1978 Australia bought the islands from the fifth John Clunies-Ross for $6.25 million. Soon there was an exodus of the Malay population, the few who stayed behind aiming at democratic government and an economy based on tourism; the copra industry was by this time almost extinct. In 1980 the Australian Labor government tightened the screws. Clunies-Ross was declared a bankrupt in 1986 after the failure of a shipping venture, and he retired to Perth. His one regret was the loss of Ocean House, located on a beautiful promontory on the Cocos lagoon.

On 6 April 1984 the Cocos Islanders, in an act of self-determination, decided to integrate with Australia. The Commonwealth assured the people that their religious beliefs, traditions and culture would be respected. Completing the political process, at least for the time being, on 7 March 1991 the Australian prime minister and leaders of the Cocos community signed a 'Memorandum of Understanding', which embodied the intention to ensure that standards of living in the Territory were equivalent to those on the mainland. The 1996 census showed a population of 655, of whom 80 per cent were resident on Home Island. The present administrator and staff have made enormous efforts to give Cocos the care it deserves, while also promoting this rare and precious group of islands as a resort. The Commonwealth government allocated $11 million from 1997/98 to 1999/2000 for upgrading water and sewerage services and other facets of the infrastructure, and to provide new marine facilities on West Island.

Perhaps the soul of Cocos was always at peace. Today all is so tranquil that the events of 1942 might never have happened. The atoll nestles in placid blue waters; exotic palms, herbs, mosses, lichen, fungi and a wealth of multicoloured tropical fish thrive, and bird life is abundant, with spoonbills, frigate birds, boobies and several species of tern nesting there.

Both Direction and Horsburgh islands, where the CLI and CGA respectively were encamped during World War Two, are now uninhabited. In 1997 Dr Martin Mowbray, the administrator of Cocos, arranged for one Matthew Bryson to take a party over to Horsburgh Island to see what remained at Rowe Battery. Bryson wrote:

> It seems that the only recognisable parts of the battery left are the guns, of which one is in two pieces and both may have been moved, a couple of rises and a rusting well. The single whole gun on the water's edge is on the south east of the other inland gun, the barrel of which is 50–100 metres further west. It seems that between the destruction by the weather and the evacuation, there is not a lot left on Horsburgh Island.[2]

At the time he was planning his mutiny, Gratien Fernando had no way of realising that the odds were already stacked against the knights of the bushido. The reasons for the failure of the Japanese, according to H P Willmott, were their inability to destroy the enemy's main forces, especially at sea, and consolidate their gains; and their dissipation of effort over a vast area in pursuit of divergent objectives.[3] The acquisition of the Cocos (Keeling) Islands might have helped to solve some of Japan's logistical problems in sustaining thrust in the Indian Ocean, and of course it would have cut an important Allied line of communication.

Willmott argued that Japan should have staked everything on a major offensive in the Indian Ocean. He agreed with the comment that 'Japan had seized a wolf by the ears and was in no position to let go.' We can never know what the outcome would have been if Japan had taken Cocos and Ceylon, and pressed on westwards. What we do know is that she surrendered in 1945.

A peace treaty was to be signed with Japan in San Francisco during September 1951, and Mr J R Jayawardena, Ceylon's finance minister, was sent by the prime minister to the Peace Conference. It was, perhaps, a provocative choice: Jayawardena had openly praised Japan as the first Asian power to challenge the West and as an equal of the Western powers. In his speech to the assembly, Mr Jayawardena said:

> We in Ceylon were fortunate that we were not invaded. But the damage caused by air raids, by the stationing of enormous armies under the South East Asian Command, and by the slaughter tapping of one of our main commodities, rubber, when we were the only producer of natural rubber for the Allies, entitle us to ask that the damage so caused should be repaired.[4]
>
> We do not intend to do so, for we believe in the words of the Great Teacher, whose message has ennobled the lives of countless millions in Asia, that 'hatred ceases not by hatred but by love.'
>
> It is the message of the Buddha, the Great Teacher, the founder of Buddhism, which spread a wave of humanism through South Asia, Burma, Laos, Cambodia, Siam, Indonesia and Ceylon, and also northwards through the Himalayas into Tibet, China and finally Japan, which bound us together for hundred of years, with a common culture and heritage …
>
> This treaty is as magnanimous as it is just to a defeated foe. We extend to Japan a hand of friendship and trust that with the closing of this chapter in the history of man, the page of which we write today, and with the beginning of the new one, the first page of which we dictate tomorrow, her people and ours may march together to enjoy life with full dignity of human life in peace and prosperity.[5]

It was nearly twenty years later when Jayawardena made another speech of note. He was by this time president of his country, and its name was now Sri Lanka. The date was 20 September 1979 and the occasion an imperial banquet held in his honour in Tokyo. In the course of his address he made a startling statement that went far towards condoning the actions of Fernando and his men:

I come from a land and represent a people in many ways as ancient as yours. The people of Sri Lanka, practising the same religion, Buddhism, speaking the same language, Sinhala, lived throughout the island as an independent nation till 1815 for 2300 years. The British monarchical rulers then replaced the local monarchs under a Convention accepted with the consent of the people, and not by conquest.

Under King George III of the United Kingdom and his descendants, the British Government ignored the Convention and ruled Sri Lanka as a colony, and as a Dominion till 1972 when we became a Republic.

Under foreign rule the faith of the people, their language and their customs almost died away. Because of this, not only we, but all Asian nations which suffered similar fates under Western Imperialism admired and looked up to Japan.

During the last 80 years Japan stood out in Asia as an Independent nation. When the Western powers dominated the whole world with their military might and their commercial enterprises, you competed with them, equalled them and often defeated them.

I do not support war or violence. I did feel however that the 1939 War would end British Imperialism. Together with my friend and colleague, the late Mr Dudley Senanayake, and ex-Prime Minister and son of our first Prime Minister, we even discussed with the Japanese Consul in our country in the 1940s how we could help the Japanese if they landed in Sri Lanka, provided they help us attain freedom. Fortunately we were saved the bloodshed consequent upon an invasion.[6]

The freedom that Fernando dreamed of came on 4 February 1948 with the declaration of Ceylon's independence from Britain. In a debate on the Ceylon Independence Bill in the House of Lords in 1947, Lord Soulbury had said:

Your Lordships are now asked to assent to the emancipation

of an ancient people, who have in the past enjoyed independent Sovereignty, and who for centuries have known civilised rule.[7]

How ironic it was that what Gratien Fernando had set out to foster by putting his life and integrity on the line should now come about so quickly and so easily. Some have found it easy to take the view that the bombardier had been merely giving expression to his personal grievances, and in the process endangering those he dragged along with him. But a fair assessment of the evidence in this book would lead, I suggest, to a different conclusion. To those who decry the action as a futile gesture it may be replied that, yes, the odds were stacked against its success, but this does not mean that he was playing a wild card. With a touch more commitment on the part of his colleagues and a more reliable machine gun, there might conceivably have been a different outcome.

We have noted that some commentators believe the Field General Court Martial conducted by Captain Gardiner was seriously flawed and that the accused did not get fair trials. Though critical of the proceedings, the Judge Advocate General in New Delhi had no alternative but to accept the reports and evidence that Gardiner and his court martial provided; the mitigating circumstances that might have affected the verdict were certainly not addressed. It may be observed in this connection that Lieutenant Van Twest's scathing report never reached New Delhi, and my efforts to find it in the Public Record Office and the Imperial War Museum met with no success. The disappearance of this vital indictment of the military bureaucracy is a mystery, though it is open to speculation that someone in the system deliberately and quietly disposed of it.

With the passage of time and 'freedom of information' disturbing what were previously rigid rules, many are re-assessing the court martial decisions of the world wars. In May

1998 Lorna Duckworth, the political correspondent of the *Sunday Mail*, reported that 'the death sentence for desertion, mutiny and treachery in the Armed Forces was to be scrapped in Britain.' British Armed Service Minister John Reid even considered the pardon of 307 soldiers shot for cowardice in World War One.[8] The British debate saw Tory ministers wanting the death penalty retained for misconduct in action, helping the enemy, obstructing operations with intent to help the enemy, mutiny and failure to suppress a mutiny.

In Australia attempts are being made to reconsider the court martial files of the two world wars and even one from the Boer War. Anthony Hoy in the *Sydney Morning Herald* of 13 April 1999 wrote: 'The honour of Harry Breaker Morant and his co-accused Peter Handcock, executed by the British in the Boer War, may be restored …' According to researcher Nick Bleszynsky, 'It has been clearly established that it was standard practice during the Boer War to shoot prisoners. Morant and Handcock were singled out, [whereas] new evidence confirm[s] that Kitchener himself gave the order "No Prisoners".' He added that the commander-in-chief's behaviour 'had been cowardly and questionable in disappearing for four days after his "death by firing squad" order [on Morant and Handcock], so no appeal could be considered.'

There is also a campaign concerned to clear the names of some of the men executed after courts martial, on the basis that there had been serious flaws in procedure. The New Zealand writer Christopher Dore has told the story of Victor Spencer, who, after surviving the horrors of Gallipoli, served in Turkey and later on the Western Front.[9] He was charged with cowardice and executed by his own unit. Spencer and some companions had got drunk and left their battalions without leave, and this is not disputed, but Dore contends that they were all 'shell-shocked.' One of them, Jack Braithwaite, was accused of leading a mutiny, which he claimed he was in fact trying to defuse. The court martial trial lasted only fifteen minutes and all faced the firing-squad.

Of 127 Australians sentenced to death in World War One, only two, Privates John King and John Sweeny, who fought with the New Zealand army, were actually executed. According to Christopher Doe, the Australian government would not sanction the executions ordered by the Imperial Forces leader, Field Marshal Douglas Haig, but New Zealand did. The government of that country has begun an inquiry to determine whether the executed men should receive a posthumous pardon. There is a feeling that many of these soldiers suffered a miscarriage of justice at the hands of military authorities, insofar as the latter completely failed to take into account war-related psychological disorders.

Military justice did not always result in extreme punishment. Nearly two hundred men of the British 8th Army who downed weapons in the battle for Salerno in southern Italy during 1943 were condemned to punishments ranging from seven years to death after court martial, but all sentences were suspended after intervention by Adjutant General Sir Ronald Adam, who was horrified at what he read in the court martial files. It was a close call, however.

The Cocos mutiny must be viewed in the context of the larger picture. The young Ceylonese volunteers, fresh from school, had to learn the hard way that the days of playing war games were over: when the enemy is at the door everything takes on a new significance. That Lieutenant Henry Stephens was only nineteen when he got his commission illustrates just how much responsibility was being placed on youth — it must always have been a real question as to whether Stephens had the maturity and experience to control seasoned troops who had seen tough times in Seychelles.

But the spotlight necessarily always returns to Gardiner: it was only during his tour of duty that unrest flared up. While Koch and Wickramasuriya were in command, there was a contented, loyal Rowe Battery, and one that remained so even in the face of a Japanese bombardment. Clearly Gardiner and Stephens failed to establish communication with their troops, a cardinal sin of military leadership. And it is a serious dereliction of duty for a commander and his second in charge not to perceive that a revolt is brewing.

Yet mutiny can never be condoned, and in the armed forces it is one of the gravest crimes, as such imposing a serious responsibility on all officers who have to deal with it. While acknowledging this, it must be recognised also that the very nature of the court martial process creates many opportunities for the denial of natural justice, raising the question of a possible need for military law reform.

Having followed the Cocos story for over three decades, I am also at a journey's end. I have seen the full range of human emotion experienced by the officers and men who were involved in the uprising at Cocos Keeling; I have seen the politics of army factions and the readiness of some to exploit and distort the basic events of the mutiny; I have observed the conflict between authority and expectation, between leaders and those who lose their way, between the Asian dream and colonial fulfilment, between the 'white man's burden' and the deeper quest for enduring values.

Bombardier Gratien Fernando dreamt of the 'Isle of Fate.' Little did he realise that Cocos Keeling would emerge from its isolation and its troubled wartime history to offer one of the world's enthralling opportunities for enjoying an unspoilt environment.

> *Blue waters rippling at the atolls,*
> *The gentle surf lapping the coral reef …*
> *Ghosts of those who saw death and life*
> *However brief to tell their tale …*
> *Of blood and tears and the shadows*
> *That haunt the beauty of the breaking dawn*
> *In an Indian Ocean …*

Acknowledgements

This book could not have been written without the assistance of many who helped me in different ways. I would like to thank especially:

Lt Col Lyn Wickramasuriya for reading the original manuscript, for giving me constructive criticism and advice, and for providing a foreword.

Dr Richard Cashman of the Department of History, University of New South Wales, and Dr Max Harcourt, who supervised my MA thesis on the mutiny. In the course of my research I was helped by Professor Frank Crowley, Dr Michael McKernan and Dr Ian Bickerton.

Alan Gill for his consistent support and help, for reading the initial drafts and for making very valuable suggestions. It was Alan and his wife, Daisy, who sponsored my family into Australia from Sri Lanka twenty-five years ago.

H P Willmott, the noted British military historian and author of *Empires in the Balance* (Orbis, 1982), for generously allowing me to quote from his book, and for all the encouragement he has given me. It is a rare privilege to sit under the shadow of one of the world's eminent military historians.

The Literature Board of the Australia Council for a special grant in 1978 to help in writing this account of the Cocos mutiny; to Michael Costigan, who showed a keen interest in the project; and to Edmund Campion, SJ, former Chair of the Literature Board, for his encouragement during the anxious days when I was peddling my script among publishers. Thank you, Edmund, for sharing your conviction that 'a good story will eventually find a good publisher.'

Lucy Meo, author of *Japan's Radio War on Australia* (Melbourne University Press, 1968), who willingly shared her expertise on the radio war and its implications for the Cocos mutineers. She, too, was generous in allowing me to quote from her outstanding work.

Ken Mullen, author of *Cocos Keeling: the Islands Time Forgot* (Angus & Robertson, 1974), for helping me to fill in the gaps and for allowing me to quote from his book.

Edgar Harcourt, wireless navigator in the RAAF in World War Two, for invaluable advice and for permission to quote from *Taming the Tyrant* (Allen & Unwin, 1987).

Lionel Allen for sharing his recollections of his years on Cocos and providing valuable leads.

Maurice Matthysz for assisting me with information relevant to submarine cables and to the operation of the Cocos cable station and the OTC network.

The BBC, London, and Claire Choudhury for information from Dai Richards's production *Timewatch: a Very British Mutiny* (3BM Television for BBC 2).

Deb Blaskett, Deputy Administrator of the Territory of the Cocos (Keeling) Islands, and Paul Sparke for providing information about Cocos today and a picture of the coral atoll on the eve of the millennium.

Peter Hastings, former Research Fellow in the Strategic and Defence Centre, Australian National University, and one-time Foreign Editor of the *Sydney Morning Herald*, who with Ian Hicks invited me to write up the mutiny story for the 'Good Weekend' magazine. Peter gave me useful advice and leads in pursuing my research.

F E W Felsinger, former Librarian of the Repatriation Department Library in Canberra and Librarian, Northern Territory Library Services, for his encouragement and expertise in directing me in my work.

The Director, Classical Archival Records Review, Defence

Corporate Legal Office, Canberra, for permission to use World War Two Defence Top Secret Documents in chapter 3. They are reproduced and published with permission of the Australian government.

The Controller of Her Majesty's Stationery Office for permission to make extensive use of copyright material in the Public Record Office, and Copyright Officer Tim Padfield for his assistance.

The officers at the Public Record Office at Kew, London, for their unstinting support in tracing documents in the Cocos mutiny files.

The Director, Reprographic Ordering Section, Public Record Office, for expediting at short notice the provision of copies of documents in the Field General Court Martial files.

Anthony P Richards, Archivist of the Department of Documents, Imperial War Museum, London, and Julie Robertshaw for assistance in tracing primary sources on World War Two mutinies.

Peter Duncan and Kenneth Myers of the BBC, London, for arranging interviews about the Cocos mutiny on *In Town Tonight*.

The Director of the Australian War Memorial, Canberra; the Senior Archivist, Australian Archives, Dickson, ACT; and the Senior Archivist, Australian Archives, Brighton, Victoria, for helping to obtain documents pertaining to Cocos and its defence. Also to Beth Rogers of the Access Services, National Archives, Canberra, for information re obtaining access to military primary sources.

Winston G Ramsey, Editor-in-Chief of *After the Battle*, for permission to quote from Wing Commander Derek Martin's article 'The Cocos mutiny' and Marcus Fernando's follow-up story. Also for the use of Matthew Bryson's photographs of the Cocos Islands and the guns at Horsburgh.

Buchan & Enright, London, for permission to quote from Lawrence James's *Mutiny*, 1987.

Dr J T L C Rajah Fernando of Edmonton, Alberta, Canada, for generous assistance in securing documents, and for providing details of the life of his cousin Gunner G Benny de Silva.

Editors of the *Sydney Morning Herald, Ceylon Sunday Times, Sunday Island, Sunday Observer*, Independent Newspapers Ltd *Weekend* and *Star, Australian Advocate* and *Asian Times* for quotes from my articles in these publications on the mutiny.

Readers Digest for permission to draw on Lawrence Elliott's article on Squadron Leader Leonard Birchall, and to Chief Sub Editor George Rupesinghe for his advice.

James Bulner, author of *The Eurasian* and *Where have all the Aussies Gone?* (Albion Press), for advice to Teserine Publications, Sydney/Colombo.

Victor Melder for helping me with documents from his library in Melbourne, and for documents on the Japanese air raid on Colombo. Victor's treasure-house of Sri Lankan archives was of immense help.

Mr R J Linford, Administrator of Cocos (Keeling) Islands in 1977, for details of the mutiny available at that time.

Clarence Corera, a World War Two veteran and indefatigable Secretary of the Ceylon Artillery Association who has done extensive research on the services during World War Two, for help in identifying CGA personnel.

Gnr Bertie Claessen (CGA) for sharing his experiences as a member of the first contingent on Cocos, and for his correspondence with the British Ministry of Defence.

Gnr Aubrey Corterling, a schoolmate at St Peter's College, Colombo, and a loyal soldier who acted in support of Capt. Gardiner at the peak of the mutiny, for his observations on Cocos.

British World War Two veteran Lt W F Rook, who saw action in Ceylon during the time of Admiral Layton and Lord Louis Mountbatten. Thank you, Frank, for your notes on Colonel Mervyn Joseph and his concern for the condemned mutineers, and for your cooperation generally.

Special thanks for the personal interviews given to me by: Lt George Koch, Lt Douglas Aluwihare, Lt Henry Stephens, Gnr Ken Porritt, Gnr Donald Patterson, Gnr Gerry Anandappa, Gnr

Mark Hopman, Gnr Alfred Edema, Gnr Mervyn de Rooy, Cpl Lucian Koch, Bdr T N A Ousmand, Lt Owen Wambeek, Lt I D M Van Twest, Lt Henry de Sylva, Lt Col. Dr Trevor Van Twest, Pte Eric Van Rooyen, Lt Col. Cecil Fernando, Lt R D C Jonklaas, L/Sgt O M D W Perera and Pte Calixtus P J Seneviratne; also war chaplains Fr Adrian Brennan, OMI; Fr Claude Lawrence, OMI; Fr Emmanuel Alles, OMI; Fr John Gardiner and Fr A Culkin.

I must mention the assistance of Totsy Collinson (the sister of Gnr Carlo Gauder), who with C D Collinson and Norman Don gave me details of Gauder's last days.

I owe a debt of gratitude to Eva and Helen Fernando, sisters of the leader of the mutiny, Gnr Gratien H Fernando. Eva provided documents, photographs and details of her brother's fatal involvement. Also thanks to Indra Chandrasekera and Robert Crusz, who helped in the May 1999 interview with Helen.

Patricia Stephens, daughter of Lt Henry Stephens, who gave me photographs of her father at the time of his enlistment.

Mr K C Selvadurai of Singapore, who photographed for me the headstone of the grave of Gnr Samuel Jayasekera, whose remains were taken from Cocos to the Kranji War Cemetery.

Among the media men who paved the way in my quest were D B Dhanapala, Eric Devanarayana, Rex de Silva, Douglas Grenier, Sinha Ratnatunga, Rainie Wickrematunga, Louis Benedict and Greg Roszkowski.

Lalin Fernando and Len Pereira for assisting me with their computing expertise.

My brothers Prof. Hilary Crusz (University of Ceylon, Peradeniya), Rienzi (Canadian poet) and Jerome (photographer), all of whom helped me in my research. I record also a debt of gratitude to my late parents, Michael and Cleta Crusz, who introduced us at an early age to the world of books. We cannot forget the ten volumes of Arthur Mee's *Book of Knowledge.*

My nephew, film producer Robert Crusz, and Ceylonese director Prasanna Vithanage, who are developing a script for an international production on the Cocos mutiny, based on the first draft I wrote for Sankofa Film & Video (Ltd) United Kingdom.

Last but not least I owe much to the encouragement and assistance given to me by my wife, Tirzah, in Ceylon, Australia and London. She showed great patience and understanding during the many hours spent for many years in chasing this story. She has been a tower of strength to me in proofreading the manuscripts and transferring them to the computer.

It is with regret that I must mention that not a few who helped me in writing this book and whose names are mentioned above have passed on. That this should be so is not surprising in the case of a project that has taken over thirty years to complete.

While acknowledging all of the above, I would stress that I bear all responsibility for any of the shortcomings in the story I have told.

I am deeply grateful to my editor, Allan Watson of Perth Editorial Service, who has helped me in no small measure to tell my story. Apart from his copy editing, his constructive criticism helped me to sift the evidence in a way that was essential to the project. Thank you, Allan, for the faxes and the phone calls and the checking that went into this book.

Thank you too, Ray Coffey and Fremantle Arts Centre Press, for the decision to publish the story of the mutiny. Fremantle Arts Centre Press has brought completion to a project that began in 1942.

Endnotes

PREFACE

1   General Wavell died in 1950. Viceroy and Governor-General of India from 1943 to 1947, he helped to promote the cause of self-government for that country.
2   The ages of the non-European officers in charge of Ceylonese troops at the beginning of World War Two were: Lyn Wickramasuriya (24), George Koch (45), J A Pye (35), R D C Jonklaas (23), D Aluwihare (19), Henry Stephens (19) and Henry de Sylva (35).
3   Mr Clunies-Ross was the great-great-grandson of the original settler.
4   Susuma Nishiura, Chief of the War Office, National Defence Agency, told me that most of the historical records were destroyed by Allied bombing. Only some of the plans of the long-range submarines were salvaged.

CHAPTER 1

1   Notes supplied by Lieutenant Mervyn Vanderwert and Lieutenant Colonel Cecil Fernando.
2   Report of the Rt Hon. W G A Ormsby Gore, MP, on his visit to Ceylon, Malaya and Java in 1928, pp. 97–98.
3   Oscar M Abeyratna, *The History of the Ceylon Light Infantry*, Colombo, 1945. The Battle of Lys took place at the river of that name in NE France and Belgium.
4   Eric Van Rooyen, a private in the CLI, enlisted in May 1932. Some details of the units were provided by him.
5   Weerawardana, *Ceylon General Election*, 1956, p. 60. Those who went to prison were Dr N M Perera, Philip Gunewardena and Dr Colvin R de Silva. They escaped during the Japanese Easter Sunday air raid of 5 April 1942.
6   S A Pakeman, *Ceylon*, London, Ernest Benn, 1964. Pakeman lived

for thirty-one years in Ceylon. He was Professor of History at the University College until 1942.

7 In 1971 I interviewed Eva Fernando, Gratien's eldest sister, in Mount Lavinia. She provided valuable primary sources in the form of photographs, family documents and correspondence. In April 1999 his youngest sister, Helen, answered further questions regarding his involvement.

8 Quoted in a letter from 'The Comrades of the Great War' to the Secretary of State, Lord Lloyd, 4 June 1940.

9 One of the tanks was set ablaze in April 1942 by Japanese Zeros.

10 Their gist can be gathered from 'Message from the Workers and Peasants of Ceylon,' issued by the Lanka Sama Samaja Party section of the Bolshevik Workers Party of India, Burma and Ceylon (Fourth International) in April 1942.

11 S A Pakeman, *Ceylon*, London, Ernest Benn, 1964.

12 *Sunday Times* (Ceylon), 29 April 1992.

CHAPTER 2

1 The motto on the garrison's coat of arms was 'Ubique quo fas et gloria dicunt' (Everywhere where right and glory lead).

2 Seychelles had become a British colony in 1903.

3 Also present at the ceremony were Vice-Admiral Ralph Leatham, CIC of the East Indies Squadron, Lieutenant Colonel O B Forbes, Commander of the CGA First Heavy Regiment, and Major F C de Saram.

4 Nauru was shelled on 27 December 1941 by a vessel bearing a Japanese name and flag but which was in fact the German ship *Komet*. With the *Orion*, she sank five ships engaged in phosphate transport. (Lionel Wigmore, *The Japanese Thrust*, Canberra, Australian War Memorial, 1957, p. 52.)

5 Quoted in the *Ceylon Daily News*, Colombo, January 1942. Sir Andrew Caldecott had succeeded Sir Edward Stubbs as governor in 1937.

6 The officiating priest was Fr Aidanus Peter Brennan, OMI, who in the course of his sermon spoke of the outstanding virtues of a soldier — obedience and courage in the service of his sovereign — virtues that must characterise the Christian in the warfare that he as a soldier of Christ was called upon to wage in the service of his heavenly king. After the ceremony each of the thirty CGA men was presented with a rosary and a specially autographed prayer book from the Archbishop of Colombo, the Most Rev. Dr Jean Marie Masson, OMI. Fr Brennan later attended the executions of the mutineers.

7 The Right Reverend Cecil Horsley, Bishop of Colombo and senior

chaplain to the forces in Ceylon, addressed the men. As quoted in the *Ceylon Daily News*, January 1942, he said among other things: 'In your long hours of watching and waiting, you will pray for those you love and have left behind here in Ceylon. You will pray to be worthy of the traditions of the Ceylon Garrison Artillery, and add lustre to its record.' In the congregation were Colonel R S M White (Commandant Ceylon's Defence Force), Lieutenant Colonel O B Forbes (Commander CGA First Heavy Regiment), Lieutenant Colonel Stanley Fernando (Commander Ceylon Engineers), Major J O Widdows (Staff Officer Ceylon Command), Major Mervyn Joseph, Major R L Bartholomeusz and Major Neil Schokman.

8 Journalist Janaka Perera in the *Ceylon Observer* (27 June 1976) interviewed Lieutenant Harold Van Cuylenberg, who provided details of army life in wartime Seychelles.

9 I interviewed Mark Hopman in Colombo on 3 May 1970. He later migrated to Australia and refused further interviews.

10 They returned on the *Ispingo*, which was attacked by Japanese submarines off Batticaloa but escaped with minor damage.

11 Files MP 729/6 16/401/273 of the Australian Archives contain a summary of the strength of the Australian units on Cocos in November 1940. File MP 42/918 (16/431/6) deals with the financing of the Cocos garrison. Australia had to pay one third of the capital and maintenance and the United Kingdom and the Straits administration two thirds. The Cocos atoll was attached to Ceylon from 1939 to 1945 while Singapore was under Japanese occupation. It became an Australian Territory in 1955.

12 Noticing the wreck of the *Emden*, which the Germans had scuttled in 1914 after its encounter with the Australian cruiser *Sydney*, Seneviratne and his companions boarded it and ripped off pieces of brass as souvenirs. 'I gave a piece of brass to a Malay mechanic on Direction Island,' he said, 'and asked him to turn it into a miniature shield and mount it on a piece of *gonga* wood. He did a wonderful job with the inscription of my name, date (5.9.41) and name of the ship. The souvenir is still with me.' A protection law now forbids this kind of activity.

CHAPTER 3

1 Ken Mullen, *Cocos Keeling: The Islands Time Forgot*, Sydney, Angus & Robertson, 1974, p. 68.

2 In 1926 a more modern cable was laid from Cocos to Australia.

3 The names of some of the smaller islands are Button, Rice, Alison, Ross, Long, Misery, Goat, Pool, Scott, Hare, Turtle, Cemetery and Turk's Head.

4 Troops were warned that a copra bug was to be flicked off rather

than squeezed on the flesh lest painful blisters develop.

5   CA 19 Department of Defence (11) 1936–1939; CA 36 Department of Army (1939–1945); Australian Archives accession MP 729/6: Secret correspondence files 16/401/273, Cocos Island Garrison 1936–45; CA 36 Department of Army file 16/431/6 'Keeling Island'. Used with permission of the Australian government.

6   On 1 March 1942 the light cruiser HMAS *Perth* was lost in the battle of the Sunda Strait. The *Perth* and the American cruiser *Houston* were attacked by the entire Japanese invasion fleet. The *Perth* was struck by Japanese torpedoes, and orders were given to abandon ship. Only 320 of *Perth*'s 680 crew were rescued by the Japanese, and of these 105 were to die as prisoners of war. The *Houston* was sunk with 600 of the crew. On 15 September 1944 survivors from the *Perth* and other British ships were rescued from the Japanese transport *Rakuyo Maru*, which had been sunk by the American submarine *Sealion*.

7   This opinion was confirmed by the medical officers of HMAS *Perth*. Australian Archives, MP 729/8, File 16/431/6.

8   The *Emden* was scuttled by the Germans after an encounter with the *Sydney* at North Keeling Island.

9   Born in 1919, George Koch studied at Royal College where he was in the cadet battalion. He was a Ceylon golf champion and played rugby for the Havelocks team. He died in 1984 at the age of 65.

10 James Prior in the *Sydney Morning Herald* 'Good Weekend,' 3 December 1977.

11 If Ramshaw's alert had been heeded, the Americans would have been aware of Japan's move against the Malay Peninsula, and would certainly have been ready at Pearl Harbor and in the Philippines. James Prior feels that 'the Day of Infamy might have become the Day of Disaster for the Forces of the Rising Sun. Obviously Britain wanted the United States of America to come into the war and felt that, if Britain struck the first blow against Japan, it would hinder their cause.'

CHAPTER 4

1   The name of the carrier was not revealed. Wickramasuriya said it was probably HMS *Invincible* or *Indomitable*. He was interviewed in Colombo in June 1970 and again in September 1992.

2   One of the Japanese destroyers was the *Kuma*, which operated from Penang. It was later sunk by the British submarine *Tally-ho*.

3   'After the fall of Singapore, traffic could still flow through Darwin via Java, Cocos Islands and South Africa, but that lasted for only four days. On 19th February 1942 the Japanese bombing raid on Darwin destroyed the cable station [but] cable communication was

restored within 24 hours. A radio message was then transmitted to Batavia saying in plain language that Cocos had been permanently put out of action. The Japanese accepted this at face value, for Cocos was not attacked again.' Edgar Harcourt, *Taming the Tyrant*, London, Allen & Unwin, 1987.

4   Sorana Estate (Horana) in low-country Ceylon was reputed for its rubber production. The author interviewed Lieutenant Henry Stephens there in 1962, having previously interviewed him in 1950.

5   Corporal Lucian Koch, detailed as a medical NCO in the third detachment, kept a diary of his service in Cocos. On the subject of the canteen he wrote: 'The ... canteen provided liquor, cigarettes and chocolates. Hankies and perfumes were also available, all sold on account as we did not have any cash. Salaries were paid to us less our monthly accounts after we reached Colombo, as we had no need for cash in Cocos.' Koch now resides in Melbourne.

6   *Sunday Times* (Ceylon), 6 September 1998.

7   Hideki Tojo was Commander of Japan's Imperial Army and Prime Minister from 1941 to 1943. Known as the 'Razor of Japan,' he directed and ordered the Pearl Harbor attack. The International Military Tribunal for the Far East sentenced him to death and he was hanged after a botched suicide attempt.

8   *Ceylon Weekend*, 21 July 1986.

9   De Bary, *Sources of Japanese Tradition*, Vol. 2, pp. 294–5.

10 Cf. R Storry, *The Double Patriots*, Boston, 1957.

11 Public Record Office, London, WO 208/871.

12 L D Meo, *Japan's Radio War on Australia 1941–1945*, Melbourne, Melbourne University Press, 1968. I was fortunate in coming to know Lucy Meo, whose well-researched book is widely accepted as a scholarly account of this aspect of the war.

13 H P Willmott, *Empires in the Balance*, London, Orbis, 1982, p. 91.

14 Broadcast by Ken Goto, 29 January 1942.

15 Broadcast from Tokyo, 3 March 1942, Australian Listening Post.

16 According to Toshio Kojima, the Imperial Japanese Army had 6.4 million men and 2889 planes, while the Imperial Navy had 1.86 million men, 524 ships (total tonnage 1.4 million) and 10,819 planes. *Weekend News Magazine* (Ceylon), 21 July 1985.

17 D H Lawrence observed in 1922, after spending six months in Australia: 'They are terribly afraid of the Japanese, and especially Sydney feels that once there is a fall in England so that the great powers could not interfere, Japan would at once walk in and occupy the place.' (D H Lawrence, *Collected Letters*, ed. H T Moore. London, Heinemann, 1962, p. 707.)

18 *New York Times*, 28 January 1942, p. 6.

19 The War Tribunal heard how in Penang two women were tied by a

rope to a motorcycle and towed naked around the prison yard.

20 *New York Times,* 13 April 1942, p. 2.
21 ibid. 19 April 1942, p. 36.
22 Meo, op. cit., p. 5.
23 ibid.
24 ibid., p. 5.

CHAPTER 5

1   Quoted in Arthur Zich, *Time Life World War Two: The Rising Sun.* On 24 February Churchill told King George VI that Burma, Ceylon, Calcutta and Madras in India and part of Australia might fall into enemy hands. The same day, he gave his support to an Admiralty plan for Dutch naval units to be moved from Java to Ceylon rather than have them tucked away in Australia — quoted in Martin Gilbert, *Road to Victory,* p. 60.
2   Quoted in Lionel Wigmore, *The Japanese Thrust,* Canberra, Australian War Memorial, 1953, p. 173.
3   Jan Morris, *Hong Kong,* Harmondsworth, Penguin, 1988.
4   Winston S Churchill, *The Second World War,* Vol. 4, London, Cassell, 1951, p. 156.
5   Cf. Lionel Wigmore, *The Japanese Thrust,* Canberra, Australian War Memorial, 1968, p. 460.
6   Cable No. 4231, Prem: 3/15/1, Public Record Office.
7   Wavell: Despatch Operations in Eastern Theatre based in India for March 1942–31 December 1942.
8   Layton had served in HMS *Renown* in 1933–34. In 1938 he commanded a battle cruiser squadron, and in 1939 was Vice-admiral commanding the First Battle Squadron and second in command of the Mediterranean fleet.
9   *Churchill and the Admirals,* quoted in E F C Ludowyk, *The Modern History of Ceylon,* London, Faber, 1966.
10 This refers to the Japanese shelling of Cocos on 3 March 1942.
11 There is a story that Horsburgh was also known as Virgin Island because in bygone years the virgins of Home Island were kept there by eunuchs, with instructions to harpoon any man who came there without the permission of the governor.
12 Nagumo was a torpedo specialist, not an aviation specialist, and was not confident as a carrier admiral. He had no faith in Yamamoto's Pearl Harbor strategy. At Midway he lost all four carriers, which were caught on deck with their aircraft being fuelled and re-armed. He committed suicide when he saw that the American assault in the battles of the Eastern Solomons and Santa Cruz were succeeding.

13 Steven L Carruthers, *Australia Under Siege*, Sydney, Solus, 1982, p. 40.
14 Francis H Hinsley, *Hitler's Strategy: the Naval Evidence*, Cambridge, Cambridge University Press, 1951, p. 199.
15 Winston S Churchill, *The Second World War*, Vol. 3, London, Cassell, p. 551.
16 Lord Russell of Liverpool, in *The Knights of Bushido* (London, Cassell, 1958), wrote: 'Of all those who suffered under Japanese military occupation, no people had better reason to remember its barbarism than the inhabitants of the Andaman Islands, where many thousands met death at the hands of Japanese forces. "Useless mouths" were deported to the NE coast of South Andamans, a jungle-covered uninhabitable spot. The aged and infirm classified as undesirables were transported.' (p. 37)
17 The *Argus* (Melbourne), 13 March 1942 (AAP dispatch). Vichy radio had quoted Tokyo. (Wigmore op. cit., p. 106)
18 After World War Two the Christmas Island mutineers were arrested in Java, and seven faced a court martial in December 1946. The death sentence was imposed on one mutineer but it was later commuted to life imprisonment, while the others got long terms of penal servitude.
19 Cf. Lawrence James, *Mutiny*, London, Buchan & Enright, 1987, p. 233.
20 The *Argus* (Melbourne), 28 March 1942 (Reuters cable). Cf. Douglas Lockwood, *Australia's Pearl Harbour*, Melbourne, Cassell Australia, 1966, pp. 210 ff.
21 Addu Atoll was turned into a makeshift fleet base with an airfield. There were other bases at Diego Garcia, the Seychelles (with Ceylonese troops) and Mauritius.
22 Cf. Zeylanicus, *Ceylon: Between Orient and Occident*, London, Elek, p. 189.
23 G Hermon Gill, *Royal Australian Navy 1942–1945*, Canberra, Australian War Memorial, 1957.
24 Cf. S A Pakeman, *Ceylon*, op. cit., p. 137. Attention to Cocos was in fact included in the Japanese plan, though obviously not as a high priority concern.
25 Willmott, op. cit., p. 438.

CHAPTER 6

1 Steven L Carruthers, *Australia Under Siege*, Sydney, Solus, 1982, pp. 37–40.
2 In my school days I patronised Ono & Co. and befriended Numano's sons Alan and Joe, who studied at St Joseph's and St

Peter's colleges. Mr Numano always gave Japanese bicycles as prizes for sports meets of Catholic schools. Greg Roszkowski, a Japanese radio personality and owner of the famous Hotel Nippon in Colombo, told the author that he very much doubted the veracity of the spying allegations. Another myth regarding the Numano family was that it was Alan who led the Japanese air attack on Colombo on 5 April 1942.

3   Sir John Kotelawala, a former pilot and army man known as 'the laird of Kandawela,' was a well-known political figure who later became prime minister.

4   Cf. David Hay, *Nothing Over Us*, Canberra, Australian War Memorial, p. 226. Ten years later, in 1952, I had the nostalgic experience of going to England on the Orient Line ship *Otranto*, which was decked with photographs and souvenirs of the troops who were transported in it during the war.

5   ibid. p. 229.

6   *Ceylon Daily News*, 19 March 1942 (Colombo Archives).

7   Augustus Agar, *Footprints in the Sea*, London, Evans Bros, 1948. This son of a Ceylon tea planter, Captain Augustus Agar, VC (RN), was present at that meeting.

8   *Keesing's Contemporary Archives*, 4–11 April 1942, p. 5127.

9   Isoruku Yamamoto was a Harvard graduate and one-time Japanese naval attaché in Washington. He was killed in 1943 when he was ambushed by American planes. In Japan Yamamoto was second in prestige to the emperor.

10   Lawrence Elliott, *The Canadian Who Saved Ceylon*, London, Readers Digest, 1983; *Ceylon News*, 10 November 1977 (Kirthie Abeysekera in an interview with Leonard Birchall in Toronto).

11   Michael Tomlinson, *The Most Dangerous Moment*, London, Kimber, 1976. A brother of actor David Tomlinson, Michael Tomlinson joined the RAF Volunteers in August 1940 and became a personal assistant to Sir Arthur Harris (No. 5 Bomber Group). He was the Station Intelligence Officer at Ratmalana and later at China Bay. After the war he became a tea planter at Fordyce Estate Dickoya in Ceylon. He returned to London in 1970 and died in May 1993, a few months after he had revised his book on the Ceylon raid.

12   ibid. p. 88.

13   Sir John's egg-hopper parties were widely appreciated. He died on 1 October 1980, ten days before the formal opening of the Kandawela Defence Academy. He had donated his fifty-acre estate for this purpose. Cf. *Sunday Times* (Ceylon), 10 April 1994: 'Kandawela: a lasting legend of the military' by Hiranthi Fernando and Nirmala Abeysekera.

14   Galle is my birthplace, and I was in the St Francis Xavier Seminary

(of the Oblate Fathers) in Bambalapitiya, Colombo, when I gazed at the spectacle of the approaching planes. The anti-aircraft shelling from a unit in the seminary gardens compelled me to get into an air-raid shelter.

15 Noel Crusz, 'Bluff, blunder and bombs,' *Sunday Times* (Ceylon), 4 April 1993, p. 15.

16 In spite of early warnings, thirty-four merchant and war ships were still in the Colombo harbour on 5 April.

17 Tomlinson, op. cit. p. 111.

18 They were commanded respectively by Captains A W S Angar and P C W Mainwaring.

19 Tomlinson, op. cit. p. 101.

20 *Ceylon Daily News*, 6 April 1942 (Colombo Archives).

21 The Australian roll of honour is: Sergeant W E Pearce (Squadrons 64 and 261) from Sydney; Navigator O G S Burgan, a transport driver from South Australia; Sergeant M C Gray (Squadron 11); Flying Officer D H Evans (Squadron 11), a farmer from Western Australia; Sergeant L E McAuley (Squadron 11), a grazier from Queensland; Sergeant H A Mackennan (Squadron 11), a bank officer from Brisbane; Sergeant A E Travers (Squadrons 211 and 11), a farmer from Tasmania; Flight Sergeant F J G Nell (Squadron 11), a bank officer from Melbourne; Warrant Officer N L Stevenson (Squadrons 223 and 11), an accountant from Adelaide; Squadron Leader K Ault (Squadrons 139, 218 and 11); Sergeant G K Eckersley (Squadron 11), an accountant from Queensland.

22 Tomlinson, op. cit., p. 136.

23 Willmott, op. cit., p. 447.

24 The SS *Mauritania* and *Aquitania* were said to have recovered the bodies of the *Hermes'* victims. In fact they were collected by motorboats and, after embalming, were transported by train to Colombo for burial with naval and military honours.

25 Anton Muttukumaru, *The Military History of Ceylon*, New Delhi, Navarang, 1987, p. 120.

26 Cf. John Deane Potter, *Admiral of the Pacific: the Life of Yamamoto*, London, Heinemann, 1965.

27 Tomlinson, op. cit., p. 149.

28 *Ceylon Daily News*, 12 April 1942.

29 Quoted in Kirthi Abeysekera, 'The man who saved us from the Japs,' *Ceylon News*, 10 November 1977.

30 Birchall's prison diary was used in the Tokyo War Trials. He was responsible for a memorial pillar in Koggala for the eighteen servicemen who lost their lives between 1942 and 1945. It was unveiled in April 1995.

31 Journalist K D Jayasekera notes that few relics of the Japanese raids

on Trincomalee remain. At the War Cemetery near Alles Gardens in the north there is a headstone of a British soldier: 'A L Shewell, who died on 9th April 1942, aged 30.' There is also the burnt oil tank of the Admiralty's fuel depot at China Bay. The Essential Service Corps had to bury many civilian casualties in the dockyard.

CHAPTER 7

1 Obtained from his eldest sister, Eva, along with other correspondence, in Colombo on 13 June 1970.
2 James, op. cit., p. 231.
3 ibid.
4 In an article entitled 'When Britain practised apartheid here' published in the *Sunday Island* (Colombo), on 14 March 1999, Joe Segera said that Tarzie Vittachi of the *Ceylon Observer* had led a campaign to end the segregation. He also told the story of how Ceylonese journalists were banned from the Darawella Club when the Queen made her first official visit there in the 1950s. And a British Bank offered chairs for Europeans while Ceylonese had to sit on long wooden benches! 'Like all colonial powers the feeling that the white man was superior was somehow ingrained in them.'
5 William Joseph Slim rose to the rank of brigadier in the Indian Army in 1940, and commanded British forces in India. In 1942 he went to Burma as Corps Commander and led the British Army in the reconquest of Burma. He was made Field Marshal in 1949, and served as Governor-General of Australia from 1953 to 1960.
6 Philip Mason, *A Matter of Honour*, London, Jonathan Cape, 1974.
7 Cf. G Mant, *You'll be Sorry*, Sydney, Frank Johnson, c.1944.
8 Mark Hopman, interview, Colombo, 1970.
9 In interview, Porritt, Hopman, Anandappa and Patterson all attested to the fact that Perera was frequently challenged about his favouritism.
10 Donald Patterson in later years confirmed that sexual congress with island women did take place, but it was by no means easy to arrange.
11 Interview 1970 and correspondence 5 October 1977 and 30 December 1977.
12 The Public Record Office in Kew, London, opened the Cocos mutiny files in May 1994. The Crown copyright material in this book is reproduced by permission of the Controller of Her Majesty's Stationery Office. File WO 71/741.
13 Porritt and De Rooy both attested to this.
14 Ravindra Varma, *Australia and South East Asia*, New Delhi, Combined Inter-Services Historical Section, 1974.
15 *Keesing's Contemporary Archives*, April 1942, p. 5061.

16 ibid., p. 4965.
17 ibid.
18 From interviews with Ken Porritt in Colombo, 8 June 1970. Porritt rang Independent Newspapers Ltd offering an interview following the publication of Marie Tirzah's serial 'The Cocos Island Mutiny' in the evening daily the *Star*, which I edited. Porritt provided the very rare group photograph of the Cocos contingent.
19 Aung Sang in January 1947 successfully negotiated Burma's independence, which came in 1948. He was assassinated in July 1947, and his daughter Suu Kyi, the 1991 Nobel Peace Prize winner, now leads the Opposition with the 'National League for Democracy.' She won the elections in 1990 but was not allowed to assume power. Cf. Martin Gilbert, *The Day the War Ended*, London, HarperCollins, 1995, p. 352.
20 Anil Seal, Indian Nationalism: 1918–1939' in *Purnell's History of the 20th Century*, ed. A J P Taylor, London, Purnell, 1971–72, p. 849.
21 From interviews with Lieutenant Colonel Lyn Wickramasuriya, Kirillapone, Ceylon, June–July 1970.

CHAPTER 8

1 From interviews with Charles Wijenayake at the BSSI, Colombo, 18 June 1970.
2 In later years Dubney said that the mutiny occurred in the weekend and that it was not until the Monday that he realised what had happened. (From correspondence with R J Linford, 27 September 1977. Linford was Administrator of Cocos and spoke to Dubney Bin Bohin about the mutiny and the motor boat. He says that no written records were left about the uprising.)
3 Captain Senior's death on Christmas Island was confirmed by Henry Stephens, who had known Senior personally. Henry de Sylva believed that the two mutinies were connected, a view that had no foundation.
4 Gerry Anandappa outlined the details to the author in a long interview at Wellawatta, a suburb of Colombo, on 14 June 1970.
5 The Bren gun on Cocos was a light gas-operated air-cooled machine fired from the shoulder. It got its name from *Br*no, a city in Czechoslovakia, and *En*field, a town in England.
6 Ken Porritt, Mark Hopman and Donald Patterson all attested that a shot was fired.

CHAPTER 9

1 The sequence and details of all these movements I compiled from personal interviews with many of the surviving mutineers and loyal troops along with the signed and authenticated documents of

the Field General Court Martial, File WO/71/741, in the Public Record Office in London released in May 1994. The evidence is not entirely consistent, and this narrative represents my best endeavour at synthesising the various strands. Archivist Anthony Richards and Julie Robertshaw of the Imperial War Museum in London were of immense help in tracing relevant military sources.

2   Public Record Office WO 71/741 SSS 15.

3   The Bren gun weighed about twenty-three pounds and was capable of firing five hundred rounds per minute.

4   A suburb of Galle in the south of Ceylon where the Dutch built their forts during their occupation. Lachlan Macquarie was sent to Galle from India to accept the surrender of the country to the British. He then came to Australia. I take pride in having been born in this historic place.

5   Interview and correspondence with Corporal Lucian P Koch, March 1999. Koch's evidence is valuable, as he is one of the few, if not only, surviving members' of the medical team on Cocos during the mutiny.

6   Public Record Office, London, File WO/71/741(SSS15). Lance Sergeant O M D W Perera was in later years to make some extraordinary claims, which neither oral evidence nor Public Record Office files could substantiate. He died in Melbourne of a massive heart attack on 29 November 1999.

CHAPTER 10

1   Quoted by Janaka Perera, 'The Cocos mutiny: old soldier confesses,' *Sunday Observer* (Ceylon), 5 July 1977.

2   Public Record Office WO/71/741. A photo transcript of Lieutenant Menon's certificate was available.

3   Donald Patterson died of a heart attack at the age of 76 on 22 March 1996.

4   The arecanut is the fruit of the Cocos palm, which often reached over 60 feet in height. The small nuts were used by villagers in Ceylon to chew betel leaves.

5   The General Cemetery Kanatta in Colombo, where the Raymonds were well-known funeral directors. Some of the service casualties of two world wars are buried there, including victims of the *Hermes* disaster.

6   The Jayasekeras of Galle were well known to my parents. The army photograph in full uniform of Gunner Samuel Jayasekera was submitted, along with some documents, by the family to Independent Newspapers Ltd's evening daily the *Star*, which ran Marie Tirzah's serial on the mutiny. Gunner Jayasekera was known as 'Samuel', though his real name was 'Samaris.'

7   All efforts to get the manuscript of 'Island of Fate' proved abortive. Anandappa and Patterson had read parts of it. Some gunners believed that the script was spirited away and destroyed. A few pages of Gratien's poems were kept by unidentified guards.

CHAPTER 11

1   Cf. *Manual of Military Law*, London, HMSO, 1952. In 1938 in Britain a Courts Martial Committee was appointed to look into the existing system of trial by court martial. (File W/O 225, Public Record Office.)
2   W F Gow, *Procedures of Courts Martial*, London, Imperial War Museum, 1965.
3   Public Record Office file WO/71/741, courtesy HM Stationery Office.
4   ibid., evidence of Lance Sergeant O M D W Perera.

CHAPTER 12

1   ibid., statements and evidence of Gunner C A Gauder.
2   ibid., Section 2.
3   ibid., FGCM records.
4   ibid., evidence and statements of Gunner Mark Hopman.
5   In his interview with the author in Colombo in 1971, Hopman made it known that he was upset at the criticism levelled at him that he had betrayed his friends and backed away after an initial commitment. This may be unfair. It may explain Hopman's migration to Australia and his refusal to comment on the part he played at Cocos. Both Hopman and Stephens faced blatant ostracism on the part of many of their army colleagues.

CHAPTER 13

1   Public Record Office file WO/71/741, evidence of Gunner A B Edema.
2   ibid., evidence and statement of Gunner A J L Peries.
3   Gerry Anandappa passed away in August 1991.
4   Public Record Office. File WO/71/741, statement and evidence of Gunner G D Anandappa.
5   ibid., evidence and statement of Sergeant I L Pereira.
6   Perera's claims will be considered in a later chapter. On his return to Ceylon, de Rooy was attached to the 13th Coast Battery at Elephant Point in Trincomalee. He later migrated to Australia and died in Perth on 28 August 1994.
7   I myself taught history at St Patrick's College, Jaffna, in 1960. Today this northern city is the scene of bitter warfare between the Sri

Lankan troops and the Tamil Tigers of Eelam. The devastation of this civil war has changed the face of Jaffna. Many Tamils have migrated to Australia and other countries.

CHAPTER 14

1 I studied economics for my Intermediate Arts at St Peter's College, Bambalapitiya, in 1939 under Mr Joseph Fernando, who was the college's head commerce teacher.
2 Public Record Office file WO/71/741, evidence and statements of Gunner G B de Silva.

CHAPTER 15

1 Admiral Layton had befriended this French secular missionary priest when an RAF plane had flown straight into the church and destroyed it. A well-known veterinary surgeon, Hector Perera, told the story that, when Layton consulted him regarding a wounded pet deer, he observed that he was 'happy the RAF pilot entered the true Church before his death.' Admiral Layton immediately rebuilt the church.
2 Public Record Office file WO/71/741.
3 Lance Sergeant 1691 Perera is wrongly identified as Lance Sergeant O M D W Perera by Wing Commander Derek Martin in a 1997 article on the Cocos mutiny in *After the Battle*. The latter was No. 1735. I have made strenuous efforts to determine which of the Pereras on Cocos at the time bore the number 1691, but without success. Most believe it was A H Perera, who was widely perceived as having been the cause of much of the tension between the batteries.

CHAPTER 16

1 Wambeek and Van Twest had been schoolmates.
2 Intriguingly, the letter was written on YMCA notepaper with an AIF (Australian Imperial Force) insignia.
3 This letter was not received by the Adjutant.
4 The Porritt brothers studied at Royal College and made their mark in sports. I remember watching the touring Australian team playing against Ceylon in April 1934 at the cricket ground in Colombo in a match where Gunner Porritt's brother F W E Porritt represented Ceylon, while Bill Ponsford and Bill Woodfull played for Australia.
5 Emphasis by Porritt.
6 All these appeal documents are from Public Record Office file WO/71/741.

CHAPTER 17

1   In contrast to the western custom, white is worn at funerals. I am grateful to Indra Chandrasekera and Robert Crusz for helping me to secure this interview with Helen Fernando. Helen worked at Visaka Vidyalaya till her retirement. Now a widow in her seventies, she lives at Mount Lavinia with her only surviving brother, Patrick, a former electrical engineer.

2   Ousmand brought this letter to Independent Newspapers Ltd in August 1970 when my evening daily newspaper, the *Star*, was running the serial story on the mutiny.

3   Some believe that the hangman was Welikade Gaol's 'Pierpoint', the gaunt Appuhamy Lewis. According to journalist Joe Segera, Lewis had many executions to his name. The last person to be executed in Ceylon by hanging was Jayasinghe Manachige Chandradasa, a 25-year-old cultivator, on 23 June 1976. The death penalty was suspended in Ceylon in May 1956, with Eric Walter Batcho escaping the hangman's noose for murdering the teenage girl who jilted him. Along with prison official Felix Ratnaike, I was summoned by Batcho to death row in a bid to gain publicity for his case with the aim of getting a reprieve. He succeeded, the sentence being commuted to life imprisonment, but he died soon after from bowel cancer. Ceylon reintroduced the death penalty on 2 October 1959, but suspended it once again in April 1999.

4   Son of Dr J T Fernando.

5   I was unable to find the grave despite a long search with Kanatta cemetery officials.

6   It was Fr Emmanuel Alles and Fr Claude Moffat Lawrence's connection with the mutineers that triggered my interest in the wartime mutiny in 1942. I was a first-year philosophy student at St Bernard's Seminary and resident at the Oblate Scholasticate at Kynsey Road, Borella. The future Cardinal Thomas Benjamin Cooray was Superior. Fr Emmanuel Alles often spoke of Gauder's last hours.

7   Ceylonese funeral director Maurice Raymond said that there is no mention in his records of burials in Kanatta from executions in the first two weeks of August 1942. Raymonds buried the victims — both servicemen and civilians — of the Japanese Easter Sunday raid and of the *Hermes* disaster. Other wartime interments were of Flight Sergeant H Smith, who died of gunshot injuries; Gunner Leonard Philip Brown of the Royal Artillery, who died at the Mount Lavinia Hospital following a fracture of the skull; Stoker Ellis, who fell from the deck of HMS *Truant* and died of injuries, and Donald Waite of the 11th Squadron, who died of brain lacerations. There are eight different war cemeteries in Ceylon, where world war servicemen

are buried or commemorated. Two of them contain World War One war graves.

8   There was doubt whether Fernando, de Silva and Gauder were officially dismissed before execution. Some are of the opinion that they were executed as soldiers paying the penalty for mutiny in His Majesty's Imperial Forces.

9   Toby Kane was a well-known tea-taster.

10 If A H Perera was the Perera named by the Assistant Judge Advocate General as possibly having failed to act against the mutiny when in a position to do so, it could be presumed that the drumming off was a consequence of that judgement being confirmed by a subsequent inquiry. (If this is so, it would follow that I L Pereira, who was also named, was found to have been not at fault, as he was not drummed off.) M M Yusuf, who had been one of the guards of the mutineers when they were in Hulftsdorf prison, and subsequently spoken of by Anandappa, was present at this ceremony.

CHAPTER 18

1   Reuters report in the *Argus*, Melbourne, 27 March 1942.

2   Bose himself later died in an airplane crash.

3   Indians were commanded to crawl along the ground as a humiliation.

4   Charles Bateson, *The War with Japan*, Sydney, Ure Smith, 1968, p. 344.

5   James, op. cit.

6   British Parliamentary Sessions: Hansard April 1935–1938.

7   Imperial War Museum, London, (Documents Section), File 87/42/1. Archivist A P Richards and Julie Robertshaw were of invaluable aid in research here.

8   The notion that the mutiny took place on a ship is a bizarre fantasy.

8   Newsletter No. 4, Celon Artillery Association, Melbourne, 1992.

CHAPTER 19

1   A loyal gunner received a reply from the British army that they 'would give no reasons why those who served on Cocos were deprived of the Star and the Pacific Star.'

2   Janaka Perera in the *Sunday Observer* (Ceylon), 12 July 1977.

3   ibid., 17 July 1977.

4   Correspondence with Lieutenant Colonel Henry de Sylva, 5 October 1977 and 30 December 1977.

5   D B Dhanapala, formerly of the *Indian Express*, is a revered figure in Ceylon journalism. His style and substance have never been

equalled. I spent eight years at Independent Newspapers Ltd under the tutelage of a man who knew his craft and who had a heart of gold.

6   Ms Bunce made unacknowledged use of the original research represented in my thesis in her book *The Cocos (Keeling) Islands: Australian Atolls in the Indian Ocean*.

7   Fr Jean-Marie Le Jeune, OMI, was a popular Oblate French priest who taught classics at St Joseph's College, Colombo. He entertained pupils in class by singing his own composition 'Naliki-va' ('Come tomorrow') to the tune of 'Danny Boy'.

8   Letter of Stephens from Fairview Park, South Australia, 10 November 1992.

CHAPTER 20

1   Ken Mullen has given a comprehensive account of developments in the Cocos atoll since the war up till the early 1970s in *Cocos Keeling: The Islands Time Forgot* (Sydney, Angus & Robertson, 1974).

2   *After the Battle*, No. 91, Battle of Britain International Ltd, Church House, London, p. 50. Matthew Bryson took the photographs of the dilapidated guns now left on Horsburgh.

3   *Empires in the Balance*, London, Orbis, 1982, pp. 436 ff. H P Willmott is one of the most reputed of contemporary military historians. A modern history MA of Liverpool University, he taught in the Department of War Studies at the Royal Military Academy in Sandhurst, served with British airborne forces between 1972 and 1979 and is the author and co-author of nine books on warfare.

4   Whereas under normal cultivation rubber trees are 'rested' between tappings, during the war indiscriminate 'slaughter' tapping was practised in the interests of maximum production in the short term, but to the detriment of the trees.

5   Record of Proceedings, Conference for the Conclusion and Signature of the Treaty of Peace with Japan, San Francisco, 4–8 September 1951, pp. 147–50. The Japanese Prime Minister, Shigeru Yoshida, burst into tears as Mr Jayawardena concluded his speech. Professor K M de Silva and Dr Howard Wriggins have written an excellent political biography, *J R Jayawardena of Sri Lanka* (Anthony Blond/Quartet, London, 1988).

6   *Ceylon News*, Vol. 44, No. 38 (1979).

7   British Parliamentary Sessions: Hansard April 1947.

8   This statistic contradicts the true count according to Public Record Office File WO/93/40, which shows that, in World War One, 186 received the death penalty, but only 18 were executed.

9   *Weekend Australian*, 24 April 1999, p. 6.

Bibliography

Abeyratna, Oscar M. *The History of the Ceylon Light Infantry*. Colombo, 1945.

Argyle, C J. *Japan at War 1937–1945*. London, Barker, 1976.

Commonwealth of Australia, Department of External Affairs. External short wave broadcasts: work of Radio Australia. *Current Notes on International Affairs*, Vol. 20, No. 7, 1949.

Australian War Memorial. *RAAF Saga*. Canberra, AWM, 1944.

Bateson, Charles. *The War with Japan*, Sydney, Ure Smith, 1968.

Bennet, R W. Military law in 1839. *Journal of the Society for Army Historical Research*, Vol. 48, 1970.

Bergamini, David. *Japan's Imperial Conspiracy*. New York, Morrow, 1967.

Bowle, John. *The Imperial Achievement*. London, London Book Club, 1974.

Braddon, Russell. *The Naked Island*. London, Pan, 1955.

Brown, David. *The Pacific Navies Dec 1941–Feb 1943*, Vol. 2. London, Alan, 1974.

Bryant, Arthur. *The Turn of the Tide 1939–1943*. London, Collins, 1957.

Bunce, Pauline. *The Cocos (Keeling) Islands: Australian Atolls in the Indian Ocean*. Brisbane, Jacaranda, 1988.

Carew, Tim. *The Longest Retreat: the Burma Campaign 1942*. London, Hamish Hamilton, 1969.

Ceylon Government. *Blue Book Administrative Reports*. Colombo, Government Press, 1938.

Churchill, Winston S. *The Gathering Storm* (Vol. 1 in *The Second World War*). London, Cassell, 1948.

Collie, Basil. *The War in the Far East*. London, Heinemann, 1969.

Davis, Burke. *Get Yamamoto*. New York, Random House, 1969.

Downs, Ray F (ed.). Japan *Yesterday and Today*. New York, Bantam, 1970.

Ferguson's *Directory 1939–1974*. Colombo, Lake House, 1974.

Firkins, Peter. *The Australians in Nine Wars.* Sydney, Rigby, 1975.

Fuchida, Mitsuo & Mastake Okumiya. *Midway: The Battle That Doomed Japan.* London, Hutchinson, 1957.

Gill, G Hermon. *Royal Australian Navy 1942–1945.* Canberra, Australian War Memorial, 1957.

Guillain, Robert. *The Japanese Challenge.* London, Hamish Hamilton, 1970.

Hale, Allan & Francis Jeffrey. Cocos Islands report. *West Australian,* 4 September 1972.

Hastings, Peter. A tale of two islands: the Cocos Christmas story. *New Guinea and Australia, the Pacific and South East Asia,* Vol. 9, No. 3, 1974, pp. 3–22.

Hoyt, Edwin P. *The Last Cruise of the Emden.* London, Andre Deutsch, 1967.

James, Lawrence. *Mutiny within British Commonwealth Forces 1797–1956.* London, Buchan & Enright, 1987.

Jayasuriya, J E. *Education in Ceylon Before and After Independence, 1939–1960.* Colombo, Colombo Associated Publications, 1969.

Lawrence, D H, *Collected Letters,* ed. H T Moore, London, Heinemann, 1962.

Lockwood, Douglas. *Australia's Pearl Harbour: Darwin 1942.* Melbourne, Cassell Australia, 1966.

Ludowyk, E F C. *The Modern History of Ceylon.* London, Faber, 1966.

Mant, Gilbert. *Grim Glory.* Sydney, The Currawong Publishing Company, 1945.

Masanori, Ito. *The End of the Imperial Japanese Navy,* trans. Andrew Y Kuroda and Roger Pineau. New York, Norton, 1962.

Mattes, J. *Constitutional Development in Two Island Territories (Cocos Keeling and Christmas Island),* Vol. 12, No. 1, 1972, pp. 23–28.

Meaney, N K (ed.). *The Awakening of Asia: Japan 1914–1976* (Vol. 2 in *The West and the World*). Sydney, 1973.

Meo, L D. *Japan's Radio War on Australia 1941–1945.* Melbourne, Melbourne University Press, 1968.

Meyer, Charles & R S B Searle (eds). *Source Materials in Asian History: Japan.* Brisbane, Jacaranda, 1957.

Montgomery, Michael. *Who Sank the Sydney?* Melbourne, Cassell Australia, 1981.

Morison, Samuel Eliot. *The Rising Sun in the Pacific, 1931–April 1942.* Boston, Little Brown & Co., 1951.

Morris, Jan. *Hong Kong.* London, Penguin, 1988.

Mullen, Ken. *Cocos Keeling: The Islands Time Forgot.* Sydney, Angus & Robertson, 1974.

Muttukumaru, Anton. *The Military History of Ceylon – an Outline.* New Delhi, Navarang, 1987.

Nadesan, P (ed.). *This Man Kotelawala.* Colombo, Nadarajah, 1962.

Osborne, G & F Mandlew. *New History: Studying Australia Today.* London, Allen & Unwin, 1970.

Pakeman, S A. *Ceylon.* London, Ernest Benn, 1964.

Parkinson, Roger. *Blood, Toil, Tears and Sweat.* London, Hart-Davis MacGibbon, 1973.

Potter, John Deane. *Admiral of the Pacific: the Life of Yamamoto.* London, Heinemann, 1965.

Prasad, S N, K D Bhargavba & P H Kehra. *The Reconquest of Burma, 2 Vols (Official History of the Indian Armed Forces in the Second World War 1939–1945).* Calcutta, Combined Inter-Services Historical Section (India & Pakistan), 1958–1959.

Records of Courts Martial. Army No. 84. Public Record Office, Kew, London.

Rivett, Rohan D. *Behind Bamboo.* Sydney, Angus & Robertson, 1946.

Roskill, Stephen. *Churchill and the Admirals.* London, Collins, 1977.

Russell, Lord, of Liverpool. *The Knights of Bushido.* London, Cassell, 1958.

Smith, J Stuart. Military law, its history, administration and practice. *Law Quarterly Review*, Vol. 85, 1969, pp. 478–504.

Smith, T E. The Cocos Keeling Islands: a demographical laboratory. *Population Studies*, Vol. 14, No. 2, 1960–1961.

Storry, Richard. *The Double Patriots.* London, Chatto & Windus, 1957.

—— *A History of Modern Japan.* New York, Penguin, 1960.

Toland, John. *But Not in Shame: the Six Months after Pearl Harbor.* New York, Random House, 1961.

Tomlinson, Michael. *The Most Dangerous Moment.* London, Kimber, 1976.

Walker, Allan S. *Middle East and Far East*, Series 5 (Vol. 2 in *Australia in the War of 1939–1945*). Canberra, Australian War Memorial, 1953.

Weerasooriya, N E. *Ceylon and her People*, Vol. 4. Colombo, Lake House, 1971.

Wigmore, Lionel. *The Japanese Thrust* (Vol. 4 in *Australia in the War of 1939–1945*). Canberra, Australian War Memorial, 1953.

Willmott, H P. *Empires in the Balance.* London, Orbis, 1982.

Winton, John. *Air Power at Sea 1939–1945.* London, London Book Club, 1977.

Zeylanicus. *Ceylon: Between Orient and Occident.* London, Elek, 1966.